I'll Never Know

The Rock & Roll Priest Looks at 80

By

Harry George Schlitt

Father Harry
11.17.22

Published by Sand Hill Review Press
www.sandhillreviewpress.com

Library of Congress Control Number: 2011904961
Nonfiction
Memoir
Christian

ISBN: 978-1-949534-29-0

Graphics by Backspace Ink

To my big sister, Della Schlitt Darling,
who has supported all my life adventures

The author is grateful for the support of the late Charles "Kip" Thieriot, Jeananne Millhon, Michael O'Leary, Jeff Arch, James Normile, Michael and Tamara Dermody, Clint and Janet Riley, Dr. Elisa Stephens, Anthony and Diane Martorana, Bert Keane and the God Squad Productions Board of Advisors: Sue Beane, John Bisordi, Lani Boucher, Joseph Cooney, Joe Cresalia, David Ghiorso, Leonard Hall, Michael Pritchard, John and Beth Schlitt, Rick and Jane Schlitt, Michael Stecher and James Swanson.

LORD, I have no idea where I am going.
I do not see the road ahead of me.
I cannot know for certain where it will end.
Nor do I really know myself.
And the fact that I think I am following your will
Does not mean that I am actually doing so.

Conjectures of a Guilty Bystander from the
diary of Trappist Father Thomas Merton

CONTENTS

Foreword

MONSIGNOR HARRY SCHLITT has rubbed shoulders at the highest levels of the Catholic Church, after studying and being ordained a priest in Rome as a young seminarian from the American Midwest. *I'll Never Know: The Rock & Roll Priest Looks at 80* is the continuing story of a remarkable post-Vatican II Catholic priest, as well as a profound homage to the priesthood itself.

Deeply influenced by Pope John XXIII's expansion of the Church to include "the people of God" and the newly sanctioned role of media in ministry, "Father Harry of the God Squad" took to the airwaves in 1968 as a rock & roll deejay, continuing his broadcasting career to this day as Sunday celebrant on TV and the internet.

I'll Never Know chronicles Father Harry's golden years, as he celebrates Pope Francis' Church of Mercy, embraces his famous parishioner Speaker Nancy Pelosi at weekly Mass, celebrates birthdays and funerals with lifelong friends, advocates eloquently for a married priesthood—while wryly sharing the laments common to octogenarians.

Father Harry is not afraid to state his deep frustration with conservative voices in the Catholic hierarchy. But his funny, sometimes acerbic, often meditative musings on his journey as a priest are profoundly relevant to any person trying to make sense of life in the modern world.

At a time when the clergy pedophilia scandal has diminished and tainted the image of the Catholic priesthood, Father Harry, simply by assembling a riveting, random diary of his life as a Catholic priest, reveals the powerful, indispensable role a great priest can play in the Christian community and the world at large.

In the Catholic tradition, the priest is not envisioned as the leader but rather as a facilitator of leadership among the laity. Many Catholics originally have been inspired by an exceptional priest. When I was 14, I entered the seminary of the Archdiocese of San Francisco and studied to be a priest for nine years. It was not to be. I dropped out and ultimately became a political consultant and later a businessman, publisher, and owner of a magazine and *The San Francisco Examiner* newspaper. Today, I have a wonderful wife and two remarkable daughters. However, my life has been hugely impacted by a number of extraordinary priests like Father Harry, who influenced and inspired me along my life's path.

I first really got to know Father Harry when he was the Vicar General of the Archdiocese of San Francisco and the right hand to Archbishop William Levada. Levada was about to become a cardinal and replace Cardinal Joseph Ratzinger as Prefect for the Doctrine of the Faith in Rome—the third ranking prelate in the Catholic Church under the Vatican Secretary of State and the Pope. Harry Schlitt really ran the archdiocese on a day-to-day basis. He had the same role under Cardinal Levada's successor, Archbishop George Niederauer. Father Harry was essentially the CEO of the extensive group of parishes, real estate, grammar schools, high schools and charitable programs controlled by the archdiocese. As chair of the board for Catholic Charities CYO—a network of 33 different social programs as well an extensive sports program—I came to greatly admire Harry's deft managerial skills and inspirational leadership style.

More than once I remember thinking that Harry would have made an extraordinary bishop himself. He became something more: Father Harry, the living embodiment of everything it means to be a Catholic priest. Read this wonderful book, savor the stories and the anecdotes, witness the joyful, powerful life of a true man of Faith.

Clinton Reilly

Preface

THERE'S A LOT I'll never know, but one thing is for certain. No one is perfect. I've learned this after going through 57 years of priesthood, not from teachers or theologians or scholars, but from living.

My life has interfaced with so many others in the 82 years I've had on this earth — people I've lived with, people I meet, those with whom I eat and drink and play and pray. Those who come to me seeking some kind of spiritual nourishment. I've been allowed to come into their lives for a day, a week or a year. But there are so many things about them that I'll never know. For the most part, I'll never know how things turned out.

As a human being, I am subject to imperfection not by choice but by my humanity. No one is perfect but to seek perfection is our calling, as Catholics, as Christians, as co-inhabitants of this fragile planet.

An old priest friend of mine once told me that I had too many notes. "You write too much. Why don't you just tear up all that paper and TELL the people how you feel about God?" It was then that I began to know what I didn't know before . . . what's really worthwhile is what comes from the heart. As Saint Francis is said to have said: "Preach the Gospel at all times. Use words if necessary."

I want to influence people for good. That's pretty much why I became a priest in the first place and one of the reasons I began working on radio and television back in 1968. It started with teens in my high school counseling and teaching work. Then broadcasting gave me access to so many more people, those who needed more than they were getting. Now it's, well, who really knows? With the present reach of my Sunday Mass on TV and the internet, and now with my new podcasts coming from fatherharry. org into the famous cloud of information, the sky is not really the limit.

My humanity guides me to one thing or another, but I work and pray to reach out beyond my humanity, asking that spiritual being to guide my imperfection and help me do whatever I can, to be as close to being right, as close to perfect, as I can. Not everyone has the privilege of a place where they can make a retreat or spend time in prayer; that's a luxury for the priest. Prayer, contemplation and meditation give me space to be quiet, open my mind and take time to build a relationship with mystery and the unknown. Some little twist makes me different and I'm able to project to those who see someone more like them than a holier than thou.

I want to help bring change for the good, to help people choosing between right and wrong make a better choice. Not one of us will ever be perfect and there's no such thing as "the perfect family". Not even the Holy Family. If you recall, Joseph and Mary had a non-traditional start and then had their hands full when Jesus was a pre-teen runaway.

Catholics believe that God sent his only son to save humanity, as scripture says, once and for all. People who trust this, who live this, find their minds are a lot more open to happiness and helping others. When evil knocks on the door and faith answers, the devil turns tail.

Since my seminary days at the North American College in Rome, I have been a child of Vatican II and I am close to despair at what is happening today to undermine those teachings. My ministry as a broadcaster stemmed from the Vatican II pronouncement that media should be used to spread the Gospel. Vatican II also held forth the promise of allowing priests to marry, but the untimely death of Pope John XXIII and the rise of his predecessor Pope Paul VI dashed that hope.

I'm out to make it better for the Church of the future, if there is one without priests. Well, dammit, ordain some married men or allow young men to be priests and be married. It's sour grapes to think this is not fair. The end game is to spread the Gospel, to do and live what Jesus left us to do.

It means we have to unload a lot of historical baggage and see our Church, our faith, as a garden to be worked and cultivated rather than a museum simply to be guarded and protected. It's a big request. I'll admit, I haven't really made it part of my prayer life. I suppose I'm like most other retired priests: we ran the race, we fought the good fight and now we hope to be accepted into eternal life for what has been gifted to us to do.

The Holy Spirit continues to work in mysterious ways that I'll never know. Songs I played in my early days as a radio deejay seem to have come prophetically true for this old rock & roll priest.

"To everything there is a season."
Turn, Turn, Turn, The Byrds
"It's better to burn out than to fade away"
Out of the Blue, Neil Young
"My occupation's just not around."
A Pirate Looks at Forty, Jimmy Buffett
"Imagine there's no heaven
It's easy if you try
No hell below us
Above us only sky"
Imagine, John Lennon

I'll never know how close my relationship has been or will be with God, not until I'm on the other side of the grass. But with 80 receding fast in my rearview mirror, I'm finding truth where I least expected. I'm realizing all the things in this realm that I'll never know.

PART I

Paradise Lost

"But by the grace of God I am what I am,
and his grace to me has not been ineffective."
(1 Corinthians 15:10)

* * *

"Don't it always seem to go
That you don't know what you got
Till it's gone"
Joni Mitchell

CHAPTER 1

Fade to Black

IT WAS IN the middle of June and I was just returning from a week or ten days on Martha's Vineyard visiting my sister, Della Darling. It was a quiet visit and one filled with memories and stories of her late husband, Pete. After landing at SFO, I picked up my car at my friend Jan's house in South City where I often left it when traveling. It was a short cab ride from baggage claim to her place where my vehicle awaited me for the drive to my relatively new home at the beach. I had only been there six months and from the Atlantic to the Pacific, gee the world was terrific. There's no place like home.

Father Miles O'Brien Riley came bouncing out his door into the backyard as I dragged my roller-wheel bag through the gravel. He greeted me with a warm hug and said breathlessly, "We have to talk."

We lived side by side in two halves of a beach house Miles co-owned with his sister Ann just south of San Francisco. I moved there from the City after the spanking scandal at the Shrine of Saint Francis. (You'll have to read my first book.) I had gone though my chemotherapy for colon cancer while living at the shrine and the 47 steps were really difficult as I was so weak from the treatments. I spent most of my time in a cushioned chair just trying to heal. When I left North Beach to come to Miramar, it felt like a great relief.

There was a deck at the rear of my bedroom and a couple of chairs, so we sat down. Miles asked about my trip and my sister (they've known each other for more than 50 years) and then launched into the tale of a dream gone black, just like the end of a 1950s TV show when the picture on the screen suddenly disappears. He told me that I would have to vacate my apartment by next week, as construction people were coming to evaluate the building and begin a project he thought would take a year to complete.

"Is there somewhere you can go? Do you have friends who could take you in? Maybe you could go to your sister's place on the island (where you just came from)?" Gee thanks. And from a guy I've known since 1961, who once had been my closest friend.

"I'm going to have to leave as well," he added, but failing to mention the place was scheduled to be red-tagged. "I'm planning on going to Stinson Beach where my sister has a second beach home."

"Miles, I can't be out of here in a week!" I hadn't even been in the door yet and still had my roller-bag in my hand. My brain raced, or what passed for that these days. *"Impossible!"* I think. *"I'll need most of the summer to find another home. Construction people can work around me or behind me. I don't care. I've put too much into this place to suddenly pick up and leave."*

I was angry and huffed into the house, jerking my bag across the threshold behind me and trying to settle down as I unpacked and looked around. The gentleman who occupied the rooms before me had decorated the kitchen as if it were a ship's galley. The ceiling was lowered and there were brass fittings on the dark woodwork to give the indication that you were in the cabin of a sailing vessel. The windows were small portholes with brass locks.

I was just getting used to this place. It was a piece of paradise. For the first time in my 76 years of life, I had a home. I wasn't in my parents' house, the seminary, a rectory, a studio apartment in New York City, or an archbishop's residence — all the places where I'd lived before now. I was home, and it was my home.

It never occurred to me that Miles' health was failing. When I had arrived the previous December, we were both recently retired as priests but still very active — he holding court for his beachside community, serving as their de facto chaplain, and I doing a lot of weekend preaching, occasional baptisms, marriages and increasing numbers of funerals, and pretending I was still an athlete on the Olympic Club handball court. He was on a walking regimen of over an hour a day. Now, just six months later, he could barely make it up the block to the restaurant on the corner. He was unable to manage the eight short stairs up to his bedroom. He really wasn't the same guy I had met at the seminary in Rome. But then look who's talking.

My memoir, *I'll Never Tell*, has more than you would want to know about our friendship and how I found myself moving from Missouri to San Francisco to work with him seven years after we graduated from the North American College in Rome and became priests. I went from being a high school teacher in the Ozarks to Father Harry of the God Squad in the City by the Bay. But that's a different story.

Anyway, in hindsight, I'm sure his sister Ann was looking out for him. They would have decided it was too difficult for him at the beach and that he should have more secure quarters where someone could look after him. So I don't blame Miles or Ann. I should have known it wasn't going to work, but I am the one who chose to move there and give it a try. I do recall asking for a piece of paper that I never got, spelling out the details of me making the move. For example, if he were sick and left, or perhaps was called by God, what would happen to the place? What would happen to me and my paradise by the beach? I hadn't yet grasped that I would never be returning.

My good friend announced that he was going to re-do his place and perhaps make a shrine out of the quarters I occupied. Not a shrine to me or because of me but a place where he could pray. He even showed me samples of stained glass windows that he thought might replace the large picture window, which allowed one to see the expanse of the ocean as well as the playing porpoises and the gray whales as they migrated. I thought to myself that this was a huge waste of money and also a slap in the face of the Almighty who had already gifted this lovely domain a breathtaking vista of the Pacific Ocean. It never came to pass but my eviction still loomed. The time, like the tide, relentlessly came closer and closer and I realized the bitter truth that I would have to abandon ship and head for higher ground.

CHAPTER 2

What to Do?

FATHER KEN WAS the pastor of St. Vincent de Paul parish in the City. It's located at the foot of Pacific Heights and goes into a neighborhood called Cow Hollow and the Marina area. It's rather affluent as parishes go. The church was on the corner of Green and Steiner Streets, conveniently near my longtime Union Street watering holes. It's a beautiful church and over 100 years old.

Father Ken had been a deacon at Sacred Heart parish when I was living there in the early 1970s. The pastor was Irish and the parish was Black. We didn't know about African Americans at that time. I think it was said best by Burl Toler's son, when the University of San Francisco named a hall after his dad.

"When he played for the San Francisco Dons, he was colored, when he became an NFL referee, he was a Negro. When he became the principal of Benjamin Franklin Middle School, he was Black. And when he died, he was African American."

Oh yes, the Dons were probably the best college football team in the country in 1951, but the players refused a chance to play in the Orange Bowl because the people who ran the game wouldn't let them take the field with an African American on the team.

Ken was originally from Washington D.C. and moved here to serve the people of San Francisco. I'm not sure what kind of impact I had on him in those days, but he became one of the most influential priests in the archdiocese. I spoke to Father Ken about returning to the City when I learned that I would be leaving the beach. He was happy to welcome me back as a housemate and there was not the slightest hesitation about my relocation. My search for a place to live after I was de-beached ended with his courteous and generous invitation to move into his rectory.

It's not unusual when you live in the same house with someone and see them every day you don't see color, you don't hear accents, you don't feel any difference. It was not my expectation to, but people have asked me about it since my roots are in the South. The pastor and I have been friends for more than 40 years, since we lived at Sacred Heart parish with Father Dan Sullivan (RIP), a fire department chaplain, recovering alcoholic and a profound influence in my life. I had been at Sacred Heart two years when Ken arrived, the only African-American priest in the archdiocese at the time. I helped him adjust to the real world of parish life and now he kindly offered me hospitality during my waning years. He is pretty much the same guy that he was when I first got to know him. He is kind, loud, and direct, and if you can't understand what he says or means, it's your drawback, not his.

I had lived in St. Vincent de Paul parish before for a couple of years in the early 1980s, when the pastor was one Monsignor Colonel William Clasby. I wrote about him in my earlier book. If you recall, he was very loud and in charge, a burly monsignor who loved to bark orders. The former pastor, now deceased, fancied himself an architect and, by golly, he proved it. He remodeled the church inside and out and it's just a wonderful place to worship. The stained glass windows are exquisite (and befitting the setting, the complete opposite of those planned for my erstwhile seaside home) and the simplicity of everything else makes it easier to feel God's presence whether you're alone or with a community. Too often we overlook the underpinnings of a parish thinking that the altar is there, the crucifix and tabernacle are there and, like opening up your fingers when you were a little kid, it works. Remember that one? "Here is the church and here is the steeple, open the doors and here are the people." If you haven't seen this childhood classic, ask any old Catholic and surely they'll recall. I liked the church so much that I celebrated my 50th ordination anniversary there. I had some friends from another parish do the music and one of my nieces, Sheila, sang like an angel. Lots of friends and family came to celebrate, including my former housemate Cardinal William Levada.

Back to the Colonel. Once workers trimming the trees out front accidentally cut power to the rectory. It so happened that this *sacerdos magnus* (Latin for high priest or heavy priest or fat monsignor) had just boarded the sole mini skinny elevator to ascend to his third floor apartment. With an abrupt jerk the elevator stalled.

Mrs. Matteucci was the longtime long-suffering housekeeper who was cleaning up after the monsignor's lunch. I happened to be bounding down the stairs when I heard his desperate bellow for help. "Matteucci, get my big butt outta here!" "Father Harry," she asked, "What should I do?" I shrugged! Before words could come to my tongue, she blurted out that she would leave him in there a spell, if for no other reason than his sins or the poor souls in purgatory. She smiled quietly, after many years of hearing him yell. "Now, he's stuck between heaven and hell and I must seem like a goddess to him. I'm free and he's caged."

They both are now enjoying eternal life, probably still laughing about the time he was stuck in the elevator at St. Vincent de Paul.

Pragmatic as I was, I went outside to check with the linemen and tell them we had no power inside. Unlike Pope Francis, who recently experienced the same inconvenience and was stuck in a Vatican elevator for 25 minutes, the Colonel did not ask for a round of applause for his rescuers when the power was restored.

There was a young adult club at the parish and they called themselves the "Greensteiners". I remember one of my Jewish handball buddies responded to me when I said, maybe in a hurry, that I lived at Green and Steiner. "I didn't know we had a temple there. Is there a Saint Steiner?"

The first time I was living at St. Vincent de Paul, we were three priests in residence — himself and two assistants. One of them was Italian and I believe, as I write, the oldest priest in the archdiocese. (He has since passed.) The other passed away a long time ago. He had the Irish flu for many years. More than once I had to trudge the three flights to knock on his door to remind him that he had the 7:30 a.m. Mass and the people were waiting. When he peeked through the narrow slot in the door, I could see his bleary eyes and told him to go back to bed, I had no problem saying the Mass.

I recall listening to him preach once as he told the story of how he forgave a bishop who took him out of an assignment 20 years ago. He had harbored evil thoughts and had grown old with a hardened heart. He carried it around with him like a dark cloud for many years. At the bishop's deathbed he held his hand and said, "I forgive you." It was the ultimate catharsis for him and very impressive for all of us in the chapel listening to him unload.

One of God's greatest gifts to humankind is to be able to say we're sorry. It doesn't happen enough for some of us. The human species seems to harbor thoughts rather than let them float away with the tide and be forgotten.

I now occupy the room where that associate pastor once lived. Today, besides the pastor, Ken, there are three of us in residence at the parish, all retired, all working and all happy to be together. Both of the others also have served the Black community in previous assignments. One of them, Father Kirk, who is now in his mid-80s, served at Our Lady of Lourdes in the Bayview/Hunter's Point neighborhood for many, many years. The other, a Sulpician father, taught in seminaries in Zambia. Father Michael is my age. The rectory has a remarkably different atmosphere from when I lived there the first time — one of good humor, occasional laughter and each trying to help the other. It is a pleasant home. We're eager to support one another and rarely get bent out of shape about what comes along. We reinforce one another on a daily basis and give our pastor the same kind of respect and assistance we were given in our combined 155 years of service to the Church.

I read where the cucumber will be cool as long as it is connected to the vine, thus the saying "cool as a cucumber". I think our house is a bit like that. We all know that Ken is the pastor and we are happy to have a place to live where we can count on one another to pick each other up when there are falls. When you get to be 80, health is always a concern. Hearing, seeing and patience are cut short. All three of us were blessed by having lived in less than ideal circumstances, yet that time we spent has served us all well. We are now in a friendly, upscale neighborhood with a beautiful church in which to pray. Our needs for the most part are met or can be met, if we but ask. If you've never lived a blessing, this is one and still growing.

CHAPTER 3

Heyday

SACRED HEART WAS a mostly African-American parish in the 1970s, with a few gay couples whose dual incomes made them capable of restoring a number of the old Victorian homes that were in the neighborhood. Little by little the Black community sold their large homes and moved elsewhere. The City had become too expensive. It's a shame, as it changed the culture of the Fillmore and Fell neighborhood that had been theirs. San Francisco statistics put the Black community at about five percent of the total population within the 49 square miles; in the 1970s it was over 13%. Willie Brown, State Assemblyman and later the City's first African-American mayor, began many major projects in the neighborhood to help develop new homes and places where ordinary families could live. It was still a challenge and the Black population continued to fade.

Most of my life has been spent in areas where the African-American population was miniscule. In my hometown of Cape Girardeau, Missouri, we were stretching to reach 25,000 people when I left home and maybe five percent were Black, and they all lived in Smelterville, the area down by the river surrounding the cement plant. The Whites ventured into south Cape on occasion, drawn by the irresistible aroma emanating from the Blue

Hole barbecue joint. The quarries left behind from the cement operation eventually filled with water and the rib shack got its name from those crystalline swimming holes. There were no Black men in my St. Louis seminary, ditto for the one in Rome. At St. Agnes High School in Springfield, Missouri, where I taught when I was first a priest, there was exactly one Black family. And all of a sudden I found myself living in the middle of what could be called a ghetto but I never, ever felt it. It was a bit scary in the beginning when I had no place to park my car. I had to put it on the street where it was subjected to break-ins and scratches and an occasional towing.

The rectory of Sacred Heart was three stories and painted inside by very artistic and talented painters who also happened to be firemen. Most were recovering alcoholics who would stay with us for a time until the San Francisco Fire Department chaplain and my pastor, Father Dan Sullivan, would give them the okay to go back into service. While they were there, Father Dan would put them to work. It was beautifully decorated.

The basement was another story. The boys in the 'hood had a club and they met there regularly. They also had a pistol. Every now and then on a Sunday night while watching TV, I would hear the sound of a firearm being discharged. It wasn't happening at the football game on the tube, so it must be nearby. It was — target practice in the basement of the rectory for the boys who were learning how to shoot. Different pictures on the door would be marked with holes the next day, when I had the courage to go down and check it out. Angela Davis was one that I remember.

One particular leader, Marcellus by name, was really the master of controlling his crowd and when he finally went to jail, the whole neighborhood experienced a change. Whatever strong and demanding influence he had on all the kids dissipated when he was hauled off to incarceration. There were no longer the fears that once controlled so many actions. The Dominican Sisters who ran the school had a good reputation and were eager to discipline everyone, but I recall one of the sisters telling me that Marcellus was a special case and would probably end up in jail before he finished school. And so it was.

The longer I lived at Sacred Heart, the braver I got. I tore out a wall in the garage so I could angle my car into a safe place for the night. While cleaning out the room, I discovered that it was the former office for the Black Panthers. They once served free breakfast to children there at the invitation of the pastor, Father Eugene Boyle, an impassioned civil rights advocate of that time. Father Boyle championed the United Farmworkers, worked for fair housing and also welcomed Vietnam War protestors and labor activists into the church. He had a 1956 radio show on KCBS called *Underscore: Catholic Views in Review*, exploring church-state relations, social justice and civil rights. He beat me onto the airwaves by more than a decade. The Black Panthers also left some of their propaganda behind in the garage, like a coloring book that depicted police officers as pigs. It wasn't hard to figure out why, when the cops were called to that Fillmore address, they took their time.

There was a pay phone on the corner of the church. Some ladies of the night used to gather there and after a few weeks I said hello. One night I came home about 9:30 and it was drizzling and I struck up a conversation with a woman called Pat, whom I'd encountered before. It didn't last very long. She told me she could no longer speak to me. "See that man in the big Cadillac across the street?" she said pointing. I nodded. "Well, he says you are bad for business and to stay away from you."

Some years later I was serving as a chaplain on a *Cursillo de Cristianidad*, a retreat facilitated by 30 women for 30 other women. Numbers and genders varied but essentially it was the building of a community in a closed weekend atmosphere that allowed each participant to dig deeper into their personal lives and see how God fits in and how they fit in with each other. I have been chaplain (called Spirit) on a number of these retreats and they have always left me with more than I was ever able to give. While still forming the Cursillo team, we met at one of the retreat member's homes in San Francisco's Forest Hills neighborhood and this lady, sitting on the floor in the large living room of the beautiful house, began to tell the story of how she had been a drug addict, and a serious one. Then, in order to pay for her habit, she became a prostitute. She had on a thick turtleneck sweater and Levi's with sneakers. I will never forget her soft-spoken delivery as she narrated her early life and how she finally discovered that I AM, GOD IS, WE ARE. She detailed her years of addiction by saying, "One day I am okay, another day I am in the pits. One day God is there and I feel him, another day and he's in hiding somewhere."

Sometimes we are together, in sync, agreeable and willing to make sacrifices for each other in order to help one another live better lives. But this is not always the case. Too often selfishness rises to the top and along with the cream we see only ourselves. It's not the way Jesus was nor the way Christians should be.

As tears began to roll down her cheeks and several of the women offered her tissues, she looked directly at me across the room and said, "Hi Father Harry. Remember the man told me I couldn't talk to you because of our business? I'm Pat."

Sacred Heart church is now closed, a casualty of changing demographics and post-Loma Prieta earthquake building codes. It's a large yellow-brick structure at the corner of Fillmore and Fell. The bell tower, a City landmark, has a slight lean to it, as if at any time it may tumble onto the one-way Fell Street traffic heading west, all four lanes. The archdiocese was unable to retrofit it. The church was on the market for a number of years until a very generous Catholic stepped up and purchased it, along with the rectory, the school and the convent.

The philanthropist invited about 20 people to the upper room of a restaurant on Washington Square called Moose's (no longer there). I knew the owner, Ed Moose, from my Penny Pitch days at the Washbag (Washington Square Bar & Grill), his first North Beach restaurant just across the park from Moose's, his last. The San Francisco mayor Willie Brown said that Ed "was the ultimate tavern owner in a period when tavern owners were celebrities. He was part of the character of the City." Moose's was known for its characters and its celebrities and counted newsmen Walter Cronkite and Tom Brokaw, columnist Herb Caen and future Speaker of the House Nancy Pelosi among its regulars. When I arrived with my boss, then Archbishop Levada, we were ushered upstairs to a private dining room. There was our host, Fred Furth, smoking a rather large cigar and on a leash was his giant Great Dane. I said to Ed, "I thought smoking was not allowed in San Francisco restaurants and, uh, what about dogs?" He looked at me like I obviously didn't know our host. I really didn't at that time. "He could buy and sell me," said Ed, "so I might as well let him smoke. Besides, he has his own food for the dog."

During the course of the dinner we were all given a couple of minutes to introduce ourselves and after that Fred Furth spoke very briefly and to what I can't remember. I was still trying to breathe with all the smoke in the room. He was sitting next to the future cardinal and I saw him with pen in hand writing a check on the table. Archbishop Levada took it, didn't look, and put it in his pocket. We said our farewells and waited for the valet to bring the car. I drove. The archbishop reached in his pocket, looked at the check, gave a sigh, handed it to me and said, "Harry, make some calls in the morning and see exactly what this buys." I almost lost control of my Ford Escape as I entered the Broadway tunnel on the return trip to the cathedral: the check was for five million dollars.

Yes, the generous man bought all of Sacred Heart, lock, stock and barrel, and saved the archdiocese from a huge headache and the buildings from demolition. The convent became a home for battered women. The school became a campus of the Megan Furth Academy, named for his daughter who tragically died at 31 and serving the children of the Western Addition neighborhood. The church, hate to say it, but it never made it back to anything except a roller rink. The ceiling is still falling. In fact there is a net to catch the occasional piece of plaster that is eager to knock someone out. A roller rink, can you believe it? A couple of my priest friends went to dinner one night and then moseyed over to the former church to see if it was a fact. It was. It's known as the Church of 8 Wheels and bills itself as "a fellowship of people that celebrates life on wheels." Their "Holy Rollers" are dedicated to the spread of "Rolligion". I couldn't agree more when they say, "A church is not the building but the people."

The relentless plaster finally rendered the rink kaput and for now the sacred space is shuttered.

CHAPTER 4

Strangers I Have Known

CHARACTERS HAVE COME and gone in my life and for the most part they've left something of themselves for me to admire and improve my own lot. As some wise mind once remarked, "If you are bored with your lot in life, build a service station on it." That's what I've tried to do. Sometimes I am drawn to those who tell me they're bad and I just keep coming. Robert was one.

We met off Market Street one Friday afternoon, when we both discovered we were going to see the Oakland A's play at the Coliseum. Neither of us had wheels so we were going to take BART (Bay Area Rapid Transit). Robert kept his money in his boots. I don't know how much he had or what he was walking on but the buck seventy-five for BART made for a lot of change from his hondo. At the same time, he made fun of my black shoes saying they were just like prison issue. I didn't know it at our first meeting but later he revealed to me that he had done some hard time for gambling. I thought, "Gambling! You don't do time for gambling." So I expect I didn't get the whole story. It must have been something more because lots of people gamble. Our church basements are filled every week with people yelling "Bingo!"

I had tickets for the game from KNBR radio. It's the sports station now but back when I was doing a Sunday morning show there it was just a fun format with great on-air guys like Carter B. Smith, Mike Cleary and Frank Dill. My engineer at that time had been doing Giants games since the mid-'70s and just retired. Lee helped me grow in radio. He corrected me with kindness before something went to tape. Robert had his own ticket and it wasn't tough to get a good seat, as the Coliseum was built for football and the baseball team played second fiddle to the World Champion Oakland Raiders. So you know how times change. They are moving to Las Vegas. Oh well.

Robert and I usually would leave around the seventh inning, when a man with a handlebar mustache and all kinds of "stuff" came in to save the game. Rollie Fingers had everything a closer on a baseball team needs, plus an impressive 'stache. If you had a bet and the A's were ahead in the seventh, it was a cinch you'd be a winner. "Here comes the fingered man, let's hit BART." It didn't take many of these trips to tighten our friendship.

It wasn't long before I had Robert going to Mass on Sunday. I even got a couple of dates for him with nice Catholic girls. That was a mistake. One of them said "never again". Don't call me, I'll call you. The other never talked to me again. So no more blind dates for my buddy Robert. Eventually he found a wonderful lady and they moved in together but it wasn't before he hit me up for some cash. I had it, in the bank. I really cared for him and grubbed him during a bad streak. I'll never forget the day he called to say he wanted to repay me. We met on the corner of Gough and Market. Used to be a bar there that served lunch. We stood at the bar, ordered a beer, and he leans over to the familiar black boot and pulls out ten hondos, slips them in my jacket pocket and says, "We're good, right?" I sighed deeply and agreed, "We're good."

So it turns out that Robert was from the East and had a college scholarship in basketball. He found it easier to sell drugs than to go to practice and do the hard work required to be a college athlete. He was kicked off the team, never finished college and had been working the streets ever since. I didn't see him for a while and then discovered him in a small bar on Polk Street. He was serving his girlfriend, when I came in with a couple of my guests from the taping we had just finished at KRON-TV. I still had makeup on as he again gave me the once over and the mocking laugh for looking so strange.

It was getting late and my guests had long gone; the neighborhood was not the best. I offered to give his girlfriend a ride. "No thanks. I'll get her a taxi, if you leave a gratuity on the bar," he replied. I tried again. "What do you say I don't leave a gratuity and just give the poor girl a ride?" It was not far. Robert had an engaging way about him and his smile made you feel like the next Andrew Jackson you pulled from your pocket was going to be his in the end.

Early one morning he phoned me and asked if I would take him to the airport. He said someone had taken a shot at him. By that time he was making book — and not with the approval of whoever approves those things — and he was frightened for his life. He showed up with no luggage, nothing except a small paper bag. When we left Sacred Heart where I lived, he asked me to go around the block a couple of times before going to the airport. He wanted to make sure we were not being followed. I did as he said.

At SFO, I parked and walked in with him. He never told me where he was going or what he was going to do. He didn't want me to know what was in the paper bag but I presumed his boots were full of cash and he had no other place to stuff bills. Robert was tall and skinny and had that New York flip to his speech which always made you feel that he was one up on everyone, no matter who it was. It's a New York thing. You have to live there to get it. What's the guy in the leather jacket from Jersey always saying? "Fuggedaboutit!" I shook Robert's hand and watched him walk down the ramp to a flight to somewhere where they wouldn't want to kill him.

It was a couple years later when I had a call from a woman in upstate New York telling me she was Robert's mother. She wanted to thank me for all I did for him while he was in California. *What? Did for him?* "You were his friend," she said, "and you were the only one he talked about when I last saw him."

So what did I learn from my friend Robert? Maybe some things about life on the streets, or what not to do for a living, or simply how to befriend someone who didn't have the same family values and strong resolve to do the right thing. There is no right way to do a wrong thing. There are many Roberts running around and I'm sure you'll meet one or two on your journey. Friendship is more important to a poor hustler than hustling for a living. The hustle is not really life.

CHAPTER 5

Surprise, Surprise, Surprise

KYUU-FM was an NBC radio affiliate in San Francisco from 1978 to 1988. During my time there, it was located down by the wharf across from Pier 23. The "ON AIR" booth was all glass and on the second floor, where you could look out and see the motorcycle cop hiding behind a red brick building waiting for someone to run the red light. When I was on air I used to announce, "Hey motorists, if you're listening to me and you're driving north on the Embarcadero, make sure you stop at that light off Greenwich. There's a motorcycle guy waiting for you to run it. If you hear me, honk your horn. I'm behind the glass here at KYUU-FM just trying to help." Once in a while I would hear the beep and knew that someone was listening. I did Saturday mornings from six to nine and Sunday evenings from nine to midnight. I had a lot of freedom and the show sold commercials so I thought everyone was happy.

One Tuesday John, the general manager, asked me to come in to see him. I liked him. He was originally from Buffalo, New York, and didn't have a problem with a priest being on the radio. There was both good news and bad news that he had to deliver. "Father Harry, the NBC FM network has decided to streamline its Sunday night programming, so I'll have to cancel your Sunday show. However, we love you and hope you will stay with us for the Saturday morning stint." I wasn't sure what streamlining meant but I soon found out.

So I retired from KYUU, as I didn't think just the Saturday morning was worth the preparation and the trouble. You can imagine my anxiety and curiosity the following Sunday night as I'm driving in my car with the radio on. I had no idea what NBC had done to change the programming. So I'm on pins and needles eager to know who is taking my place. Finally, nine o'clock comes around and on comes the voice of a little old lady with a German accent to talk about sex.

Yeah, sex! In her thick Teutonic intonation she asked the first question to her listeners who were calling in from all over the country, "Now honey, where was the most unusual place you ever 'did it'?" Dr. Ruth Westheimer, the groundbreaking sex therapist broadcaster, approved of the caller's response. "The kitchen table is certainly what I would call an unusual place. Thank you, dear."

As Johnny Carson used to quip, anyone who could pass as your grandmother can certainly talk about anything she wants on his show or on the airwaves. He wasn't going to correct them. I drove slowly home and parked my car. Sat in the silence of the front seat and tried to be thankful for the years I'd had at KYUU and that I didn't have to "streamline" my show. Just the Sunday night before I had interviewed the Temptations, who were performing at the Fairmont Hotel. After that I interviewed a charity organization in Berkeley. Now my audience was getting a sex doctor who is streamlining her grandmother voice into the many cars and radios wanting to know who Father Harry might be featuring this week. Oh no, the kitchen table! Fuggedaboutit!

CHAPTER 6

Spike Heels and Confession

I WAS AN ordained priest for just about three months when the pastor of a huge parish around EUR, a new area for living and working outside of Rome, invited me to hear confessions before the Mass on Easter Sunday. We Catholics have a thing called the "Easter duty" that traditionally requires one to make a confession annually. I had heard confessions just two times before, once in English and once in Italian. I was nervous but made my way by train to this beautiful church. It was packed. There were four priests hearing confessions. Two of us were seated on simple foldout chairs with small screens separating us from the penitents. I did not rate the small enclosed confessional box, as the older more experienced priests occupied them.

Dressed in my full priestly regalia, I took my seat and waited for people to reconcile with God. After a number of penitents had come and gone, I was feeling pretty confident with my rookie ministry. My stumbling speech, fear of the unknown and general anxiety were just about gone when along came The Challenge.

I tried to keep my eyes subdued or closed (*custodia occulorum*) as we were taught, because others in the back of the church could see what was happening. I heard the click, click, click of very high heels, maybe spike heels, or at least shoes with a slight, sensuous beat on the marble floors in the House of God. The noise halted at the base of the screen on the other side of my chair. My olfactory curiosity was the first to respond. Wow! Whoever it is certainly has used the full complement of fragrance for the day. I don't know perfumes at all, but this was strong enough to melt the air and I hoped it would not get on me, even from her to my confessional ear. I suspected that it was probably a lady of the evening and I was hoping the Spirit would provide me with the correct vocabulary in order to give her the advice and inspiration she needed to make a good confession. After she knelt down and I made the sign of the cross on the opposite side of the screen, she began with the customary, "Bless me Father for I have sinned."

All went well and my fears dissipated, as I fully understood what she said and the kind of life she was leading. After the final absolution, I gave her penance (some prayers to say) and invited her to make an act of contrition (another prayer). Following the rite of the sacrament, I told her to go in peace and then opened my eyes. At least a dozen or so men were staring directly at me. Even though I knew none of them, I could not help but believe that they were all anxious that this wonderful, thoughtful lady might have confessed her association with one or more of these fine gentlemen looking on. Or maybe it was just the person wearing the clicking heels with the air of her perfume wafting across the rear of the church that made them look. Of course, I'll never know. But even today, after over 50 years, sitting in the confessional box at St. Vincent de Paul's, sometimes I hear the click of the heels and smell the perfume.

CHAPTER 7

Green Fever

THIS COULD BE chalked up as my most famous yet most unsuccessful fundraiser. It was an original idea to raise money for charity and in particular for the aged in the city of San Francisco. We selected the night before Saint Patrick's Day for the event and called it Green Fever.

It was when disco was at its peak and a young couple named Gary and Gloria Poole had just won Dick Clark's American Bandstand Disco Dance Competition on ABC television. They were teenage brother and sister dancers and a hot commodity. They had been guests on my television show on KRON, along with an elderly couple who were trying to raise money for food and clothing for their brothers and sisters who were living in poverty. It seemed like a good fit and so I asked my colleague Jim Swanson if he would assist me as the producer to make it happen. We had no money to offset the expense but were doing the whole thing on the come. If you're a dice player, that may mean something. We met with the Pooles and their parents and tried to come to an understanding of the finances and what their part was going to be. We agreed to pay them if there was a profit. This was my first major fundraiser in the City and I honestly was all fired up about something I knew little about.

I had my TV show for publicity and we had several well-known figures who were willing to help us out. We booked a large venue, Showplace Square. It was perfect. We had to pay for that up front. We would have a dance contest as well as entertainment from Gary and Gloria.

We gave away a trip to Ireland with two lovely Aer Lingus flight attendants on hand to draw the winning names. I worked with an owner of a liquor store who provided the spirits and personnel to run a bar that turned out to be busy all night. They were elbow to elbow waiting for drinks. You can imagine my surprise when I went to collect our profits and was told there were none. The man said by the time he paid all his help and added the figures for the drinks there was zero profit. I was pretty sure it wasn't an honest statement. I couldn't believe it and I still can't. I believe he took advantage of a young priest who really had never dealt with this kind of action. I would like to say I learned a lesson.

Okay, so here I am, packed house, bar overflowing, great music and dancing, sweet trip to Ireland and the profit doesn't show up. It gets worse. The dance contest was won by a couple over 65 who were very happy to accept their prize of a week in Tahoe, with spa and salon expenses, as well as a few other small things that I had begged for along the way. They received a grand round of applause and were bursting with excitement at their winnings. Little did I know that Gary Poole also promised them a cash gift of $500. He took the cash from the gate to pay his dancers, makeup artists and others who I believe used it to celebrate after their performance.

The next day when I went to see Gary and Gloria in their flat across from the Tenderloin park, I was met by the sister who said Gary was ill and had used all the cash to pay his people . . . whoever they were. She was doped up and didn't make much sense. So, now I'm two down and only one to go. Thanks to an elderly gentleman named Larry who took the cash that was left over home with him, there was something to give to the poor.

Now back to the couple who won the dance contest. I received a letter from an attorney suing me for non-payment of $500 that was promised them the night of the event. Yes, they did go to Tahoe and, yes, they accepted all the perks we had given them and, no, they were not satisfied with what they had. It was a problem for the archdiocese, as I had to appear and defend what I had done because of the lawsuit. I also had to go to court and face the judge. I told him I didn't have that kind of money and admitted it was my fault, as I had no control over the man on stage with the microphone making promises I couldn't keep. "I'm sorry your honor but you can't get blood out of a turnip."

"Father, you'll have to do something," said the judge. "I suggest you send them $25 dollars a month until the $500 is paid in full. The check writing itself will be a good lesson for you not to expose yourself to such a predicament." Thank you, your honor. Case dismissed.

I wrote that check begrudgingly for almost six months. I never saw nor heard about the couple again. Finally, I just quit writing the checks. Let them come after me. I'll go to jail. All of this occurred 40 years ago. I'm still waiting for a call that I owe them more.

CHAPTER 8

Trick or Treat

I'VE LOVED TRAVELLING by ship ever since my very first trip in 1961, when I took the *SS Cristoforo Colombo* from New York to Naples, Italy, en route to attending college in Rome. It was exciting to be on the high seas, miles from nowhere, bobbing up and down to the rhythm of the water. Since then I've had other opportunities to sail on ocean liners, but I have to write about the most memorable cruise that I never took.

Some years back I signed up to be the chaplain on a cruise ship. My only obligations were to say Mass on Sunday and hold a Protestant service the same day. I did a lot of writing on my first book on that cruise. It was fun, relaxing, spiritually fulfilling and I would do it again. So the next year in April I signed up to be a chaplain for a Halloween cruise that was to leave from San Diego at the end of October. It was a Mexican Riviera cruise, so the temperatures would be good and perhaps I could use the time to begin writing a follow-up to my first work.

Summer went and fall arrived and soon I was in my car driving from San Francisco to San Diego. Since it's more than an 11-hour drive, I thought I would spend a night along the way. But I felt good, the weather was lovely, the radio entertainment was excellent and I knew that I would be on the sea for five days with an easy, predictable routine, so I pressed on. I arrived in San Diego in late afternoon and checked into a Best Western, just blocks from the docked ship.

I was to board the next morning. I took my time, parked my car in the lot provided for those on the cruise and wheeled my bags to the first checkpoint. The security guard looked at my passport and my black suit and collar and asked if I was sure this was my cruise.

"Why do you ask? Of course I'm sure. See my ticket? I'm the Catholic chaplain for the cruise." At any rate, that's who I thought I was and what I was supposed to be doing. I checked my bags and proceeded to the first line. I showed my credentials, went through the metal detector and for the first time noticed a large group of gay men conversing about sneaking alcohol in their luggage and taking a chance on being detected. "They can only take it away," rationalized one young man. "What's the concern?"

I went into the large rotunda where there were hundreds of passengers waiting to get their room assignments and their ID cards that would give them buying privileges. My eyes began to widen as I surveyed the large crowd, not seeing a single female nor a child. Well it is October, kids are in school but women and wives are not. Hmmmm . . . I sat down for a few minutes and wondered if I would have to wait in these long lines. After all, I was the chaplain and I did have certain privileges.

So I inquired from one of the hosts who took me through a side door and down to the crew entrance. Along the way, I noticed three African-American women going through the rotunda. I thought, "This could be the Supremes or look-alikes for the ship's entertainment." I waited on the dock for about 30 minutes in the hot sun. My black suit was soaking up the rays and causing my armpits to be soaked. A very kind lady security guard offered me her chair in the shade. She didn't have to, but did, and it felt good to see such kindness around the ship. Finally, the purser came down the plank and approached me in a very serious manner.

"I'm sorry, Father, but there is no room for you on the ship." I was told that this charter was a gay men's cruise and they didn't order a Catholic chaplain. I thought to myself, "Thank you Jesus." Then I showed him my ticket and told him how frustrating my day had been and it wasn't yet 1:00 pm. He apologized profusely and said there must be some mistake. Duh!

Did I mention that Halloween would be celebrated aboard ship? I could just imagine how much this chaplain would have been photographed aboard a gay men's cruise. I also imagined that I would have had to declare my straightness more than a few times. I learned that from Paul Lynde when we had breakfast together after the ABC morning show in Chicago around 1973. The show's producers had warned me that he was gay and would be wanting more than conversation over a plate of bacon and eggs. But Paul Lynde was so charming and funny, and I thought I was funny, so I went with him anyway. When he came on to me, it took more than a few tries before he was convinced that I was straight.

So I thanked the purser for his trouble and asked for a favor. "My two bags are probably in storage somewhere and I would really appreciate it they were returned to me this afternoon before you sail." He said he didn't think it was possible but he would try. A lady came down to show me to a waiting room where I could pray for the safe return of my bags. After two hours waiting and just about 15 minutes before the ship sailed, here comes a porter wheeling my two bags. I gave another thank you to him with a tip and another "Thank you Jesus!" and made my way off the docks, past my friend the security guard (the same one who questioned me about this trip when I first entered the gate to the dock), who simply smiled. For some reason, he already knew there was no room for a Catholic chaplain on this cruise.

CHAPTER 9

Eve of Destruction

OF ALL THE musicians I've known or interviewed over the years, none was more enlightening than Barry McGuire. He was cast on Broadway in *Hair*, a musical performed mostly in the nude and by people who were for the most part doing serious drugs. It was an unusual hit and so gained notice and fame for many of the cast. After that Barry became a traveling musician appearing wherever he could get booked. He had one solid hit over the years that was played by most radio stations called *Eve Of Destruction*. It was during the time of the Vietnam War and just to introduce or re-acquaint you here are the lyrics:

"The eastern world, it is explodin',
Violence flarin', bullets loadin',
You're old enough to kill but not for votin',
You don't believe in war, but what's that gun you're totin',
And even the Jordan River has bodies floatin',
But you tell me over and over and over again my friend,
Ah, you don't believe we're on the eve of destruction.
Don't you understand, what I'm trying to say?
And can't you feel the fears I'm feeling today?
If the button is pushed, there's no runnin' away,

There'll be no one to save with the world in a grave,
Take a look around you, boy, it's bound to scare you, boy,
And you tell me over and over and over again my friend,
Ah, you don't believe we're on the eve of destruction.
Yeah, my blood's so mad, feels like coagulatin',
I'm sittin' here, just contemplatin',
I can't twist the truth, it knows no regulation,
Handful of Senators don't pass legislation,
And marches alone can't bring integration,
When human respect is disintegratin',
This whole crazy world is just too frustratin',
And you tell me over and over and over again my friend,
Ah, you don't believe we're on the eve of destruction.
Think of all the hate there is in Red China!
Then take a look around to Selma, Alabama!
Ah, you may leave here, for four days in space,
But when your return, it's the same old place,
The poundin' of the drums, the pride and disgrace,
You can bury your dead, but don't leave a trace,
Hate your next door neighbor, but don't forget to say grace,
And you tell me over and over and over and over again my friend,
You don't believe we're on the eve of destruction.
No, no, you don't believe we're on the eve of destruction."

℗ 1965 UMG Recordings, Inc. Producer: Lou Adler
Producer: Barry McGuire Composer Lyricist: P.F. Sloan

I ran into Barry McGuire again at the Sonoma County Fair. He was a headliner for a Jesus concert and now a self-described Jesus freak. He had worked and performed with the likes of Janis Joplin, Jimmy Hendrix and Mama Cass. They're all dead. He had this to say: "I did the same drugs, drank the same booze, lived the same kind of life on the run and I'm still here. I'm not sure why, except that I went to a shrink one day and was waiting in the lobby and I picked up this paperback called *The Way*. It was the New Testament of the Bible. I had tried various institutions and gimmicks to overcome my drug and alcohol problems. After *I'm OK—You're OK*, it was transcendental meditation and the Maharishi Mahesh Yogi, who took credit for putting the Beatles back on the right road. I used every other form of drug I could in order to realize who I was and what I was supposed to do in life. I read and re-read *The Way* and discovered for myself for the first time that JESUS REALLY IS WHO HE SAYS HE IS."

Barry McGuire's words still ring true today and are just as meaningful. We can say many things about our individual journey but more than a few of us have been slapped upside the head.

Maybe, God does work in mysterious ways. I'm living proof of that as I go about my work today. I was just reflecting about my colon cancer, stage four, in 2012. By the use of miracle drugs and doctors who know what they're doing and researchers who put in long hours looking through microscopes and shaking millions of test tubes and (trumpet blast) a drug that allows me to put in this many more years in the Lord's Vineyard having the opportunity to move so many more people closer to the Almighty. I smile as I walk the streets of Cow Hollow and the Chestnut many years after close friends have been called and turned in their life-in-this-world badges.

CHAPTER 10

Family Man

MY DAD PASSED when I was 14 and Mom went to God just after my 21st birthday. I knew them both well enough to appreciate what it took for them to have a family and to work to make it a good one. Besides growing up in a home with outstanding parents, I was also blessed with a sister and two brothers. Both my brothers also have died but they left me lots of nephews and nieces, as has my sister, who survived cancer. I love them all and have had special bonds with a number of them. None lives close to me so it's a matter of visits and reunions that bring us together to laugh and celebrate life. It means a lot to all of us to come together as family whether the occasion is happy or sad. The memorial for my brother-in-law, Pete Darling, in Martha's Vineyard, Massachusetts, was the last reunion, as he was laid to rest after 87 years of life. My dear sister has set aside her grief now and adjusted quite well in her new condo near her children and grandchildren.

Shortly after Vatican II had concluded the 1965 session, I had thought, as a newly ordained priest at the North American College in Rome, I was going back to Southern Missouri to be an associate pastor for a time and then would have the privilege of receiving the sacrament of matrimony and soon have a family of my own.

I believe that I've become a poor replacement for both my brothers, as their children's children did not get to experience Charlie and Johnny as grandfathers for very long. I accept that vicarious position as a compliment. It has been such a joy to celebrate Mass in their homes, to officiate at their marriages and to baptize their children, even to the point where at last I was titled great-great Uncle Harry.

I could write quite a bit about nephews and nieces but not all of them. Some I know better than others and it's like doing a fundraiser and having to thank all the volunteers who helped. Surely you will overlook or forget one or something they did and it throws a pall over the event itself. My memoir, *I'll Never Tell*, highlighted a few of their lives but without much detail. Here's a story I thought would be helpful for any of you who have had your reputation ruined or have been the victim of false accusation.

It's as if it happened yesterday. I was driving from San Francisco to Pajaro Dunes near Castroville to visit the Murphy family on New Year's Day 1994. Ben and Noreen and their seven children vacationed there every year. I knew Ben from handball and Noreen was the school principal at Holy Name parish in the Sunset district where I lived in the early 1990s. They'd rented a house on the beach and all the kids and grandkids were surfers. Their son Marty was a pro and could teach the others all he knew, and he did. My pager buzzed and I was surprised that my brother-in-law, Pete, was trying to reach me. I had to pull off the road and find a phone booth to call him. I felt that warm flush spread over my body and the beginning of nausea when he told me that his youngest son had been accused of rape and arrested.

The night before, on New Year's Eve, the lobster plant where my nephew worked had closed early and the employees were celebrating the arrival of 1994 with drink. If any of you have been around fishermen or you've watched the movie *Perfect Storm* or seen the TV series *Dangerous Catch*, you know what I'm talking about. It's a very difficult life and is filled with danger. The high seas are not to be taken lightly by anyone. Fishermen work hard and play harder. When it was time to go home, my nephew called a taxi. The driver was female and she had driven him before, but this time she invited him to sit beside her up front. When they arrived at his apartment there was kissing and petting in the front seat. He realized the compromising position that he found himself in, exited the taxi and went into his apartment and immediately to bed.

He was awakened in the middle of the night by the local police who, after inquiring about his taxi ride, said he was wanted for assault and rape. He spent a few months behind bars before the trial. It didn't end well as the lady taxi driver presented her torn shirt as evidence. Her boyfriend had recently been released from prison and thought my nephew would be a likely victim for a plan to get rich quick, as they knew he came from a good family and a close family who would play ball in order to protect their son.

It was a quick trial and the judge found my nephew guilty of assault but innocent of rape. He spent a short time in jail and months in therapy and counseling. He gave up drinking and has since not touched a drop. He has gone through years of reporting as a sex offender. He still gets nervous if he sees a police car. He has not been able to have a good relationship with a woman. He told me that he had one serious relationship with a neighbor woman, who served in the military and who, when she discovered that he had a record, ended the affair. He didn't even know that the law had come to his place to check on him because there was a sex crime in the area. Since he was not at home, they inquired from his neighbor, his friend, and now she knew.

Thanks be to God he has been able to adjust to life even though lonely and filled with fear. It just doesn't seem fair. Where was our God in all of this? How can you not get to the truth of a scam? What a way to bring in the New Year! He knows his drinking was the cause of his misfortune and he has apologized to all concerned. But the fact remains that he was falsely accused.

It reminds me of the story of Joakim's wife Susanna (Daniel 13), when the two judges watched her bathe naked and then tried to have intercourse with her. She refused and they accused her of adultery. When they went to court, the wise judge separated them one from the other and inquired under which tree in the garden did they have illicit relations. They were unable to get their story straight and when faced with the question one said oak and the other mastic. The judge Daniel dismissed the case against Susanna and punished the lying falsely accusing judges so that they were put to death.

Father Harry has listened to many tales of woe, particularly from those behind bars who are all innocent. But it's a whole new set of feelings that come into play when it's Uncle Harry and a nephew.

The next story was a major tragedy in the state of Florida. The plane had been cleared for takeoff after waiting some hours in Tallahassee. But then the small airplane went down in the Gulf of Mexico with an experienced pilot, a medical doctor and his passenger (also a pilot), as they were returning from a football game between the Seminoles and the Gators.

My phone rang in the middle of the night, as my nephew began crying and relating the incident that had occurred that early evening. He begged me to storm the heavens and implore the Almighty to spare his son. I got alongside of the bed and was going to the chapel in the Archbishop's residence where I lived and felt so stunned that I just knelt there. I prayed and I prayed that my 28-year-old great-nephew would be found and rescued. After a full search by the Coast Guard, the action was not search and rescue but search and recovery. Some remnants of Zach's pants with his wallet were discovered in the area where the storm had not yet subsided. It was a major shock to the family and it's a mention that still brings tears to the eyes of his father on any occasion when it's talked about.

I flew to Florida to have the funeral and I recall some of the thoughts that I had of my great-nephew, whom I never really got to know as an adult. This was my eulogy. Again, it's Father Harry speaking to his family and friends as Uncle Harry.

God's resources are greater than our needs. "I will not reject anyone who comes to me, because I come from heaven," says Jesus. We are all resources to each other in great times of tragedy, like the loss of Zachary Blain Schlitt. In all relationships, we should be looking for God. Now we look to each other, as God has provided us close family and friends.

Zach had a great zest for life. It was always high on his menu, which also included any and all things on the menu. I recall taking him to a ballgame when he was very young. I promised him I would pay for whatever he ate. It cost me over $100 that afternoon. Another time in southern Missouri it was all you can eat frog legs. I was spared a huge tab, as it was a church dinner where they only hit you once for a donation. They could not have enjoyed any more than the rest of us how many frog legs this little guy could eat. We expected him to hop home.

His Mom was his best friend and he would telephone her almost every day. She wrote this about him for the funeral:

"The warmth of your loving hands, the happiness of your constant smile, the joy of your unequivocal love, the peace of your intuitive spirit, will forever fill my heart. I love you Zach. I know that your protective arms are wrapped around me always. Mom"

His Dad had similar tender words:

"Zachary, you have been my companion since your birth. You brought energy and excitement to every day. I taught you to tie your shoes, to hunt, to fish. You taught me to see the good in all people. You were with me through many adventures. Lost in a swamp, hunting in South America, comforting me after our motorcycle crash until help arrived. I only wish that I had been with you to guide that last flight home. I love you. Dad"

Every child is a blessing to its family. Benedictum *in Latin means "well said". For 28 years, Zach was a blessing on earth for his family. But blessings last forever and all of us can now cherish what a blessing he was to all.*

In football, which he loved, there is the huddle. Its purpose is to get information, to form a plan, security, to make sure all are protected from the other team, and inspiration, to do the right thing that will inspire a win. Helplessly, we huddle to memorialize a good man, a young man, a man of worth and promise. God's resources are greater than our needs. Amen.

Those of you who know me know how much I would have loved to have children, a family, and especially grandchildren. I thought all of that might be possible down the line in 1964 when I was ordained a priest. It didn't happen and that's that but it still pulls at my heartstrings when I see the beauty and the love that families have for one another. It's bigger than life and more interesting than a fairytale because it's real. Such a family as this, I'll never know.

CHAPTER 11

Janikins

IT WAS A scorcher in Sonoma County on the Fourth of July weekend when about 35 of us were making a three-day retreat at the Silver Penny Farm. There was a pool and I spent most of the afternoon in the water. Jan and I were talking when she said, "You have a little black mark on your chest and it should be looked at." I knew she was the daughter of a doctor, so I believed her but like most men did nothing about it. It was smaller than a cigarette burn but obviously not that. About two weeks later she called to tell me that she was making an appointment for me with my doctor, whom she knew, to have him take a biopsy and check it out.

So she does, I do, and Dr. Jim tells me if it had gone a week or two more and into my lymph nodes, we would not be sitting here today. Thank God, thank Jan, it was caught and removed in time. He cut one piece one day and had me return the next for a second cut, much deeper into the flesh. So the score was one save for Jan and one giant thank you from me.

Knowing the history of cancer in my family, both parents and all three siblings, Jan once again encouraged me to go to my doctor and see about a colonoscopy. I went on Tuesday and the following Friday I was scheduled for major surgery of the colon.

The doctor removed several inches of it and said I was good to go but suggested I go see an oncologist to get another opinion. After looking more closely at the biopsy, it was decided that I should have extended chemotherapy for six months just to make sure.

As an aside, the oncologist was Japanese by birth and when I went for my first interview he inquired if I had ever lived by the Mississippi River. Strange question from this man. "Why yes, I grew up on the river in Cape Girardeau," I replied, "and spent a lot of time boating and water skiing on the Mississippi." He said he asked all his patients the same question because he felt there might be some correlation. I then told him a bit of the family history and his quirky hunch was verified by yet another person. I haven't done any research but in the years gone by almost every major company in St. Louis (like chemical companies) deposited their waste materials directly into the river and felt that it would purify itself on its way to New Orleans and eventually the ocean. Little did they know nor care about stiffs like me just wanting to cool off in any body of water in the summer.

So, there I was every Tuesday morning in the Wellness Center at St. Mary's Hospital hooked up to IVs through the port in my neck. From early morn till late afternoon I was being infused. After the last batch of poison, they gave me a canister and a little shoulder strap carrier knitted by former patients to carry around with me until Thursday, when I would return to have it exported and then freedom for a week and a half. Sleeping with a beer can of poison gives one pause for serious thought. I was always afraid it would pull out, so I really didn't sleep well Tuesday or Wednesday. I was lower than whale waste following the infusion, as I was subject to neuropathy, diarrhea and not much taste for foods. But hey, it did the trick and I'm here to talk about it.

Janikins, as her 4'5"Aunt Betty called her, became a very close friend. She picked me up and took me to every infusion session in spite of her boss at the chancery office complaining and constantly checking up on her. She listened to the doctors and nurses and knew what I needed. Over the years we have grown to be as close as a priest can be to another.

At one point neuropathy set in from the drug called Oxaliplatin. It was a particularly insidious poison that numbed my fingers and toes. I could not pick up anything cold and even cold water from the tap shot electrical shocks up my arms. I got to the point where I had to wear gloves to pick up almost anything. The toes were another problem but there was not much I could do about them. I wasn't wearing shoes anyway because I couldn't really walk anywhere. It was 47 steps from the front door at the old rectory of the Shrine of Saint Francis where I was living. I was on the third floor that had been renovated by the priest who took my place at the chancery office. It was a very nice suite and comfortable, just noisy from the late night crowds of North Beach spilling out of the bars and nightclubs. More than a few times I was awakened by a barrage of verbal abuse aimed at one party or another and filthy language that penetrated the walls of the church.

Jan was not only my nurse through all this but was my medical advocate, which I now believe that everyone should have. So hats off to all those who have been given a sidebar ministry to care for the sick. If you check the dedication in my memoir, you'll see that it goes to Jan for twice saving my life. I really believe it!

I got to know Jan at St. Gabriel's parish where I was the pastor, as she and Sister Bernice Garcia did the prep work for the second graders for first reconciliation and communion. They were a great team and it was always a treat to see the little guys and gals come all dressed up to ask for forgiveness and receive the body and blood of Christ. One little guy from a poor family didn't have a white shirt and he was the only one. So, Jan sent me to my room before Mass and I selected one for him that I thought I had outgrown. They rolled the sleeves back, attached rubber bands and taped four inches of the collar and voilà, he had a white shirt like every other boy. He was so proud of it. I lost a shirt that day but gained a first communicant as a friend.

* * *

I got closer to Jan when she saw me right before a funeral service and said that she had never received her mother's ashes after her funeral. "Could you please ask Mr. Duggan the funeral director to search for them?" No problem. A week later at another funeral at the parish Mr. Duggan says to me, "Oh that urn of ashes for the mother of your friend. It's in the front seat of the hearse. I'll get it for you." After we returned from the burial at the cemetery, I took the urn and on my way to the rectory I spotted Ms. Jan on the playground with her second graders.

Not thinking about the emotion connected to the ashes of your dead mother, I approached her and presented to her this small package with a cover over it. "The mortuary found your mother's ashes." I handed the urn to her and she fled into the school asking her assistant to take over. It wasn't until later I discovered how traumatic this was for her. She still has not established a permanent place for the ashes. Her eldest daughter once remarked, tongue in cheek, that Grandma was in the basement, not with the regular wine collection but on a case of premium vintage.

Jan has made it possible for me to do so many good and helpful things to and for people who have followed the Catholic TV Mass, which she produces. It reaches over 35,000 people each Sunday. That's a pretty big "parish" by any standard. I have witnessed the marriage of one of Jan's daughters and baptized most of her grandchildren. She continues to help make the God Squad viable and successful. She manages all the mail and deals with the phone calls from the television Mass viewers. It's a labor of love, along with all the other tasks she undertakes on behalf of the production team and me.

It's no wonder that I have asked her to take care of me when it's time to go into a retirement home or have the kind of home care that I will not be able to get in a rectory of unwed fathers. Of course, God's plans are not always our plans. But I'm trying to make it easy on everyone when it's my turn to hand over the keys and prepare to meet my Maker.

CHAPTER 12

"I Do"

IT USUALLY GETS a great laugh at a baptism, when two young people are the godparents for a friend's child and they are already making eyes at one another. The priest says something to this effect, "Do you promise to help the parents of this child carry out their responsibilities as parents?" The answer is, of course, "I do." I always check the male first to see if he is squirming at all then I say, "Don't worry, Jack, it's not the vow of matrimony." That usually helps everyone relax.

It's been a common thread of conversation, when I talk about marriage, that most think since I was not married I know little or nothing about it. My usual answer is that they have only one marriage. I get exposed to the problems and quirks of many. "You're married to one woman, I've been conversant with hundreds of wives." You don't have to have cancer to understand how debilitating it is or what it takes to survive it. As a priest, you can't solve all marital problems, but like any of us you can be empathetic and hopeful for them.

Over the years I've had some unusual experiences when witnessing the marriage vows. This is one sacrament in the Church that a priest only witnesses, just like parents, relatives, family and friends. We're all there like parsley, just plate dressing for the main dish. It's the couple themselves who administer the sacrament to each other when they say, "I do." It's more than just crossword filler when the words are spoken. It's a contract, a promise, a vow and it's made not to be broken. We all know how that works, especially in California. Sometimes, I even stand out with the congregation and have the couple look at me as we all listen to their vows.

Marriages are too often just "done" not celebrated. There are too few opportunities in life to demonstrate how we all feel about love and the solemn commitment that two people make to go from one and one, to a couple. It has been one of the high points of my priesthood. And I say that having had to calm down mothers; insist that no one drink before the ceremony; toss the photographer out of the sanctuary; send the flower girl back to her mother (wherever she might be — one of the mothers I'm sure was hiding after the performance of her little cutie); tell everyone to turn off their phones, and ask a young man and his girlfriend to leave the church if they must dispute their love for each other in God's house. You get the drift. Marriages are not always celebrations of love.

Planning is the key to a successful wedding. We know that weddings are brief and marriages are forever. It's the first part that I have had experience with. People still say, "What do you know about marriage?" But believe me, in the counseling process, filling out papers for the preparation and, for a number of years, being the chaplain for Engaged Encounter (a prerequisite for Catholic marriage), I can say that I've pretty much heard most of what can be expected of two people preparing to tie the knot.

When I was broadcasting in San Francisco and people knew me from the airwaves, it was not unusual for me to get calls from all over, asking if I could perform at their marriage party. All the words were wrong so I had a clue. I didn't perform as much as witness. I didn't party as much as celebrate their love for one another, which is now being made public to family and friends after a time of engagement and getting to know each other more intimately. "Marrying Harry" some people called me. When I think about how many years I prepared for the priesthood and how quickly some people choose to make a lifetime commitment, it bothers me. Again, all the preparation in the world gives no guarantee that it will work.

Planning on a grand scale for the one-day event can be overwhelming. That's why it takes a family or a maid of honor to help bear the burden of invitations, dates, cakes, flowers, clothes, photographers, videographers, a place to party (excuse me, celebrate), limos and who will be in the wedding party. Oh, did I forget the location — the church, the garden, the living room, the ball field, the vineyard, the meadow of a friend in the country, under the old oak tree — again, you get the picture. I always lobbied for the church because of the solemnity of the vows. People tend to be a bit more serious in that setting, although I've had weddings where the bride nervously giggled throughout. The young priest with me was ready to give her a "time out" when I gave him the glance that said, "I've been here before and it's not the champagne she toasted with in the limo. It's an emotion that is honest and true. Her very being knows what is about to take place and she has lost control of this part of herself."

God has included both of you in God's plan; it would be good for you to include God in your plan. You just didn't find each other. Your love for one another grew once you met and had a chance to "fall" in love. Falling has a negative connotation. But when it's with two people, perhaps it could be considered helpful to each one of them. After all, they are a catch to each other. Falling then begins a time of faith and trust in each other. That's a lot different than a fall from grace. So, I would encourage the vow-taking in a church to let God know that God is going to be part of your plan for the rest of your life.

Some couples get so close to the day, the time, the procession up the aisle and still it falls apart. My most memorable experience was in the Midwest when the bride came all the way down the aisle with the organ blasting, "Here comes the bride!" and she let go of her father's hand and walked up to me and asked if she could use the microphone. I'm paraphrasing but her speech went something like this:

"There will be no marriage to this man today nor probably ever, as I have discovered just this morning that in the past week he slept with my maid of honor (tears now flowing from more than just the bride-to-be). Daddy, I apologize. I know you have booked for a large party. Please have it without me! I will be spending some time sulking and dealing with my anger. I also will be returning any gifts that I have received. As for these two, don't bother with pleas of apology over meaningless sex. I'm not stupid! I'm sorry. Thank you all for your support."

At that, she grabbed the hem of her dress, whirled around and gave a look not only of the dagger proportion but daggers with blood on them toward her former fiancé and erstwhile maid of honor.

* * *

One would think that more marriage ceremonies would be marred because of alcohol and the inability for young people to have the discipline to abstain for a few hours before it all begins. The excitement of it all makes it very difficult to toe the mark. I once had a limo pull up to the rear door of the church where the groomsmen were waiting to process out into the sanctuary. The driver stood there with the trunk open offering a small toddy to deal with the nerves before it all began or was over. I quickly told him where to go and what he could do with his limo of libations.

At another marriage I had, the groom came to the sacristy of the church fully intoxicated. He was not a drinker nor were his four brothers. I guess they all thought it was kind of cute that they do their celebrating with alcohol before the marriage vows. I can still see his bloodshot eyes and his red nose and noted a slight stagger as he approached me to shake hands and say he was ready to go. I told him and his brothers to go home and take a nap. I'll deal with the people in church and the bride and her parents. Lucky for this guy, his parents had long passed and he didn't have to deal with anyone who could read him the riot act. The banishment from the church for three hours was enough embarrassment to last a lifetime. After some rest and I can't imagine how many cups of coffee, they all returned and the marriage went off without a hitch. Of course, the cake got stale, the managers of the venue for the party/celebration were furious and fumed enough to light all the candles without a match.

It was like the three hours that Jesus spent on the cross for that young man, but it was a good lesson for all. Oh, I didn't mention how everyone in the church including the bride and her father felt after I announced that the groom had taken sick and his brothers took him home to rest. "He assured me that it was not serious and he could be back by three," I told them, "so why don't you talk among yourselves or go have some lunch. The lights will be on and the candles re-lighted at three o'clock and we'll proceed." I then asked the bride to come to the sacristy with me and I tried to explain how her husband-to-be was coaxed by his brothers into the cups and after catching a few winks could return and we would go ahead with it all. They understood, I think, but I'll never know.

* * *

The marriage was scheduled for 10:00 a.m. and it was now 14 minutes past. While it is fashionable for the bride to be late, I was beginning to get worried. The pastor of Ss. Peter and Paul parish always worried that the crowds would be gone by the time the noon Mass took place. I assured him there would be no problem, as I would cut the time of the photographer or ask him to conclude with his work on the steps in front of the church or across the street in Washington Square Park as many couples did. I looked at my watch and it was now 10:25 a.m. "That's it," I said. "Now I'm concerned."

I'm in the sacristy with the groom and his posse of six including the best man. "Go back and see what's going on," I said in a gruff and worried voice to the bestie. Five minutes went by and he returned with the news that there was no bride. The family was all there. The bridesmaids were present. All accounted for except the bride. Who is going to get the blame for this one?

Of all people, the limo driver. He picked up the women and delivered them and there was no instruction as to getting the bride. She was in her apartment fully dressed and sobbing that she had been forgotten. She called the church but it was Saturday and the pastor was in the sacristy with me wringing his hands and chewing his nails concerned about his noon Mass. She called the limo company and got voicemail. The driver was on the sidewalk and his phone in the car. (These were the days before ride sharing.) She tried several people she thought would be there but they had been instructed at five minutes to ten to turn off their cell phones. I had to go before the waiting congregation and again ask them to talk among themselves until the bride was delivered. At 10:45 that morning, she came down the aisle with a huge smile knowing that this was all going to happen. The picture taking had to be shortened but I didn't have to do it, the pastor did. They are still married and have two grown children. They never asked me to have the marriages of their kids. Wonder why?

* * *

Weddings can be very expensive. In a day and age where a number of young people think they have to outdo each other, they just keep piling on the costs. And it's not the vows nor the commitment nor the heart nor the emotion. It's all the little things that add up and never seem to end. I told a friend the other day, after he was telling me about a "destination" wedding that he attended, that if the couple really appreciated the priest, the church, the instructions, they might give 1% of what they were spending to the priest or the parish. He told me I ought to do weddings for a living. He said that the one he attended cost the bride's father over $300K. Let's see 1% for the priest. I could do ten a year and make more than I'm making now. Oh well.

There was a bed and breakfast place by the ocean. It also had a tavern and a banquet room a four-hour drive from San Francisco. The proprietor was a brother to a friend of mine. I drove up one Sunday to visit and have abalone, which was a favorite on his menu and hard to get at a reasonable price. During the table conversation he approached me and asked if I was interested in doing weddings on the weekend. He said he would write it into the fee for the couple for $100. He said he could do about three or four on a weekend. That was a few years ago and the rules of the Church wouldn't allow me to do the work. But it sure seemed like a good way to pad my pockets. If I were interested in that, I would not have chosen the priesthood. As I used to say, if I had money I'd be dangerous, but I'll never know.

* * *

I wrote about performing weddings as different from witnessing weddings. It was a beautiful day in Carmel and the sun shone over the blue of the water and the white of the waves with just a tinge of green as it splashed against the rocks. We were behind a mansion whose backyard was the open Bay of Carmel, only a mile down the coast from the famous golf course where the Crosby Clambake used to be held. It's called something else today. The owner of the home was a distant friend and asked me on behalf of the couple if I would witness their vows.

I was facing the couple and the very small elite group of family and friends in attendance. As I said the words, "I give you Mr. and Mrs. So-and-So, you may kiss the bride," the tail of a huge gray whale did a salute to the couple by rising out of the water and flashing or fluking as I think it's called. I did not see it but I watched the expressions on the faces of the folks facing me and they were all amazed and elated. My friend knowing that I delved a bit into show business in San Francisco, as he had seen my television show, remarked, "Just like you to stage a whale appearance to impress everyone. Nice job." The answer is "no" I didn't get 1% of what was spent on that wedding and I had nothing to do with the whale salute from Moby. But it was memorable and it will never happen again.

* * *

Over the years, I've made a few road trips either to celebrate marriages or to be a witness in the group gathered to do just that. This event took place in a normal neighborhood of Los Angeles. It was in a temple and there was a plethora of sweet smelling incense permeating the place packed with pillows on the floor, no pews. We were all in our places with sunshiny faces eagerly awaiting the entrance of the wedding party, which happened to be having lunch with a famous "guru" flown in from Colorado to perform the ceremony. After an hour had passed, the pillows began to feel like the concrete floor on which they were placed. There was a loud gong and a robed man entered stage left to announce that the guru and the wedding party had finished their lunch and would be along shortly. "Until they arrive," he said, "you are all invited to exit the sanctuary and go to the hall for an adult beverage. We will crash the cymbals when they arrive and then we will return to this place." A huge sigh of relief that I believe was audible as we bent our knees and backs, returning to the upright position and advancing toward the bar, not really a bar, but another room where a bar had been set up. This was all new to me, as I had never witnessed a Buddhist wedding in a Buddhist Temple.

It was probably 45 minutes later when the gong sounded and we returned to our pillowed places. A very handsome Caucasian-American man walked in, bedecked in priestly robes followed by the bride and groom to be joined in holy matrimony. There were, of course, apologies for the late arrival and a humorous story to begin the ceremony. It was a beautiful expression of two people doing and saying what they should in order to bring about a long-lasting and never-ending life together. The guru was exceptional. His words were poignant and to the point. His manner and delivery were eye-catching and mesmerizing. There was only the occasional interruption of a young lady with a pitcher of clear liquid poured into a tall thin glass that would quench his thirst.

It was during the reception when I inquired from one of the people who seemed to know the temple and the guru if I could visit with him. I let them know I was a Roman Catholic priest and a close friend of the groom. I wanted to thank him and express my praise for the way he conducted the ceremony and his impeccable delivery. I was told to wait in a given spot and my message would be delivered. Two minutes later the messenger returned with the disappointing news that the guru was "indisposed". Later the groom informed me that the clear liquid being poured from the pitcher was a brand of vodka that I could not afford. I was shocked for a few minutes but soon got over it.

As a priest, I would never go to dinner or lunch with the couple about to be married. I'm sure there are stories about priests with an alcohol affliction who've done worse. One priest (a close friend) told me he had too much at the rehearsal dinner the night before and went off with a couple of guys to Las Vegas. The next day the flights from Vegas to San Fran were canceled because of weather. He missed the sound of the gong for the wedding in his own parish. He was able to alert a sub to go over and do the ceremony. He had a lot of apologies to make to the family. Indisposed is a good word, but doesn't really tell the whole story.

* * *

Michael and Mary Jo Pritchard are now much older than when they came to me and asked to be married. Mike was from St. Louis and had attended the same seminary where I began my preparation for the priesthood, although a decade later. He was thrown out for ringing the chapel bells in the middle of the night, a cut-up even then.

I first met him after he had received much publicity for winning the San Francisco Comedy Competition. That wasn't such a big thing but the fact that he won first place and Robin Williams won second does make a difference. I booked him on my radio program at KYUU-FM and in our discussion discovered that we were both raised in the Midwest and he had gone to the seminary to become a priest. That was the beginning of a friendship lasting to this day.

After I got to know Michael and his girlfriend Mary Jo, they asked about marriage. We prepared all the paperwork and set a date in Sacred Heart church. I went over early to prep the altar, light the candles, turn on the lights, and waited. After 20 minutes, I blew out the candles, went outside to look up and down the streets and no wedding party. After 30 minutes, I turned out the lights, and locked the doors. This is before cell phones and instant communications.

It turned out that Michael was performing at the Greek Theatre in Berkeley. It was Joan Baez's Bread and Roses concert, which raised money to bring musicians and comedians to jails, prisons, hospitals, children's wards and institutions that didn't have much access to entertainment. The festival was stuffed with laughs: The Smothers Brothers, Howard Hesseman, Don Novello (Father Guido Sarducci) and Robin Williams all showed up, in addition to Pritchard. Mike had done his half hour and was to be followed by the star of *WKRP in Cincinnati*, Johnny Fever (Howard Hesseman). Johnny had more than a fever (indisposed, perhaps) and was not to be found backstage, so Joan Baez asked Michael if he would go back on stage to fill the time before she appeared. Well, that was the time he was supposed to be in church making his solemn vows with his fiancée. Mary Jo was also backstage and both of them agreed that they could get married anytime and that this was more important. That made my time insignificant . . . I assumed the "chopped liver" role on this decision.

The wedding took place a couple of weeks later just as we planned and nothing was ever said, that is until I had a public forum like this to tell everyone how I was slighted for bread and roses.

Short of a miracle, I'll never know the pleasures of marriage. But here's one thing I know for sure. During your lifetime you are going to find that special someone, that person who makes you light up, who turns you on. You'll know it's not an angel — you know how? No wings!

CHAPTER 13

Cancer

I WAS COMING OUT of the hospital a few weeks ago when I ran into Nurse Cheri who is a godsend to all cancer patients and especially those who have to do radiation or chemotherapy. She had been the one who prepped me for the whole shebang when I was battling colon cancer a few years back. She is short in stature and when greeting me with a big hug, the top of her head was just above my belt buckle.

"Oh, Harry, you look so good, I think you're the only one still living from your infusion days!" I gulped and said thank you, I think. Then I remembered that a friend who lectors on the TV Mass is also a survivor and doing great. "Oh, then there are two of you," she said.

If you have experienced cancer in your family, and who has not, you are aware of how concerned you become when anyone mentions the "Big C". Suddenly a whole new vocabulary comes into play and you're off and running with this story or that one. A handball buddy of mine who lost his wife recently can't even talk about it without welling up and then having to walk away because he didn't want to be seen crying over something that happened and is over. But for two people who've spent most of their lives together, it is never over. The painful memories are always there.

Some years back, I had a telephone call from Dr. Jordan of Stanford University. He was an oncologist specializing in children's cancer. He wanted to know whether or not I could muster the original crew at KRON TV and put together a follow-up to the show we did 35 years ago called *The Kids From Company C.* It was a half-hour documentary following Dr. Jordan and his assistants and their work at the Pacific Medical Center with this disease and how it affected children and their families. This man was not only gifted as a physician but also as a communicator and a great responder to parents and children with the age-old questions, "Why me? Why our family? Doesn't God know that these are just little kids who've never had a chance?"

One of the highlights of our video was to see these kids in transit as we went to Volkswagen car dealers and asked them to supply us with three small convertibles so that these kids could be loaded with their movable poles and drips sticking out the top of the cars. It was quite a sight and one that I'll never forget as we paraded in a mini-procession to the San Francisco Zoo, only to be treated as royalty by the staff once there, as they had never had such a strange looking group of visitors to the zoo. It was a grand afternoon.

I pitched the idea of the follow-up program to the executive producer at the TV station. He was the same fellow who, as a newbie in TV production, went to Lourdes to do the documentary on the apparent cure of Dr. Don Rose, a famous deejay when rock radio was at its peak. Jim said the station didn't have the kind of budget it would take to follow up on Dr. Jordan's patients who both lived and died under his care.

The good doctor had kept careful records and I still think the work could have been done. I filed the idea and a few notes under "to do". Within six months I read that Dr. Jordan had passed away. Once again, I'm a day late and a dollar short of doing something good for the people whose family and friends have had to deal with the "Big C". I'll never know what good I could have done.

CHAPTER 14

Papal Visit

MY GOOD FRIEND Michael Pritchard, the comedian turned "do gooder" for the world, cannot help himself when it comes to talking about opening for the pope at Candlestick Park in 1989. He has opened for many big celebrities and entertainers but this one from Vatican City really tops his list.

I felt pretty much the same way when I was invited by KPIX TV, the CBS affiliate in San Francisco, to work on the six o'clock news for a week prior to the pope's arrival in San Francisco. John Paul II, who later was made a saint, was working his way westward after a brief stop in Denver. For years I tried to get the smallest budget to do this or that for a couple of shows I hosted there but to no avail. So, upon my arrival from New York the news director says, "Whatever you need, Father Harry, camera, crew, chopper. It's all at your disposal. We are going to lead all competition in our coverage of this one-time visitor."

They housed me at a five-star hotel and picked me up early AM and delivered me late PM in a limo. First time I'd traveled in that style and, yes, I could get used to it. My particular task was to monitor the pope's moves and appearances across the country and give a brief report on the 6:00 p.m. news. It was at that time hosted by Dave McElhatton and Wendy Tokuda. Both of them were the best in the City and professional in everything they said and did. It's difficult to make the evening news unless there is a disaster or you kill someone. Sexual abuse among the Catholic clergy had not yet made its way into the headlines.

Archbishop John Rafael Quinn was the leader of the Catholic community in our three-county archdiocese. He was instrumental in providing an opportunity for Sister Helen Garvey, president-elect of the Leadership Conference of Women Religious, who spoke in the cathedral directly to the Holy Father about the plight of women religious and the direction women's participation in the Catholic Church was going. Shortly after that audience between the pope and 3,000 nuns and brothers, John Quinn was summoned to Rome to meet privately with Pope John Paul II to discuss what Sister Garvey had said in her proposals to the Holy Father. Archbishop Quinn was admired by women religious around the world for his courage in helping aid their plight.

I recall the famous pasta dinner I had with the archbishop upon his return from Rome. I was living in an apartment in Manhattan and he spent the night in New York instead of going directly back to San Francisco. We went to a very elegant Italian restaurant and he dared asked the waiter what kind of pasta they were serving. The tuxedoed server's brash reply was that our pasta is the best in the city and it doesn't matter what kind of noodle it might be. After he left our table, John told me that the night before he had dined with the pope whose cook inquired if there was particular pasta that he would like. It was only funny when we left the table and passed a couple of my pals at the bar who noticed and said, "How was the pasta?"

The papal parade arrived at St. Mary's Cathedral right on time. A good friend of mine, a politician, couldn't help but badger me with the expense San Francisco was undertaking to welcome such a guest. "Do you know we had to pull up every sewer covering on Geary Street?" I didn't know that. "Did you get dirty?" I asked. He knew I wasn't impressed by whatever preparations had to be made for a papal visit.

So, there I sat atop a large apartment house across the street from the cathedral observing the every move of the papal entourage as they made their way through the crowds and into the place of worship. It's amazing what the eye of the camera might catch when you're nowhere near it and then be asked to comment about what we're seeing. You have to admire those people who work without a script at such events.

Of course, we were more than occupied with demonstrations and anti-papal people, who cared about more about what was being done and said than the manhole covers on Geary Boulevard. As it turned out, there were very few and most of them were a block away and didn't get much publicity.

The most memorable event was the pope holding and blessing a little boy at Mission Dolores who had AIDS. It was a picture that went around the globe at a time when AIDS was a major topic and challenge for the world. I can still see that photo with Monsignor John O'Connor, pastor of Mission Dolores, and Archbishop John Quinn in the background, as the Holy Father held up the small child with AIDS. Brendan O'Rourke died three years later at just seven years old.

The specifics of the day are long gone to my memory. I'll never know what I said except to acknowledge that, like my friend Pritch, I opened for the pope in San Francisco in 1989. That was a lasting memory.

* * *

Poor Junipero Serra, who did so much in establishing the California missions up and down the coast. He found, fed, and many believe fleeced the Indian population so much so that in 1987, when Pope John Paul II made a trip to San Francisco, about as close as he got to making a saint of the priest was to go to the Old Mission on Dolores Street and welcome the gay community as he reached out to people with AIDS.

It's always easier in retrospect to make judgments from the recliner as we do when watching sports. The same is true with much of our history. We now have a whole new perspective when looking at slave owners in the South or missionary priests who taught people how to plant corn and might have saved thousands from starvation, while all along teaching them about Jesus who was God.

Kevin Starr has a tome about the missionary fathers, Society of Jesus, coming into California. I'll not forget the night I attended a talk at the University of San Francisco and he and the president of the university had an open forum on his book, *Continental Ambitions: Roman Catholics in North America: The Colonial Experience.* After the presentation and discussion I got in line for Kevin to sign my newly purchased copy. He wrote out my name on a piece of scratch paper and inquired if this is the correct spelling. I nodded and he proceeded to write a little note and signed it. I said, "Kevin, you know my name and how to spell it, why did you ask?" He said he has had a number of book signings in his life and you can't afford to eat a $40 book if you make a mistake with someone's name. I took a page from his book.

CHAPTER 15

Role Model

I TAUGHT HOMILETICS at St. Patrick's for two years. I was the pastor of St. Gabriel's at the time and the one full day away at the seminary was both an outlet and escape from the parish and the chancery office, where I served as the director of development. I knew where and for what reason I would be busy every Wednesday of the school year. It was a 45-minute drive each way on the freeway, which has a sign that reads: "Most Beautiful Drive In California" or something close to that. It gave the mind time to process what had taken place and how to put it into perspective.

There was much to be learned from the students and much that I took in which made me fearful for the future. I was sure that the Holy Spirit was going to have to work overtime to bring the bunch that I taught up to speed. One man, no matter how slowly he spoke, could not be understood. I sill have trouble with him today, as he rushes to greet me and ask how I'm doing. After he finished the course I asked him to do three things. First, take a course in English pronunciation. Second, never talk more than five minutes from the pulpit. Third, write out and read slowly what you have written. Others I taught have had the challenge of not being boring. Nothing has changed that much since last I heard them in the seminary. One fellow who was a practicing attorney before he came to the seminary was excellent. He deserved an A for every homily he gave. Unfortunately, he was the exception and not the rule.

Another one of my students once proclaimed on Christmas Eve at the 5:00 p.m. Mass, expressly planned for young children and their families, that there was no Santa Claus. The pastor nearly fainted. Of course, the young priest's purpose was to bring Christ back into Christmas and to draw attention away from Jolly Saint Nick. Just a few months ago I was relating this same tale from the pulpit and after I said "no Santa Claus" there was no reaction. So I repeated it. One lady left her children and raced over to the rectory to report to the pastor what I had said. She and her husband (who later throttled me on the steps of the church) did not hear the whole story, with an emphasis on story. I couldn't defend myself nor could I accuse them of not paying attention. I took it. I apologized. I waited for the letter to come. It did. I tore it up. I apologized in writing later that day. It will be difficult to face that family when I return to the early Mass in the parish. I had not been lambasted for anything I've said from the pulpit for years. It was a shock and upsetting but as I gave it more thought, I settled down and realized that others did "get it" and reacted as normal.

Priestly pulpit tales come across differently to different people. Any of you who have done public speaking or been exposed in the media know what I'm saying. You can talk for years and offer opinions and give advice and time goes by. But let one negative out where you get flogged, flagellated and thrown under the bus, and the hurt lasts a while. I can be complimented and in a matter of minutes, forget what it was. But the criticism digs in like a splinter and begins to fester, if you let it.

The term "classmate" among priests is often used as a name for a person with whom you might have a special relationship. It's more than just a friend or someone who shared the same year of ordination or age group. Classmates often go on vacation together not unlike the three guys I just mentioned. Many of them, during my 50+ years as a priest, maintained their priesthood commitment because of the encouragement and special relationship they have with a classmate.

As seminary students, we were always warned about "particular friendships". At the time the statement was made, I didn't have a clue that it meant boys with boys. Now that I look back, it was pretty silly then and it seems even more ludicrous now. The Church seems to be farsighted in this matter. (Isn't that when you can't see distance?) I was told by a gay priest once that even though he doesn't "hang out" or is not a practicing gay man, he loves to wear long robes and the kind of garments that priests do to celebrate the liturgy. But more importantly, just like the rest of us, they enjoy reading the scriptures and preaching the gospel.

Sex hits the headlines when anything near to it is exposed with the Church and, more pointedly, boys who are studying to be priests. Most of these men are not practicing gay men but still gay men who find a life of ministry suits them and their individual sexual lifestyle. They, too, like dressing up and putting on robes and preaching the gospel.

There seemed to be a whole different atmosphere at St. Patrick's Seminary in Menlo Park, California. When I taught there, I knew for a fact that there were at least a half dozen guys who were gay and came to the seminary not denying their personal lifestyle. I was not on campus, only in the classroom one morning a week, but it was enough to listen to these men give homilies and recognize from their background and stories intermingled with the scriptures that they had a completely different upbringing than I had. There were few sports anecdotes and hardly any quips about hanging out with the "guys" and other such man-cave happenings. It's worth noting that most of these men were senior and had been in the working world and had finished a secular education. For the most part, they had come to pursue the priesthood because of a personal calling and the love for preaching the gospel.

One such lad was a banker and an attorney before he came to the seminary. He was a brilliant man and I gave him A's for all his work. He was as good a homilist as most seasoned priests but without the experience. I recall when he was first assigned as a young priest. He telephoned to ask about going to another parish. He was posted at a large, mostly White, wealthy parish where he was only allowed to preach once every five weeks. All the men took turns and there was a bishop who lived in the neighborhood who took his turn along with the three others in the rectory. It was sad because my student had the gifts and was not allowed to use them. I suggested that he go to priests' personnel and ask for a change. He did, it happened.

The same guy, now deceased, had a difficult time wherever he went. He once went for an interview with the archbishop to complain about a very legitimate action and took along a court reporter to record the conversation. He was asked to leave and never was able to make his point. He never seemed to capture the now-and-again satisfaction that every human being wants and deserves. Enough was enough and finally he was asked to retire early. He went on to become a sheriff's deputy. Go figure. He was given a stipend and a place to live with two garages. I know because for years I signed his check. It was a choice that others above me made. We could go to court and possibly lose and have to pay damages, or ask him to go quietly into an apartment without an assignment and we would pay for it. It was not a pleasant experience.

I was the administrator of the parish where he lived and he threatened the secretary, in fact, he locked the door behind him in her office and castigated her for something she had no idea existed. I could have called the police and had him arrested. Instead, I patiently talked to him and asked if he would apologize.

He did. The woman quit her job after many years of service to the parish. When the pastor returned from Ireland, he was furious. I took the heat and the blame. In fact, he would not talk to me for about three years. We had been friends before all this. I finally sucked it up one Saturday and drove to his new parish. I was nervous but intent on setting the record straight and clearing my conscience. He met me at the door and very formally we went into the common room. Most old rectories have a large sitting room with books, a large television, a small table with after hour libations and comfortable chairs. Usually it's off the dining room or the kitchen. We sat down and I told my side of the story and then proceeded to let him know that I was truly sorry for the loss of his parish secretary. He listened and told me how hurtful it was because that woman had been with him for years and was a true and honest servant of the Church who liked her job so much that she would have worked for nothing. I nodded, agreed, and repeated my apology. There was a cold handshake at the end and I drove back down the coast to my residence.

There is a story about each one of the guys I taught but none as elaborate as this banker-lawyer-priest-sheriff's deputy. I remember going to his funeral and when his sister, who gave the eulogy at Most Holy Redeemer parish in the Castro neighborhood, remarked that he had asked her if she knew that he was a gay man, the entire congregation roared with laughter. 'Nuff said.

CHAPTER 16

Student Life

IT WAS MISTING when I walked out of the church just off St. Stephen's Green in Dublin. I flipped up my rain hoody and continued walking down the street. I had had a wonderful meditation in the little chapel where Father John Henry Newman (1801-1890) used to preside and where he lectured. He was the impetus behind the "Newman Centers" that have sprung up all across our country to assist college students who are Catholic and away from home with no way of keeping their connections to their faith. I prayed earnestly and with fervor as I recalled the few things I knew about this Englishman who became such a memorable Catholic, cardinal, and saint, and was so influential in the growth of the Catholic faith during his days.

I had a short stint at being a Newman chaplain at San Francisco State University. I hadn't really spent much time around there. I knew they had a wonderful and successful communications department. My colleague and longtime friend Mike O'Leary had gone to school there. I didn't really know anyone there, whether faculty or students. When I returned from my seven years in New York, Archbishop Quinn never really asked me about what I might want to do, he simply assigned me as the chaplain to State.

There is no place to live there but they do own a house on 74 Banbury and it's essentially yours and you can do what you want with it. The garage had been made into a chapel. It was dark and dank and not very welcoming to the few who might come by. That was all that ever came by, a few. There were no regulars whom I got to know or could count on, just a few drop-ins. The university was handy and very useful for young people who lived in the Bay Area. They all had cars and they came and went according to a class schedule. Those who lived on campus were from other countries and were not keen on practicing Roman Catholicism. Some were "born again" while many others were Buddhists or Muslims from the Middle East.

The few Catholics who did live in the dorms usually went home on the weekends. I presumed they went to their parish churches where they grew up. Suffice it to say it was a commuter school with little interest in Newman Centers or Newman chaplains. I think Archbishop Quinn, who assigned me there, knew I had a reputation for working with young people and thought that I would thrive in that atmosphere. Well, I probably would have but the only way I could relate to them is to hang out in the Student Union or go to a game and sit with them in the bleachers. It didn't take more than a year for me to realize what I was up against. I recall the archdiocesan Vocation Director at the time, who was a young vibrant priest with lots of personality. He used to drop by and let me know that the two of us had the worst jobs in the archdiocese. Students and young people in general were simply not interested in going to Mass or into religious life or the seminary. It was a down time for that kind of thinking. So Father Mario and I would sip on Diet Pepsis and wonder what was next for the two of us.

The few students I could coax to Banbury Street on a Friday night were the kind who couldn't or didn't want dates and had nothing to do. The first few months there were two or three young girls who came and wanted to pray the rosary in the chapel before we ate. Oh, I provided pizza, pasta, popcorn and pop so you could satisfy your hunger and hopefully get into a discussion with the chaplain or your peers and grow in your Catholic spirituality. I even invited kids from another parish who I knew were okay and fun to be around. But they were really not into the recitation of the rosary before pasta. Those Friday nights were daunting. Now, as soon as word got around that there were young women coming to the Newman Center a few old guys started coming. By old I mean in their 40s who were still taking classes and looking for the college life that for one reason or another had passed them by. When I saw them coming on to the girls, I had to ask them not to return. It wasn't my idea; some of the young women came to me in private and said they were afraid. Sometimes they were followed back to the dorms. Okay, that's it. No more of this. So we're not talking big groups, we're talking eight or ten altogether. I learned quickly not to cook too much pasta or order too much pizza. I was not planning on eating cold pizza and pasta for the week.

I had not lost my knack of attracting young people and feeling I was doing some good. Then I discovered a retired priest living just the next house over was planning to open up an oratorium, a center for young men who might be considering the priesthood. The Congregation of the Oratory of Saint Philip Neri is a pontifical society of apostolic life of Catholic priests and lay brothers who live together in a community bound together by no formal vows but only with the bond of charity. The concept stemmed from the religious order called Oratorians who were interested in training young men to become priests. Wikipedia says, "Founded: 1575, Founded at: Rome". There they were, good looking young men in black cassocks handing out rosaries at a state university and asking students to come and pray with them. Their leader was a man who had had a successful career as a science teacher at the University of San Francisco, so he knew much about student life. He was married and had several children. When his kids grew up and his wife passed away, he entered the seminary. Archbishop Quinn ordained him to the priesthood. It's not my place nor my wish to denigrate him, but let it be said that he was ultra-conservative and had not been exposed to the changes that Vatican II brought to our changing Church. So, I not only had to fight for a place at the table for just a few young people who came to the center but for anyone else looking for all the great things that came with Vatican II and the new definition of the Catholic Church.

I was living at Holy Name parish and commuting to the campus every day including weekends. I didn't know what a day off was and I didn't have priest friends to pal around with. While I was in New York, I'd really lost track of the few guys I had known before I left. I remember the archbishop asking me to return for that reason. He said, as you grow older it becomes more and more difficult to make and maintain friendships that will take you into your twilight years. He was wise and correct in his evaluation. I never really did endear myself to the local clergy nor did I have the kind of friendships that you have if you are studying for years with the same guys in the same seminary. My ties were to the North American College in Rome and my priestly friendships were with the guys I spent four years with in Europe never coming home until you were ordained.

Monsignor James McKay was the Vicar General under Archbishop Quinn and invited three retired deacons who were all married and had been successful businessmen to join him as a committee to evaluate and make suggestions about how they could serve the people of Northern California and how best to use their priests. It was around this time that the pinch of priests who were leaving active ministry for marriage or other careers began to surface into a major problem for priest personnel (human resources in a diocesan structure). These three were exceptional and it came to the fore that more and more committees began to appear with lay men and lay women as advisors and entering into the management structure of the Church.

It wasn't long before they met me at 74 Banbury and said, "What are you doing and how is it going and do you think this ministry is worth having a priest assigned full time?" It was music to my ears. I basically outlined for them what I wrote in this chapter, which concluded with a statement about the waste of priest personnel at a commuter college where there were only a handful of students who would make use of a Newman Center. That was the beginning of the end to the Banbury drop-in Newman Center that was my first assignment following my return to California from New York.

Leaving State to work in the chancery was the first time in my priesthood that I would be working in an atmosphere with adults and mostly clergy. While the idea of office work didn't bother me, losing my connection to the youth of the Church did. I always had no self-doubt that I was able to both communicate with young people and understand them in a special way. I practiced it and was comfortable in my own skin when it came to an opinion about it. But without some kind of connection, I worried it would destroy the strong ties that I had through popular music and my radio work. I was still commuting to New York to record for ABC radio. I had an inkling that it would soon cease, as there was going to be too much to do.

PART II

Last Days in the Garden of Eden

"Unless a grain of wheat falls to the ground and dies,
it remains just a grain of wheat; but if it dies,
it produces much fruit"
(John 12)

* * *

"Who knows how long this will last
Now we've come so far, so fast."
Don Henley

CHAPTER 17

Fundraiser

THAT COMMITTEE RETURNED to my door with another proposition as an assignment. "Father Harry," said Gerry Pera, "We think you would make a really fine contribution to the archdiocese as a development priest." They didn't say it but a fact is that people generally give to people and they figured I was an honest enough person to represent the Church to the people of God. I had been successful raising money for the God Squad. I had done ten Just for the Halibut dinners followed by Friends of Father Harry dinners. It was enough to keep the God Squad in the black but hardly credentials for keeping the archdiocese on an even keel. I had done fundraisers in both New York and Florida. That outreach was always important to supplement what we could glean in our own backyard.

So here I go, off to an office in the chancery with my black suit and Roman collar, surrounded by people with coats and ties and dresses known as administrators. Of course, the archbishop was in charge but he had essentially found committees that were much more efficient than ordained priests working with a basic foundation in theology and without any formal training in legal matters, property management, human resources, finances and development. So the idea was to find people who did know those fields and direct them so that the mission of the Church would not get lost. It was to be pastoral motivation that pushed us to recognize that business was business but ministry, if done well, also had to have a business sense to it. You just couldn't say to all the pastors who are managing schools and churches and sometimes a full block of buildings that they needed to be careful whom they hire and how they hire. Next thing you know they fire someone and have a huge legal suit against them and that kicks over to the parent company, that would be the archdiocese. Now you've got a can of worms all because Father didn't like the way the lady cleaned the house or refused to do certain things like pick up the mail as it was not in her job description.

So here comes Father Harry to an office that I'm told will be occupied by another priest who was a retired pastor and still wanted to work but they had no place to put him. He smoked a large cigar and was a very successful fundraiser. Unfortunately for me, his ideas and mine were not in sync. He liked to go to lunch every day at the Press Club and press the flesh of potential donors and look for huge gifts, while sipping scotch and puffing on those brown ropes that pass for smoking pleasure. He would leave the office around 11:30 a.m. and return around 3:00 p.m., shuffle papers to four and be gone before five. I never complained because he was an older man and was duly respected for what he had accomplished in the priesthood. He was also in his day a great pastor and just a nice guy.

My introduction to finally getting a handle on what I was doing came at the tutoring of a major fundraiser and a very competent woman from Missouri, who is now editing this book and will probably delete this part. We were a team of three and did good work for the Church. At the same time I was a pastor at St. Gabriel's parish and split my time between both assignments. The parish was always the most attractive, as there was true joy in dealing with people, the sacraments, the school and the team

I had assembled to manage the parish. We were a close-knit group and convinced that our model of collective ministry was the best. It included the principal of the school, the director of religious education, the pastoral minister who took care of the sick, a deacon I eventually had to let go because of his inability to recognize our style and the system we were following and, finally, the other priest.

Father Tom, the associate pastor, moved into the rectory about three months before I was appointed. Boxes of books were stacked outside his room for almost six months after I was there. "Hey, Tom, when are you going to shelve those books in your room?" There was plenty of book space in his room. After a few nervous twitches, which he had from living a good part of his life as an alcoholic but now was completely dry, he stammered, "Uh, oh I was waiting to see whether or not I liked you." If he didn't, he could easily just bail and look for another parish.

After I left as pastor, he was made a pastor at a rather large parish and I would periodically help out on Sundays. He told me, in confidence, that the stress was getting to him and he found himself in a liquor store shopping for alcohol, any kind. He said he prayed about it and went to the archbishop and asked to be released as a pastor, for fear he would be driven back to drink. That took some courage and some grace to know you might be falling from it again. He just died this year after major heart problems. The number of men and women whom he counseled with the same disease are too many to count but a good number showed up at his funeral service. They were men and women, old and young, used and fresh, grateful for what this man said to them and confident that they too could be helped over a huge hurdle in life known as alcoholism. Praise be to God, I'll never know.

As I was saying, the world of fundraising is not always fun. It's for the kind of guys who you want in the lead tank when you go to battle. They have to be up front and honest and unafraid of being rejected. Most intelligent people figure out what the result of something is before they do it and then, if it fails, they know they've done the preparation and it could well be a learning experience for the next foray (remember Green Fever?) Personal feelings cannot always be part of your makeup. There is too much hurt in rejection. But there is a secret in working for the Church. You are not raising money for yourself. You're not making the "ask" for personal achievement or gold stars on your report card. You are doing it for others. That's why I boldly each and every week beg my television audience to send a gift so that we can keep the ministry going without depriving others, like the very elderly on social security and the incarcerated, who do not have an income to reap the benefits of those who can give, or others who can no longer get on a bus, or who live back in the backwoods.

Over the years there has been much written about how to raise money and much quoted scriptures about what the early Christians did to help each other. We still have many people who believe if they are successful, their harvest should be shared. One old priest used to tell me that the Christians came out of the catacombs with their hands open pleading for donations. It hasn't changed much over the years. It was a big thing for me to cancel the second collections in my parish. Any second collection had to have an envelope and they would be in the pews. If parishioners wanted to give to this or that cause, they could use the envelopes but the basket was only coming by one time. I still believe it and would do it in any parish where I had the say-so.

CHAPTER 18

Cruising

I BOARDED THE *USS Enterprise* in Oakland to spend a week with the Navy at the request of the Naval Commander, in order to become more familiar with the men and women who served at sea. Armed Forces Radio Network broadcasting made it possible. I was welcomed by the chaplain aboard, who also was named Harry. That was his last name. He took me for a tour and then to my quarters. That evening I was invited to the captain's table; he could not have been more welcoming. He was in command of this huge carrier with over 5,000 men and women serving the U.S. Navy. After dinner he took me to the bridge and let me sit in his chair (covered with a thick sheepskin). He then began to query me about some political matters in the world. I think he was fishing for a staunch stance to see which side of the fence I was standing on. He even showed me an article from TIME magazine with a feature about Archbishop Hunthausen from Seattle. I can't be sure but I believe he wanted me to agree that this man was out of bounds in his theological thinking. So, wisely, I did not take the bait and played dumb (not that hard) declaring ignorance of the situation. I was a great fan of the Archbishop and believed that he was saying and doing the right things for the growth and betterment of the Church. He was a true Vatican II proponent.

Part of my duty on the ship was to offer both morning and evening prayers over the ship's PA, which could be heard in every nook and cranny of the carrier. I also spent an hour on the ship's radio station playing music and answering questions from the sailors, pilots and marines who were in charge of the security on the ship. It was really a lot of fun. Most of them knew who I was because at that time I had a weekly program called *Love on the Rock*, which was heard around the world on Armed Forces Radio Network stations as well as the many ships at sea. It was a bit like the work that Robin Williams did in the movie *Good Morning Vietnam*.

My biggest thrill on that cruise was to watch the jets take off and land. I stood on the bridge for hours. I just couldn't get enough of it. One of my nephews Ron Schlitt was a Marine pilot and he related to me that it was like approaching a stamp on a floating letter that you had to hit exactly and be caught by the tail, or you were off either into the sea or with such great thrust to circle and try again. I saw that from a few of the pilots as I gazed in amazement. Fortunately, there were no mishaps.

One of my favorite words from that trip was FOD. Every so often flights would cease and a group of sailors would go arm in arm down the entire deck looking for any stray object that might hinder or cause an accident for the pilots and planes. "F" stands for foreign, "O" object, "D" debris. Once the deck was declared free of FOD, the flight maneuvers would continue. The speed, the noise, the flames from the tails of the jets was just too much to miss. They practiced day and night.

After a week at sea, I was debriefed with the chaplains and the ExO as to my visit. My ride back from the seas to San Diego would be in a giant helicopter called a Huey. I was so excited to board. I put on the helmet amid the deafening sound of the rotary engine and took my seat on the wall and strapped in. My joy at my first helicopter ride soon turned to sorrow as I saw sick sailors coming aboard to be transferred back to land to be hospitalized. They were sick and suffering. One by one as they passed me I prayed for them and for a safe journey. My ride was like one at a carnival for fun, theirs was like an ambulance to the hospital for healing.

I was so proud of those guys. I thought I would cry when the humongous Huey powered up and my teeth began to chatter. The vibrations were unforgettable. I could only thank God for my health as I watched the others shaking. It was less than an hour to terra firma where the sick were the first to exit the aircraft. I shook hands with the pilot and boarded the jeep that had to take me to the next airplane headed for San Francisco.

It wasn't long after that when I read in the paper and saw the picture of the *USS Enterprise* stuck on a sandbar in the San Francisco Bay right before going under the Bay Bridge. There was the name, Captain Robert Kelly — the really wonderful host that I had for a week aboard his ship. I heard he was relieved of that duty and took a job in Washington. I think he was later named an admiral. But I doubt that the U.S. Navy would allow him to command another carrier.

You may recall I was once recruited to join the United States Marine Corps. I thought I could do some good in Vietnam. My bishop had other ideas. Although I'll never know what it's like to serve in the military, I'm thrilled to have had the chance to watch fighter jets taking off and landing on a ship at sea.

CHAPTER 19

What's in a Name?

MY GREAT-NEPHEW Zachary Schlitt used to say that he was the best. The many young attractive women who came to his funeral, all proclaiming that he was their main squeeze, helped to solidify his proclamation. It was really very simple for him. He lived in the United States, which was the best. He attended the University of Florida, which was the best. His fraternity there was the best. He was the leader of that fraternity, which made him the best. So there was really no argument that he was simply the best. If you knew him, you would tend to agree. "Zachary" means "God Remembers". I know he'd be pleased that his Uncle Harry remembered his Thomistic logic and deemed it worthy of reprint.

Henry was the given name of a Monsignor Schurman, the pastor of the parish where I was baptized and grew up and he is my namesake. I guess the family preferred Harry because they never used Henry, always Harry. After all, America got its name from Harry. I was reading *The Book of Saints* and discovered this:

HENRY

Note. A Teuton name latinized into Henricus (name used when I was ordained a priest in Rome). The most common variants in other languages are — German, Heinrich; French, Henri; Danish,

Eric; Spanish and Portuguese, Enrique; Hungarian, Emeric; Italian, Enrico (Arrigo, Amerigo — whence America).

So it's not such a stretch to realize that both South and North America use the derivation of my name when they refer to themselves, thus, the United States of Harry. It all made sense before Prince Harry in England began using the name on a daily basis.

CHAPTER 20

Bestselling Author

NO ONE HAS asked me about being an author but if they did I would chronicle the process beginning with the interest of California State Librarian emeritus, prolific author of books about California history, and USC professor Kevin Starr. The impetus he added by informing me that there was not another book like mine, which would lay down a part of the history of the Church from the vantage point of a priest who lived through Vatican II, was what it took for me to finally put pen to page and write the book I had talked about writing for 30 years. His passing just five months after the publication of my memoir was a huge blow to my motivation for beginning this second book and a tremendous personal loss.

While I am not a "writer" per se, I've spent most of my adult life writing scripts for radio and television and homilies and talks to church groups who were searching for common sense among the clergy. I have not even considered the thousands of letters I responded to during my 16 years in administration in the chancery office, from thank you notes to donors, to full blown apologies for an act of unkindness perpetrated by one or another of our employees.

It has felt like I've been given a talent and should not be so eager to place it under a bushel basket but rather to put it on a high place so that others might be able to see and maybe find their own way a little easier. It's a constant reminder that we're only reflections from above. So the brighter our light, the easier for the blinded to find their way. In the present climate where nuclear arms abound, the Shakespeare adage "to be or not to be" is a real question. So if we're going to be, let's make the most of what is ours to reflect to another. A light under the basket is not really a light. It's wasteful and only useful when it's allowed to shine on the path for others to advance in life.

I had finished a draft of my memoir in three years and after allowing others to peruse the manuscript it became evident that if you knew me, fine. But if you didn't know me you would have a hard time teasing out the different mini-tales and putting them together so that they made sense. I asked a former colleague Cindy Arch to work with me. She is an advanced literary student and possesses an unusual grasp of what she has heard, seen, or read. So Cindy went to work for the next two years placing events, people and happenings in some order so as to follow a sequence that would tell a story and adding significant events, like Harvey Milk's assassination, giving context to the reader who was interested in the times. For me it was just another exercise but for the reader who just might happen to buy the book, there was order. What we did must have worked, because in 2017 *I'll Never Tell: Odyssey of a Rock & Roll Priest* was awarded Best Autobiography by the Independent Press Association.

Kevin Starr had given me an introduction to his agent in Los Angeles. She was not particularly interested in the memoir of a priest. One of the other agents in the firm did read *I'll Never Tell* and felt it was worthwhile, but was unable to convince his boss that they should get behind the project. It didn't "speak" to her.

After striking out with the LA connection for publication, I was advised to call Tory Hartman. She was beginning a publication house and was looking for new authors. I had known her husband from his work in the archdiocese. Bill Hartman was a financial wizard and served on a couple of committees before he was hired to manage our capital investments office. Unfortunately, we both were discovered to have cancer about the same time. In fact, we made a trip to Lourdes together with the Knights of Malta. They are a volunteer group with a special ministry to the sick, the poor, the suffering. Every year they charter a jet to the south of France and transport the *malade* (French for sick) at no cost. They go to pray and help those suffering as much as they can. They are doctors, nurses, technicians — ordinary people who are gifted and want to share with others. Bill's cancer was more serious and more advanced than mine but he knew what was going on and we had a few laughs together while making the spiritual rounds on the grounds of the shrine to Mary, Mother of God. I kept insisting that my stage four colon cancer was over, finished, done with, until I tried to walk a few blocks on my own. The wheelchair was the way to go. Bill, on the other hand, slept more and at times didn't know the hour or the place or the surroundings.

Tory accepted my book for publication by her company, Sand Hill Review Press, and the work proceeded in haste. We signed a contract in November 2015 and it was one of the proudest days of my life. Again, everything took much longer than I thought but literature and publishing were all new to me and I had to adjust to the delays and intricacies of the print world compared to the electronic media that I felt I had a good handle on. *I'll Never Tell* was published in August of 2016.

The Academy of Art University and its president, Elisa Stephens, organized a book release party for me. I had been presiding at AAU's graduation ceremonies for nearly ten years and she and I had become friends. She had promised two years earlier to do it and it came to pass. It was unusual as the event was held in one of the closed churches in the archdiocese, which we sold to the university. They were able to retrofit the building and restore most of its original beauty. It was an Irish Catholic church dedicated to St. Brigid and she would have been proud of the new ceiling, lighting, flooring and the painting. The archdiocese had no intention of doing any of that, as there were three other parish churches within a one-mile radius of this one. It was a lovely affair and I sold quite a few books. Kevin Starr was there to address the group, as well as Dr. Stephens. Michael Pritchard was the host and I said a few words of gratitude at the conclusion.

The Coyne family had more than a passing interest. They came to see the beauty of the inside of the church as it had been closed for more than 20 years. They were amazed to view the stained glass window that their grandparents had donated to the parish over 100 years before. They are some of the most beautiful stained glass windows in the churches of all San Francisco. European countries by and large found a way to preserve and take care of their historical monuments and this included most of the churches. San Francisco just didn't have the wherewithal, the intelligence nor the will to find a way to preserve a number of our churches. The same could be said of me.

There were very few people attending the church. In fact, the pastor told me he could not get enough students to serve Mass and had trouble finding ushers to take up the collection. When they had their hearing about the parish's viability to stay open, it was attended by a few who were more interested in being on TV and being heard than they were in saving St. Brigid's. The sale to AAU would guarantee its preservation even if it were no longer an active parish.

I've had the privilege of speaking in many churches over the years but this was a little different when I introduced my book at the former St. Brigid's. I can remember opening my remarks with the surprise of what might happen if at a time when you feel you need some help from above and turn to scripture. I call it scripture roulette. First you sit down by yourself with the Bible and you close your eyes. You open to anywhere and take your index finger and point to a line or a paragraph. Then you open your eyes and read what it says. Then you simply take it to heart and follow the instruction. Imagine my surprise when I opened my eyes to the passage where it simply said: "Judas went off and hanged himself." Knowing that couldn't be what I was meant to do, I shuffled the pages, took my finger and pointed again. Oh no! It said, "Go and do likewise." It wasn't my day so I put the book down and asked for God's help. I was granted it because of the many friends who came to the former church that night to raise a glass of Prosecco and support me in this first attempt as an author.

The next month when I was traveling to Cape Girardeau for my great-niece's wedding, Linda Leicht, a freelance reporter from Springfield, Missouri, met my sister and me in St. Louis at the Drury Inn near the airport. I had no idea what to expect but when I found out that she drove four hours to have the opportunity to sit down and chat for an hour, I was impressed. She didn't seem to be pushy or overly attentive as to impress but rather laid back, like a professional woman who knew her craft. I was thrilled to death to see the full page New Year's Eve article in the Gannett-owned *Springfield News-Leader*, complete with color photos. She delivered.

I wish I could have said the same for the Catholic newspaper in Springfield called *The Mirror*. After multiple emails, calls and call-backs, nothing transpired. It could have been political or it could have just been the fact that they were not interested. Guys like me usually feel we have something to offer. But, maybe not. At least not to my old diocese.

When I was in Cape Girardeau, I also had been in contact with the local newspaper, the *Southeast Missourian*. They had told me that they would do an interview. No telephone call, no contact occurred. As I was performing my great-niece's wedding in St. Vincent's church, the man in the pew behind my sister remarked during the kiss of peace how wonderful the priest was. Della told him that she was my sister and he introduced himself as the owner of the *Southeast Missourian*. When we were outside of church he came up to me and asked if I'd had a chance to introduce my book to the people of southeast Missouri. Well, before I was able to make it to the reception, which was held on a riverboat on the Mississippi, a caller on my cell asked if I would be open to a short interview before the reception began. There I sat in the hallway of a riverboat casino with a young man who had little or no idea of what he was supposed to do or say. He had not read the book nor did he have any idea that the owner of the paper had requested his assignment. His editor must have sent him. Unlike other people who work in the press, this young man was on a learning curve and I hope by this time he has had enough experience to do the job. The printed piece came out the following week and, what can I say without being critical, it was words.

The article in the *Springfield News-Leader* stirred up some nostalgia among my former high school students and radio listeners and more than a little interest. So, the following spring during Lent I traveled back to my first diocese for a book signing. The pastor and associate pastor at St. Elizabeth Ann Seton parish were both old friends from my early days as a priest and Monsignor Reidy invited me to be the guest homilist and con-celebrant for the four weekend Masses at his booming 2,000-member parish.

I had left the Drury Inn in St. Louis in such a hurry to get to Springfield that I forgot my black pants to match my suit coat. Now, I'm in town and have to go shopping for a pair of pants just so I can look like a priest to this parish with a ministry for everyone. Father Tom Reidy has done a great job handing out work. Collaboration wins over ego any day. That's the way it should be with the shortage of priests. The more the laity can do, the more it will prove that it's their Church and their faith that will keep it going and growing. Both Tom and his associate Mike McDevitt were instrumental in making my visit a great success. They are cream of the crop priests who have borne the heat of the day and continue to channel the graces of the Church to everyone who wants or has the courage to step up and ask for it. I'm not sure I could have remained as strong in my faith and committed to the priesthood had I remained in Southern Missouri. There is a reason for everything under the sun. It was quite unusual in 1972 that I went to California and at the time I always felt that someday I would return and life in Missouri would go on. It wasn't God's plan nor mine. I'm grateful for what happened. I can look back and see what I've been able to do that never could have been done in the bible belt of Southwest Missouri.

St. Elizabeth Ann Seton parish had all the trimmings of an up-to-date service station for the faithful. It had a school and meeting rooms and more rooms so that the multiplicity of organizations could thrive and support one another in their effort to live the Gospel. As I approached the pulpit, I saw nary a face that I recognized. There upon I asked the question of who might have been taught by me at St. Agnes High School in the late 1960s. There were hands going up from almost every section of the 500-seat place of worship and I felt at home. It was a wonderful and rewarding response. Saint Elizabeth Ann Seton did her thing many years ago for Catholic education and my wee contribution warmed my heart.

I gave the same homily at all the Masses and it didn't bother me to repeat and repeat the same Jesus message that few had ever heard from me. Sometimes, I see a glazed over look on the people in the pews and no matter what I say it seems to fail to go the distance and peters out like a small Fourth of July rocket that runs out of powder. The joy of Mudville can disintegrate rapidly with just a few negative words. It's good motivation for me not to pass judgment so quickly on others, as I have felt the sting of disappointed people who are not afraid to let one have it when you make a mistake.

Crowds can be mindless, so there is always the danger of saying the wrong thing. Moses broke the Ten Commandments coming down the mountain to give them to the people. The God I know is a God of mercy and not laws. Commands make for good order but too often they condemn when we should be merciful.

No one has shown this better in my 53 years as a priest than the present pope, Francis. His little book on mercy is a treasure. I could include all kinds of quips and quotes from it. It made a difference in my struggle for life. All of us are searching for wholeness. Being a priest, a Roman Catholic and a Christian are all helpful but as scripture says, "In my father's house there are many mansions." There is room for everyone no matter who you are or where you're from or what your beliefs.

Many of my former students stayed afterwards to talk and buy *I'll Never Tell*. We took pictures and I signed books. I sold a number of books — actually sold out, as did Barnes and Noble in the mall — and I ended up mailing some 50 copies back to Springfield. It was a true joy to have some of the young men and women come to me after Mass that day to tell me how much I had meant to them as we were growing up together. Our paths had not crossed for years and yet I felt a warmth and a genuine gratitude for the time I had spent with them nearly 50 years ago.

There was a young diocesan priest who did an interview with me for his radio stations and he went to a lot of trouble, motoring over from Joplin, Missouri, and setting up his equipment in the conference room of the old high school where I had taught. It was now the diocesan chancery office. Father J Friedl was kind and interesting and more interested in his guest than himself.

After many years of being on that side of the microphone doing radio interviews, I learned the difference. More than a few times I caught myself trying to look and sound important and spellbinding, while forgetting that the reason I'm talking to another person is because I want to learn from them and about them. Over the years, it became quite an education to listen to someone espouse their main beliefs and tenets in a 15-minute period, when it might take a half a day to review the book or do the follow-up to really appreciate that unique individual. It's a rare talent that some interviewers have, to step inside another and explore the nooks and crannies of their guest's existence, and then move in and out so that all of a sudden the audience says, "Hey, that guy is special." Not everyone is out to sell something.

When I do an interview, I have to be careful that I'm not trying to peddle my book. I was offering grace one time before a benefit dinner in San Francisco and as I was praying I looked up and saw a man in the corner selling my books and without even thinking about it, I mentioned his name and what he was doing. Father Ken, my good friend and the pastor of the parish where I live, spoke up in the quiet of the prayer-filled room and reminded me that I was saying grace before the meal and that I could sign the books afterwards. I did that while on ego-pilot but it just goes to show how one's thoughts, even in prayer, can be projected somewhere else.

It was a special lunch that I had with my former seminary classmate Charlie O'Reilly while I was in town. He has been very successful with O'Reilly Auto Parts and has been generous in supporting my TV Mass ministry and the God Squad. He is a gentleman and a delight to be around. He and his lovely wife, Mary Beth, came to Mass and unfortunately I did not have time to go to dinner with them. She had serious cancer during her lifetime and the O'Reilly family came to the rescue building a cancer center in Springfield dedicated to serving the people of southern

Missouri. Charlie still has that boyish face along with his crew cut. I always gave him a flat top in the seminary. I was a student barber and tonsorial artistry helped me with expenses that my family could not afford. He also has maintained his good health and a fit and trim physique. I think he has gone for cycling in a big way. His brothers are good motivation for all of them to stay in shape.

Once again I got in such a hurry to drive back to St. Louis that I left the rectory with my billfold, all my money, cards, and driver's license in the top drawer of the desk where I had been writing. I was an hour up the road when I had to turn around and retrace my drive. Of course, that made me two hours late for a dinner scheduled with the Drurys. Charles and Shirley are longtime friends and supporters of my ministry. They had been close with my oldest brother Charlie and his wife, Mary. They did many things together. It was my brother who nicknamed Shirley "Flickers". I had known them since I was just a boy. Charles is now in his 90s and still working managing his chain of hotels. I try to visit them every time I go to the Midwest. They have been a blessing to me. I had to call and cancel. I think they were relieved. So I took my time and contemplated the entire visit to the Show Me State and life on the road as a bestselling author.

* * *

I had a chance to go to New York that December and do an interview on Sirius radio on the Catholic Channel with Father Dave Dwyer, a Paulist priest. The executive producer, Brett Seidell, set it all up for an evening. He does a show every day with Cardinal Dolan the Archbishop of New York and follows the signs of the times. The program is *Busted Halo*. I love that title. It leaves lots of room for the human condition. Father Dave was a very good interviewer and kept things moving. He still does the daily chores of a Catholic priest, but in the evenings he is devoted to the airwaves for a few hours. He was aware of my relationship with Cardinal Dolan. I was able to relate a couple of stories from *I'll Never Tell* and that seemed to be of interest.

The frosty weather and the hectic pace of the Big Apple brought me back to the first winter I lived in New York City. It was 1983 and I was working for the Catholic Communications Conference and recording my *Father Harry God Squad* spots at ABC radio. My show aired around the world and I was still something of a phenom as a rock & roll priest. I was moving in rarefied air in those days and had scored an invitation to MTV's New Year's Eve Party. I was rubbing elbows with the likes of Elton John and Cyndi Lauper and thinking how important I was. About three in the morning I headed out in my sport coat and leather shoes, walking toward home, not quite sure where that was. The snow was beautiful at first and then a major storm began to blow. I came across Grand Central Station by some miracle and found my way to my bed before daybreak, but not before catching the cold of the century. I smiled and thanked God for the Busted Halo, which was much more my speed now days.

CHAPTER 21

Land of Eire

I WAS IN and out of the Sirius studio in 30 minutes and had just enough time to meet up with my good friend Jim Normile. We met at our old hangout, the New York Athletic Club, on the handball courts. Remember I spoke about how friendships grow? Jim and I met in 1982. I had his marriage and baptized his three children. He has been a member of the God Squad board of directors all these years and a generous benefactor.

He has a second home in Glin, Ireland, on the Shannon River. It's about a 45-minute drive from Limerick. He has invited me to spend time there often to write and reflect. I'm in Dublin tonight and will take the train to Limerick tomorrow morning. My telephone doesn't work but the email does. I'm going to shower and go to dinner. I hate eating alone so it will be "fast" food. No sense in paying the big prices for a nice place when I can only stare at the other patrons.

I always look forward to the ride from the Shannon airport to Glin. I'm picked up by another Jim who drives the one taxi in the town. After I get in his car, he begins to speak and 45 minutes later I'm home at the Shannon Fort in Ballyhoolahan, with hardly a clue of what he was saying. I do know that he cares about Yanks and is delighted that my good pal Mr. Normile had purchased and redone the old structure. The Georgian house, circa 1790, was remodeled by a Normile cousin who lives nearby. He is a master carpenter and the home is in Maurice Craig's book *Classic Irish Houses of the Middle Size*. The website "Buildings of Ireland" calls Fort Shannon romantic with "picturesque massing" (built with simple lines, in varying heights with low-pitched roofs).

There is no television at Fort Shannon, no telephone, no radio, no WiFi, just the quiet whisper of the wind and the eager moos of the cattle outside the window of the room where I write. The dining room table serves as my desk and is where I say Mass daily. I've got plenty photos of this house and the River Shannon, as well as the cows in the pasture out my window. They love me. They're teenagers and run every time they think food is coming. All they do is eat and shit, eat and shit. Glad I'm not a cow.

After a walk, I finished a good book and now will try and prepare some grub. It's almost 7:30 p.m. and I've yet to eat. Looks like smoked salmon for warm up and a turkey burger or two. Tom Healy (Jim's cousin) brought me some Irish soda bread this morning. Jim arrives Saturday evening. I've got two full days without him.

As I sit here in the quiet of the countryside in the county of Limerick, I can't help but think of all the great things I've learned from the Irish people over the years. In my formative years in the seminary the lessons were numerous and precious. I'm still in my formative years as I learn something everyday. Just this morning a visitor was telling me about the fat Irishman who was trying to lose weight. His wife said, "Dearie, would you like an egg?" "Aw yes my love," he said through a smile, "but only if you include with the meal the one who laid it."

The town of Glin is a good 45-minute walk and just enough to work up an appetite and look forward to some conversation with the locals about the happenings in the area. Ireland is one place in the world that doesn't know a stranger. You go into a pub and someone will invite you to conversation. It's always worth it.

The Irish have invested heavily in education for their children and these educated people have been labeled the most expensive export of the country. It's no wonder that so many good writers and creative talent come from the Emerald Isle. I buy groceries and visit the little town of Listowel where some of the most famous writers in history have gathered to match wits and produce work that will never go away.

Jim arrived today so we're going to cook a chicken. We'll take a rest and then go to Conway's pub at 10 p.m. to meet his cousins. I know it's old and it smells but it's the place to be on a Saturday night in Glin. Normile is a common name in the area as both Jim's parents were born and raised there. He can enter almost any pub and when he announces his name someone will have known his family and his family's family. What a blessing! It's just like the TV bar "Cheers" where everybody knows your name. There is always a warm feeling when you're in a strange country and people initiate conversation. They are interested in Americans and everything we do and say. With friends like Jim, who needs to worry about life?

* * *

How to make a guy feel good . . . open your e-mail on Pentecost Sunday while you're working on a second book, thinking about all the wonderful things you might be able to say, when you see a message from an Irish bishop sent via my website fatherharry.org.

Name: Brendan Comiskey

Message: I'm a retired Bishop here in Dublin (and a naturalized US citizen). Read your book today and yesterday. Thank God for you and your courage and your great love of the church. +Brendan

Isn't that grand! Here is an honest opinion from someone who knows the Church and who has traveled around the Episcopal block a few times. It was a rare treat to get his message and I had to share the joy of this message with all of you. I hope that I'll get to meet him someday and thank him in person. The writing is coming along. The Irish weather has been great with a few clouds. It might rain today so it will make it easier to work. Now I must look him up to review his background.

Sorry to say Bishop Comiskey retired after he was accused of not doing all he could to prevent sexual abuse in his diocese.

* * *

A 30-something priest asked me to come to his Young Adult meeting to share some of my book with his club. I wasn't sure how many, if any, of them knew me and so was not expecting a crowd. There were six counting the young priest. I knew I was up against it when I mentioned Vatican II and got the never-never look. I asked how many of them knew about it. Well no one, so there goes my depth of discussion if I have to define "Church" for them according to Vatican II. How many of you have heard of Cardinal Roncalli or Pope John the 23rd? No one. So there goes my introduction to the greatest pope of my lifetime. It would take more time to introduce these two topics than it would to discuss them in the bar where the six would head off to once I was finished. Don't misunderstand, I was glad to have six. Oh, no sales pitch and no (or little) mention of the book. I just wanted to discover for myself how these young adults were fitting into the picture of the Church universal. They really were a new breed and one that an 80-year-old would have to spend more time reading about than socializing with.

Gen Z is the new nomenclature. Gone are the Baby Boomers, Millennials, the X generation — '23 skidoo, rosin on the bow and here we go! The Catholic Church could easily be accused of losing a whole generation or two of people becoming Catholics or living

Catholic lives. But a strong belief in the Holy Spirit makes me think and feel like it will be a whole new brand that is bred and guys like me will be out there in the pasture, like the cows outside my window, chewing our cud watching the rain fall and hoping the grass would stay green forever.

I did get the attention of this small group by telling them that I thought I would be married after about five years in the priesthood. I thought marriage for priests was imminent. That meant the rules would have changed by 1970. Now I'm quite positive that they'll change about five minutes after I croak. Then the scriptures will be proclaimed that the first pope, Peter, was married, as it says that Jesus took care of his mother-in-law when she had a fever. When she got better she got up and waited on him. Jesus had a number of women who were close to him during the three years he was an itinerant preacher. Our history and theology got so hung up over the years that the rightful place for women in the Church has not yet come to the fore. It will. I'm convinced. The Holy Spirit will be the enforcer. Time, like oil, is a great healer. Oil or chrism is used for baptisms, confirmations, anointing of the sick and of the newly ordained. One day it, too, will consecrate the hands of the dedicated women who are half the human race and can assist in making the Church whole.

Although my writing will never compare to that of Matthew, Mark, Luke or John and I'll never know their fame and glory, it is truly inspired by so many wonderful and holy people. The two Latin words *in* and *spiro* literally mean to "breathe into". From year one to year 80, I have had people who have not only breathed down my neck but into my heart a spirit of Godli- and goodli-ness. Those people have made it possible for me live and breathe the faith in all that I do and say, and yes write.

Jim and I are going for lunch at Adair today and we'll take a long walk by the river if it's not raining. He made scones early this morning. I got up at 6:30 a.m. because I wanted to finish off the notes I had. This place and this stay were great for writing. I have a picture from Listowel, the "Literary Capital of Ireland", of me standing alongside a statue of acclaimed playwright Mr. John B. Keane. We make a great couple.

I leave Dublin around noon tomorrow and will be home in San Francisco by 3:30 the same afternoon. Then my system will have to re-adjust. I hope to return to Fort Shannon. It's there for the asking.

CHAPTER 22

From Montana to Maui

MY OLD FRIEND and classmate Charlie O'Reilly gave me the family cabin in the woods of Montana to go fishing. It's near Yellowstone National Park. He made the generous offer when we saw each other during my book-signing trip to the Ozarks. I asked my longtime friend and handball buddy Tony Martorana to come along and he accepted my invitation and off we went.

We arrived on Sunday night. We fished all day in the rain on Monday. Tuesday we drove around looking for fresh water so the fish could see our bait. Too much rain! Wednesday, it snowed. We had hoped to drive to Yellowstone to see the wildlife but learned that the roads were all closed because of the snow. We paid United to change our flight and came home on Wednesday afternoon. The idea of sitting in a bunkhouse in the mountains watching daytime TV was just not that inviting. I told Charlie about our trip and he opened the door to next year.

I've been using other people's property my whole life. In fact, I'm looking out at the ocean from a home in Maui where I've holed up to edit what I've written so far. People are so generous with their wealth. I've been blessed.

I worked every day, mostly in the mornings from seven to noon. Then a quick dip in the ocean and a wash clean in the pool and back to writing. I did some editing and also went over about 200 radio scripts from my days as *Father Harry of the God Squad* to see if there was material that could be used in my next book. I found plenty. There are pieces that may seem far out there but as I re-read and edited they were not as bad as I imagined. I tackled three letters and delved more deeply into the priest abuse phenomenon.

It was a beautiful setting with hardly any distractions except my two housekeepers who work for my host, Kip. On Thursday, after they had done the laundry and cleaned, I asked them to lunch. It was very enjoyable. Coming out of the restaurant we're met by five aging men mostly bent over and looking like they were searching for the geriatrics ward. One guy said, "Oh my God, it's Harry Schlitt!" and I responded, "It's Charlie Murphy!" It was Bishop Todd Brown from Orange, Cardinal William Levada, Monsignor Murphy and their classmate Father Jerry. Monsignor Murphy and I had been friends since Rome. They were spending a week vacationing in Maui. I tried to make an adequate introduction but failed miserably. Seldom at a loss for words, I had a moment's pause trying to say what I was doing in paradise with two gorgeous young women. Finally Miranda introduced herself and her friend. Miranda handles all Kip's properties on the island for him.

Later on I sent Bill an e-mail and invited him to the house on Friday. He and Murphy came over and we took a dip in the ocean. We weren't very sure on our feet and had to hold onto each other when entering the waves. It was a sight. No pictures. Mahalo.

My time on Maui was drawing to a close, so I kept my Saturday schedule light. I'd say Mass, have a bite and stare at the sea a bit. I'd break for intermediate dips in the pool and later in the afternoon catch the Notre Dame/Michigan game. My old pal from Rome Wayne Ressler and I made a point of attending that match when we could, but who needs football when you can have paradise. My days as a babe magnet are dwindling fast, but there will always be sports.

CHAPTER 23

Gadgets Galore

REMEMBER HOW WE used to think that television was a distraction for young people? As a guidance counselor in the Ozarks during the last century, when I saw parents troubled by their kids I always inquired about television and just how much they were watching. This later included video games, which can occupy hours and hours of minds while bodies are resting on a couch, a recliner or even the floor. I never did an official study nor did I put it all together to draw an empirical conclusion, but others have. Forty or 50 years ago it made a difference in all our lives whether we watched or not. Most did and, like secondhand smoke, we were all affected. Even though I've been a television presenter for more than 50 years, I watch very little TV now, except sports and old movies. Honestly, now that I read what I've just written, I watch a lot so it's a little bit like a pot calling the kettle black.

But television is nothing compared to the present day devices that are in 90% of hands on the streets or in offices or homes or wherever the human being finds a place to use them. Wait — I just looked it up and it's a mind-blowing 96% of Americans who use a cell phone. Unfortunately, these devices have also been the cause of innumerable deaths in cars, as texting while driving or even talking while driving distracts the person behind the wheel from what should be their major focus, driving. Cell phones make every little byte of communication so important that instant gratification seems necessary. But it really isn't.

Ask the person who gets up early and leaves his cell phone in bed because he was using it when he fell asleep. They arrive at their desk and reach in their pocket to check e-mail or see if there were calls. Oh no! I left my iPhone in bed! Somehow, they make it through the day and as soon as they return from work, they dash to the bedroom. They pick it up and scroll the calls, the emails, the messages and, lo and behold, there was nothing important. They head for the liquor cabinet, make themselves a vodka martini with olives and plop on the couch to watch the evening news. They could leave it at home everyday but will they? Not on your life!

It's a bit like the common cold; there is no ordinary cure. Billions of dollars are spent in research and development for all kinds of ailments, but no one has yet found the cure for the common cold. Some are saying that all the particles going through the air are making a difference in our lives. Some say that brain cancer might stem from using the cellphone so close to it, so now we see so many these days with a little white ear attachment protruding from their auricular openings. In my day, "this Bud's for you" had a completely different meaning. Information even when dull, un-exciting and repetitious isn't information but only fuel for the fire pit. There is a 30-year-old man I know who lives with wires coming out of his ears. Whatever he is listening to through the wires is only penetrated by the call to dinner.

There are all kinds of studies about the lack of personal development or communication because of being enslaved to electronic devices. You can read those on your own and come to your personal conclusions.

Online dating services like Match and Christian Cafe are being used more and more these days because people can browse and read what another says. Some people even record and post videos.

But still, it's a long way through cyberspace to the soul of another human being. I used to say that the longest journey is from the head to the heart. We can convince ourselves of something but never really treasure it unless it directly affects how we feel. Since that beautiful gift of love comes from the heart, it's more important to pay close attention than to rely on technology to carry the case. Relying on a video to choose the perfect person is like sitting at the roulette table and gambling whether the pea will fall on the red or the black. Imagine your surprise when it hits the green. OMG!

CHAPTER 24

Tassels and Barbed Wire

IT'S BEEN EIGHT straight years that I've been invited to give the invocation and benediction for the Academy of Art University graduation. Over 2,000 students pass before me on the stage each year with the highest of hopes for their careers. It's been both a privilege and a pleasure for me to participate. I see young faces from all over the world accomplishing something. They are proud to be productive and to make a contribution. Art knows no boundaries and this led me this past year to concentrate on walls of separation and bridges of understanding. Not exactly the ruling party line in Washington but certainly appreciated by an audience who knows how hard it is to come to another country and get a degree, whether undergrad or grad.

My prop was a simple piece of rusted barbed wire, about a foot in length, all twisted and bent. This is how I got it.

In the college seminary in St. Louis, I had a classmate named Paul. He decided the priesthood was not for him after four years of college at the Cardinal Glennon Seminary in Shrewsbury, a small 'burb of St. Louis. After graduation I never saw him nor heard from him, until one evening in the Vatican, where I was studying theology, I got a telephone call from Berlin. The mysterious voice says to me, "Don't say my name if you recognize me, I'm undercover." Seems that the CIA was eager to recruit seminary students for their training, as they believed they were getting high moral character, mixed with strong family values and the intelligence to do their work. Obviously, much of it was clandestine. Paul fit the profile. "Could you take the train to Berlin?" he asked. "I need to talk to a friend and I heard you were at the North American College. The train is fast and inexpensive. I'll pay your way. When can you get a few days?" Without thinking I replied, "We have a break after Easter. I'll sign out for that time and will meet you." "I can't give you any details," continued the mysterious voice, "but I'll send you a ticket and just get on the train and off. Don't worry. Everything's cool."

The train was a *rapido* (Italian for fast) and comfortable. I had been to Germany the year before but never as far north as Berlin. It was there that the Iron Curtain separated East from West and over the years they had become like two countries. It was never more clear than during the Olympics, when there were two German teams. We all saw the terrible pictures of how it was.

I disembarked in West Berlin and before I could look around out of the darkness came this wispy little figure wearing sunglasses at night and non-descript clothes, walking the same way I could recall from a few years earlier when we were in the seminary. "Hey Fuzz," he said, using my nickname from school. "Good to see you. Thanks for coming." We hustled out of the Bahnhof and into a small dark Volkswagen, one of the 1963 kind that was called a beetle or a bug. Naturally, I was curious about his life and we tried to catch up during the short drive away from the lights and into the countryside. After about 30 minutes, he pulled off the road. He told me to stay put no matter what. He darkened his face and hands and took a small wirecutters and dropped to the ground and began crawling through the weeds. My window was rolled down and I could hear the faint sound of dogs barking in the distance. It was the East German police patrolling the fence. In what seemed like an age, probably about five minutes, Paul returned to the car and started the engine while wiping his face and hands on a towel in the back seat next to my bag. When we were a half mile down the road he produced a piece of barbed wire and laid it on the dashboard.

"Harry, whenever in life you feel bound, limited, not welcome, not free, a prisoner in your own country, take this barbed wire and have yourself a good meditative prayer." He said it was a very small risk that he took for a piece of wire that I might be able to use to tell the story of the Berlin Wall and influence others with whom I speak about how important freedom is to every individual.

So I say to the AAU graduates, "Let your art build bridges. Let your talents not be wasted behind walls thrown up by politicians who don't have the moxie to figure out that's what the whole world needs."

Jesus told his followers pretty much the same thing when he told them if they have talents and gifts not to hide them or put a bushel basket over them but rather put them up high for everyone to see and appreciate.

As an aside, the AAU in San Francisco has come under some sharp criticism in the past few years. The school has grown to over 14,000 students. They have campus property all over the City and a growing interest in educating people all around the world. I wrote a letter of support to the San Francisco Planning Department and submitted it to the *Chronicle*, which never printed it.

Dear President Fong,

I am a Roman Catholic priest and for the past nine years have had the pleasure of addressing almost 50,000 students, graduates, parents, family and friends of the Academy of Art University.

I have sat on the stage as these students from all over the world pass by their president, Dr. Elisa Stephens, to receive their diplomas in the Arts and so many offshoot disciplines. I marvel at their parents who have made great sacrifices to send them to the United States and to San Francisco to gain not only a skill in their chosen field, but to live and work in the environs of one of the most unique cities in the world. That in itself is a priceless education.

I have watched and admired the University (without a campus) transfer old buildings, yes, and even one of our most beautiful Catholic churches into an artistic venue for continued education. Room and board for foreign and domestic students is provided all over the City with transportation to and from classes and living quarters.

Dr. Stephens and her very large faculty have truly made something out of nothing, the classic definition of "creation".

I can't believe the short-sightedness of politicians and public figures wanting to lessen the value of a priceless education in the arts in a City that itself cries out for youthful talent to come and taste, and return to your homes with an affection for and bragging rights to have worked, lived, and studied in this outstanding place.

It is also worth telling the truth about the many aged buildings and places that could easily be torn down to the detriment of the historical significance here, structures now being occupied by students who appreciate living here and working on a degree at the same time.

God Bless the Academy of Art University for this wonderful contribution to the City of Saint Francis.

Sincerely,

Monsignor Harry G. Schlitt

* * *

The AAU awards honorary doctorates at every graduation. It's a marvelous way of showing respect and highlighting the works of those who have graduated and made it in the real world. You can witness what they've been able to accomplish from their hard work in school.

Talent in the field of art is an unusual thing, a gift really. No artist is ever finished. The critique of their work will live forever. As long as we have viewers and listeners, admirers or critics, we'll have art.

De gustibus is a Latin phrase which translates to "a matter of taste". Our likes and dislikes vary according to each one of us. That's another reason why art is so valuable to our society. It allows everyone from everywhere to have some enjoyment from what another has created.

I like to address the students as a "world class" of whatever year because in the case of the Academy, it's true. Students come from all over the world to study art and San Francisco is a world class city in which to try your hand and open your soul to return something to the world. Good, bad or indifferent, art is art and as I said before it's a matter of taste. One woman's castle is another woman's convent. Not sure where that came from.

For the past nine years it's been my privilege to witness many students who experience the joy of advancing a grade, of making something from nothing, of joining the creative universe of art. Each valedictorian says it better than the one before. They all seem to have original ideas to accompany the usual advice to their fellow classmates of hard work, late nights, disappointment, trial and error along the way. They continue to amaze me with their genuine outlook on life and what has just gone before them. With a piece of paper that says they did something, for the most part they still have no job, no immediate monetary satisfaction for what they can do outside the confines of the classroom.

In 2018, I told the story of the former Navy fighter pilot who was in command of a Southwest Airlines jet when one of the engines blew. A sharp piece of the engine hit the side of the plane and made a hole in the cabin window large enough for the woman seated there in Row 14 to be blown out. Her seatbelt saved her from being completely ejected and she was pulled back into the plane. She later died. With nerves of steel, the female pilot safely landed the badly disabled jet, saving the lives of 148 people. There was much ado about it in the media and rightly so. One interviewer asked her where she got the cool, calm and collected demeanor to land the plane without panic. She replied that she did what she'd learned about flying: aviate, navigate and communicate, adding that these are the three basic skills that compare to the ABCs of anything.

You fly, you figure out where you are and where you're going, then you tell someone so that in case of emergency they can be there to help.

I told the graduates that they are, first, artists, but they had serious and meaningful instruction. Teachers have helped them along to aviate, to fly. Now they must navigate and go where they might find a suitable place in life to work, to create, to produce. After that, it's a matter of telling people about their work. It's a challenge to get out there and do what you have to do so that someone sees your art. When you were young, your mother put it on the fridge. Now it has to be hung, sung, or seen somewhere in order for you to make a living. I asked God to guide them along the way through this process and be grateful to their parents, sponsors, teachers, instructors and fellow students who have prodded each other to this final day of graduation.

As has always been the case throughout my ministry, I never know when my words affect my listeners, unless they let me know.

A few days after that graduation, I got an email via my fatherharry. org website from one of the new grads:

"Hello Father Harry,

My name is Jonas, Thank you for coming to my graduation in the Academy of Art University and speak the truth about our heavenly father. It takes courage to speak his name in public in San Francisco, and this is the first time I have heard his name in this school, thank you for your motivational speach."

Nice for an old guy like me to have relevance with someone from Gen Z.

Let's face it, most graduations are boring, except to the students who are graduating. The ceremony goes on and on with speeches and promises that more often than not seem too lofty to be kept. One prominent exception is the speech written by the 1918 valedictorian of St. Lawrence grade school, my mother, Theckla Dirnberger:

> *New Hamburg, Mo.*
> *April 26 - 1918*
> *Rev. Father, Teachers, Parents & Friends,*
> *On a fine spring morning, 8 years ago, several kind Mamma's of New Hamburg, fitted out a little girl for what they considered an important event — the first school day. With the primer in one hand and the lunchbasket in the other, those little girls were presently on their way to school. Being one of them, I can say, our little hearts were filled with great joy and expectation. Arriving at our destination, just a little fear and awe threatened to overcome us, in spite of all our bravery. Good Sr. Wilhelmina's pleasing ways, however, soon made us forget all uneasiness. Alas! Poor Sr. Wilhelmina cannot be with us today, but I am sure her kind eyes look down upon us from heaven at this moment. Before we realized*

it we were arranged in classes and set to our task. Months and years passed. We labored on, passed from class to class and from room to room, until now our teachers think us qualified to graduate from the grades. We have reached the goal of our ambition and we rejoice. Let us not pride ourselves, however, nor attribute our success to our efforts alone. Our teachers have worked hard and patiently, and have spared no means to advance us in our studies, and fit us for the life henceforth. Let us never forget and ever remember the credit due them.

Today is, as it were, a turning point in our lives. Like a foot ball player we have reached the first goal. We are about to step from childhood into womanhood. Our life so far, flowed along calmly and serenely as well as full of ease. Thus far our parents have cared for us and supplied all our wants. From now on we must lend them a helping hand. We must share with them their cares and labors of life, and so lighten, the burden, that has rested upon their shoulders so long. In so doing, we will in part repay them for the sacrifices they brought for us, and under their wise guidance prepare ourselves for our future stations in life.

And now my dear fellow-graduates! In the presence of the Rev. Pastor, Teachers and Parents, let us promise ever to prove ourselves <u>*true*</u> *pupils of our* <u>*school*</u>*. Let us show by our conduct in the future, that the seed it has sown has fallen on fertile soil, and that the principles implanted in our hearts have taken deep root, never to be effaced.*

Knowing you all will join me in my pledge, I now bid, farewell to good old St. Lawrence School.

Theckla Dirnberger
New Hamburg, Mo.

* * *

My mother was just 12 years old when she wrote this and lived up to her pledge her entire life.

Some speeches are so political that they make the evening news and the morning papers. In fact, most graduations have politicians as speakers because they are in the news and are accustomed to speaking in front of broad audiences. And who, I might add, are usually graduates themselves from some denominational institution. They seem to fit the fare of what the faculty expects at a graduation. The difference at the Academy of Art University is that they already have product to show and tell. There is sound and light, picture and production to put on the screen. It makes for an interesting couple of hours. Everyone is complimented when they see their work on the big screen in front of thousands of people they don't know. I'm sure more than one parent remarked, "Oh this is what my kid has learned in art school. I thought he was just drawing pictures somewhere!"

Recently the university honored Jan Yanehiro for her work as the first Director of the School of Communications & Media Technologies. It was particularly interesting to me as I have known her since 1973 when she first started at KFRC in San Francisco as the Director of Public Service Broadcasting. Since the air is owned by the people, they have a right to offer services that help the community. This used to be the regulation. The FCC, Federal Communications Commission, no longer requires this so that spectrum of radio that was so rich in different colors and causes has now disappeared. Of course, this included religion and many of my earlier broadcasts were bundled into the public service package that helped stations meet their obligations to the community they served.

Jan was very helpful to me in those early days as she had personality and could charm anyone. She is Japanese by descent but was raised in Hawaii. Her earlier attempts at breaking into broadcasting were denied, as she says, because of "this face". She was turned away by every TV station in the San Francisco market. I recalled that she interviewed me on TV around 1981 as a practice reel for her future work. She finally got her start at one affiliate for a show called *Evening Magazine*. She did that for 17 years. But the real story for Jan is to witness how much her students love and respect her. They went crazy when she stepped to the podium as Doctor Jan Yanehiro. It gave me goosebumps.

I consider myself an artist, so it's not really a task to encourage others in that field to open their heart to art. The book they write might sit on the shelf, their painting might rest in the attic, their designer clothing might be hidden in a closet, but they should never forget that the creation of their art came from the heart. The heart cannot be denied unless it has died.

Over the years I've had my share of graduations. Back in Southern Missouri I gave baccalaureate speeches as well as commencement talks because I was a popular figure on the radio. It meant a lot to me to be the first Catholic priest to be welcomed in a mostly Baptist community with a number of local preachers who would have leapt at the invitation to deliver a soul-saving spiel to high school students about the dangers of life after graduation. I have saved a few of those talks just to see what I said and how I would approach it now after 60 years of life experience. The following is from Pleasant Hope, Missouri, given on May 18, 1972. The cover on the program had a quote from Dr. Martin Luther King, Jr.. This was significant because I didn't see one African-American person at the graduation.

"This is our hope . . . to transform
the jangling discords of our nation
into a beautiful symphony
of brotherhood."

I recall how I began with the story of a little baby who is so helpless and yet continues to grow with help. Then after accomplishing the great art of mobility and speech, they are often told to "sit down and shut up".

The film *The Graduate* was still in vogue and the lines from the Simon and Garfunkel tune were still meaningful, as they are today:

"We'd like to know a little bit about you for our files
We'd like to help you learn to help yourself."

I'm not in this world to live up to your expectations and you are not in this world to live up to mine. You are you. I am me. And if we find each other, it's beautiful, and if we don't, I pray it can't be helped. I used the lyric from *American Pie* about the day the music died. (Remember, I was on the radio every week and really enjoyed and used the lyrics of the songs in those days.)

I asked those young kids if a blind person would like them. They can't see your physical beauty or how tall you are and have very little to make a judgment on or about you. I gave the example of a 17-year-old on television, who was thinking about taking her life when she called in on the *Kennedy Show*, which was broadcast on ABC in Chicago. I was a regular guest. I had no immediate answer for her but simply smiled and said how grateful we were that she took the time to seek out help. I was told later on that the joy from all of us on the set made a difference in her choice to keep going.

Making a choice about self-image was big for me in those days. Most of these youngsters had heard my descriptions of my coach who used to say, "Harry, sit at the end of the bench, you're drawing flies." Or, my grade school sweetheart who was once described as a raw egg on a nail.

My conclusion was a quote from an Egyptian priest in 2000 BC: "The children love luxury, they have bad manners, contempt for authority and they show disrespect for their elders. They contradict their parents and tyrannize their teachers. The end of the world is near."

This was followed by a lyric from a Carpenters' song:

> "Sometimes not often enough
> We reflect upon the good things
> And those thoughts always center around those we love
> And I think about those people who mean so much to me
> And for so many years have made me so very happy
> And I count the times I have forgotten to say 'thank you'
> And just how much I love them."

When I was given an honorary doctorate in humane letters from Waynesburg University in Pennsylvania, I gave the Baccalaureate speech and Senator Rick Santorum gave the commencement talk. We were both Catholics but he was much more tied up in old time religion and missed out on the beauty of the Second Vatican Council. So many younger people today don't realize that by definition they are the People of God and therefore have all the rights and privileges thereof. No one can deny them their part of being and acting like someone who has been saved and appreciates the gift of forgiveness from God. Senator Santorum was an excellent speaker but he was still talking about a Church that I grew up in, not the one that has made some significant changes. For example, we now pray in our native tongue. We love and preach the scriptures. Life is to be lived, not to feel guilty about what we did in life.

The President of Waynesburg University heard me speak in Dallas, as I was given an award by the wife of a famous senator Bob Dole. Elizabeth Dole was president of the American Red

Cross at the time. The organization giving me the award was the Religious Heritage of America. It was a national interfaith organization founded by W. Clement Stone. It was instrumental in getting the phrase "one nation, under God" added to the U.S. Pledge of Allegiance.

President Thyreen invited me to Western Pennsylvania to address his students. I returned a second time as part of an evening concert. That was in 2000 after I had been made a Monsignor that summer by the Holy Father. I remember wearing my black robe with the red buttons and the red sash. I felt like Bishop Fulton Sheen but my rendering was field fodder compared to what he could do. However, it merited a third invitation and an honorary doctorate. I treasure that piece of paper, now under glass, as I had no time to return to school and work for a doctorate in communications like a number of others who were considered on-air talent.

CHAPTER 25

Pillars

ROMAN CATHOLIC SEMINARIES in general have a mantra about priestly formation that is described as four pillars. Saint John Paul II in a letter entitled *Pastores Dabo Vobis* described the principal foundations for priestly formation as human, spiritual, intellectual and pastoral. You can read about these in many places and they are pretty much described in the same way. But after 50 years of practice, permit me to advance my perspective.

"My God, Harry, you're more human than I am and as a priest, you're supposed to be on another plane." Well, that might be part of the problem. Others might think you should be but you're not. You're only human. Sometimes you feel like you are very close to God and sometimes you're not. Remember my prostitute friend Pat? And how after she changed she told me, "Some days I am, some days we are, and some days God is. A lot depends on the day."

Human for me is a *homo sapiens* with a personality, who is working to be whole and is looking for any way they can to become better than they were. They know they have to get along with others and will have to interact in one form or another in order to become whole and better. It's not like the guy who says, "I love everyone, it's individuals I can't stand." There should be a sign on every seminary door that states, "Robots and loners need not apply." The church does provide for both in special fields of church work. Robots can often be found in canon law work, where simply memorizing the book and following the letter makes you a good canon lawyer. Not so! You have to embrace the pastoral pillar or you'll find yourself clinging to laws made a long time ago that do not reflect the church of the 21st century. Loners can imagine happiness as humans if they take themselves to a monastery, where poverty, chastity, obedience and silence are required 24/7. This is really for special vocations who know themselves better than anyone else and have been tapped by some spiritual wand that gives them the grace to accept and be happy with it. There are men and women like that. You have to know them to appreciate what they're doing and why they are doing it. My few short years with the Carmelite sisters as their chaplain in Springfield, Missouri, gave me only praise and admiration for the life they had chosen. I knew I couldn't do it, even as recently as a few short years ago when my friend Wayne and I met in Chicago. He picked me up and we drove to Gethsemani to spend some time in prayer and reflection.

Gethsemani is in Kentucky. It's a Trappist monastery set back up in the hills surrounded by rich farmland and beautiful trees and fields. The monks there work the land to provide for themselves. They live a cloistered life mixed with a work, sleep, and prayer schedule that makes them unique. They do not speak, nor watch television, nor play cards. Their minds and hearts are engrossed with God. They have a singular focus, to grow in the grace of the ONE who is above all, above all. One of their brethren was Father Thomas Merton. He authored a number of books and perhaps the most noted is *The Dark Night of the Soul*. He was studying Eastern religions in Thailand when he was electrocuted by a loose wire in a fan in his cell. (Monks live in cells.) He probably influenced hundreds of vocations to the religious life. He was a beacon for those searching to find something more.

We arrived very early one beautiful day and attended morning prayer with the monks and then meditation and Mass. A little after 1:30 p.m. we both agreed that we made the right choice in not pursuing the monastic life and so we put ourselves in reverse and headed for another part of Kentucky.

There is a small town with a post office, gas station, general store and two other major edifices. You enter the village and it says quite clearly home of the Sisters of Loreto (motherhouse) and the distillery of Maker's Mark whiskey. Guess which one we visited next?

One Christmas a friend gave me a book written by the son of the founder of Maker's Mark. It was delightful reading and I was so impressed I wrote him a letter. Bill Samuels, Jr., the owner and brilliant marketing genius who ran the company, wrote me a short note to thank me and welcome me if I ever got to that part of Kentucky. Lunch was on him. We arrived a little before noon, hoping that a short tour and lunch would be in order. "Oh, I'm sorry, Mr. Samuels isn't here today." As it turned out, it was Tuesday, an election day, and there was no alcoholic beverage to be sold or drunk or given away on that day according to local laws. His secretary telephoned him and he apologized and even offered to drive from Louisville to host our lunch. We declined and returned to Bardstown. Lovely place but don't go on election Tuesdays or you won't be able to taste the delightful spirits of the local distilleries.

Back to the pillars. So once you feel like you're human, it's time to pursue the intellectual requirements that you'll need in order to be a priest. It's pretty easy. If you don't make it, you don't get the grades, you're asked to leave. If you live in a building with those who teach you in the classroom, see you on the sports field, monitor you in study hall or the library, and keep an eye on you in the refectory, it doesn't take that much observation to see if a guy can hack it. More often than not, the person will get the drift before being asked to leave. There are a number who mean well and who can be all the other things needed to be a good priest, but the brain will not serve them to study and learn rudimentary things to continue.

I began this formation when I was 14 with 113 young men, among them one named Gene Westfeld. He was serious and holy, healthy, human, with a giant heart and a smile to match. His teeth sparkled in the sun. Yet when it came to reading a book or adding some numbers or English grammar, he was a total loss. It was sad. He had to leave the life that he dreamed of because he wasn't given the gifts to pass the courses at the time. He may have helped with the cure for cancer later on in life, I don't know. God bless him for his acceptance and appreciation for what he didn't have to manage the life as a priest.

Like most careers in life, there are men and women who or are better than others. It works with the pillar of education but not with the third pillar of spirituality. The word defines itself.

The spiritual pillar is somewhat of a mystery. None of us really knows the depth of another's spiritual life. There are certain telltale signs, like going to church regularly, loving your neighbor as yourself, or going out of your way to make someone else look good. You all know the drill. But too often there are people who have a great deal of spiritual depth to them that has not been exposed. It's there and it's not there. Judgment in this area about another is precarious to say the least. Each one of us knows from experience that we can cast a shadow on someone who turns out to be one of the best people we've ever met. There are many sinners in the history of the Church who turned out to be saints. The best example is Saint Augustine, who lived a morally reprehensible existence for many years. His poor mother, Monica, prayed and prayed. She stormed the gates of heaven to bring her son back to being a decent human being. Eventually her prayer was answered. Does this sound familiar?

When my oldest brother was discharged from the Army after an extended stay in Japan, just months after the Korean conflict ended, he arrived home with a whole new set of values that both my mother and father had not experienced at 33 North Hanover Street in Cape Girardeau, Missouri. He took a job as a bouncer in a nightclub across the river in Illinois. It was called the Purple Crackle. I can't tell you how many times it caught fire. It was an easy way to collect insurance or change management. He then went to work for an atomic bomb plant in Kentucky. He had money, charm, an outgoing personality and he could hold his liquor, most of the time. His newly found behavior was just not acceptable in the home to which he returned. So my mother prayed and she prayed. Fortunately, he was able to meet the love of his life, who helped him see the light, and they lived happily ever after. Saint Augustine said his heart would not rest until it rests in thee . . . meaning his savior, Jesus Christ.

So the spiritual life can be there, be lost, be found again, or in some never have been there, nor recognized as spirituality. I often use the expression, "The menu is not the meal, the map is not the journey, religion is not the spiritual life." You need a menu, you need a map, you need religion but they are just guides to get where you want to be or help you along the way. The first Christians were called wayfarers. They were people "on their way". The word Christian did not make an appearance before the second century, when Saint Ignatius of Antioch used it to describe those on their way. Catholic was a long time after that, when Saint Ambrose recognized that it was now a universal following and therefore could be called Catholic. Roman Catholic is yet a long way from that, because of Peter and Paul spending so much time there and Peter being entombed on the Vatican Hill in the Eternal City. They were both martyred there and their blood was the seed for so many others who would be convinced to follow the teachings of Jesus.

Even that word "eternal" smarts when I think about it. Like a few others, I felt that the center of the Church I know and love should be in Jerusalem where it all began and where the founder, Jesus Christ, did the bulk of his ministry. But it's hard to leave a place or a locale once you've built a magnificent basilica with the likes of Michaelangelo himself doing most of the work. Change never comes easy, but enough about the pillar of spirituality.

The final pillar is pastoral. This follows naturally from the spiritual life and provides the motivation and wherewithal in order to be a pastoral person.

Those preparing to become priests take a year of field education. It means that they go out from the protective walls of the seminary and get involved in parishes, varied cultural experiences, elder care centers, special educational schools, social service agencies, soup kitchens, hospitals, high schools and prisons. Each one of these assignments is supervised by a field instructor. Usually it's a priest who also works at the seminary, or it can be a religious person, or a lay person who might be in charge of the ministry. For example, it could be teaching religion in a Catholic high school where the head of that department would oversee the work and activity of the individual. I never really had that advantage in Rome, although I did say Mass and hear confession at a big parish outside the city. One penitent person was of the world, if you know what I mean, and left me with an earful of her life. After I gave her absolution, I took a deep breath and realized for the first time that I was now doing the work of a priest. I was pastoral. No one had to supervise that experience. It was the opening of one soul to another in trust and love that the gift of forgiveness was more powerful than most the joys we experience as human beings, on my part at least.

Pastores Dabo Vobis (the letter from the Pope) is translated, "I will give to you shepherds." In order to understand a lot of the New Testament, you have to be familiar with the terminology that goes with sheep herding. It was a major occupation in the time of Jesus. Jesus uses many examples, among which is the story of the Good Shepherd. For example, there is the sheep gate, of course the shepherd, also the hireling, who only works for money and doesn't really care about his flock. When the wolf comes to scatter the sheep, the hireling dashes off into the night somewhere. So we have the wolf in sheep's clothing. A guy who was my boss in New York once gave me a stuffed wolf doll with a sheepskin poncho around its neck. At the time, I wasn't sure of the thinking behind the gift. Now as the age of 80 is here and gone, I'm quite sure what he was trying to tell me.

CHAPTER 26

Couples

I'LL NEVER KNOW how people who have come to me over the years, who have had such humble beginnings — as they say, without a pot to make soup in — wind up with all kinds of problems when they finally make it big. It's a mystery. One would think there are so many lessons to learn along the way. I dislike the scripture quote about it being more difficult for a rich man to pass through the eye of a needle than to get to the kingdom of heaven. I believe that to be a simple warning about putting too much confidence in having surrounded yourself with all kinds of material goods and then coming up short in the common sense realm. For me it is not a condemnation of the wealthy. Many rich people have worked long and hard for what they have. And the others who inherit are strapped with the daily doings of people who are trying to tap into their treasure or at least wanting to befriend them so as to hope to be part of the division of booty when it comes time. Remember plenty to live on . . . but nothing to live for!

Charge it. First it was the barter system, then precious metals and printed paper. Next we put it in mattresses, then safes, then we went to plastic, now we have little black lines on iPhones and bitcoin.

I guess it comes down to greed. When you don't have much, this doesn't seem to be an overwhelming obstacle to growth and stability. WRONG. But when you have a lot, much more will be expected of you. That too often seems unfair, but it's life and everyone knows life's not fair.

Now that I am 80, it occurs to me that I spent too much time participating in sports because of the competition and too little time appreciating how much fun it was and how good for the body and soul. Or *mens sana in corpore sano*, a healthy mind in a healthy body, which they tried to teach me in the seminary. That has always been important to me yet you didn't appreciate it?? I never wanted to end up an old fat monsignor who thought he knew more than he knew. I have all kinds of excuses about weight, but the best one today is the drugs I took after my colon surgery and both during and after my chemotherapy. It was truly chemical. I was never able to lose the extra pounds that I had gained.

During Mass, there's a prayer after the gospel that says, "Through the words of the gospel, may our sins be wiped away."

People used to ask me how come priests don't talk more from the pulpit about sin. I know why I don't. Remember the people building glass houses and throwing stones? No one's perfect and to stand up in front of a mixed group of people drawn by God to worship and then wax and wail about their mistakes, their evil spirits, their sins. Not me. It's like when they questioned Pope Francis on one of his visits around the world about homosexual people going to heaven. "Who am I to judge?" he replied.

Behind the altar in all of her chapels are the simple words "I thirst". According to scripture, Jesus said this while hanging on the cross. He was looking for relief, any kind of relief. Eventually a soldier attached a hyssop, or sponge, to a spear, dipped it in vinegar and offered it to him. Saint Mother Teresa says that Jesus was thirsting for souls. That was her simple message to her followers. They too should be thirsting for souls. I was so moved by the explanation that I pass it on.

If that's the focus and the plan, there is little time for self-pity, egoism and jealousy over what you don't have. She also said that the less we have the more we give. Saint Mother Teresa was the founder of the Missionary Sisters of Charity and while this is certainly true for most of these women religious, I can't say it has worked that way for me. I've always said that if I had lots of money I'd be dangerous. Not much chance of that with my monthly salary of $2,000 (but then, I get free room and board). Working for God pays little, but the benefits are out of this world.

The long-running comic strip Peanuts used to have a Complaint Department. Charles Schulz's character Lucy was famous for complaining. "Why shouldn't I complain?" she demanded. "It's the only thing I'm really good at!" This reminds me of people who complain about a rose bush having thorns and a thorn bush having roses. They don't appreciate the roses as much as they are aware of the thorns. Thorn bushes with roses or rose bushes with thorns, "I can't get no satisfaction". Mick Jagger and the Rolling Stones knew what they were singing about when they came up with that little tune.

Here's the prayer the priest says in private after he takes communion: "May the reception of your body and blood not bring me to judgment and condemnation but through your loving mercy be for me protection in mind and body and a healing remedy."

CHAPTER 27

Home from Missouri

UNITED AIRLINES, Flyover States, October 30 — Returning home from Missouri in seat 21-A, I thought I would jot down a few happenings of the weekend.

My first experience was an accident. I was at the counter at Avis and an older fellow walked in front of me in line. The clerk saw the whole thing. I didn't complain nor cause a scene as I was in no hurry and the old guy looked nervous. So when he was done and I stepped up, the guy behind the counter said, "I noticed that. Can I offer you an upgrade?" "Sure," says I. He pointed, "It's that beauty right in front." It was a Toyota truck of some kind and I thought it was perfect for going to the country. "I'll give it a try," I said with a smile, thinking to myself, "Oh boy, now I'm a trucker." The Schlitt boys would be so proud of me as they all drive trucks. When I come rolling in with this baby, all eyes will see the shiny new pick-up and say, "Who's that guy without a gun rack?"

So I inspect it from the outside. I step up (very high) and buckle in only to discover when I fire up the engine it has just 55 miles on it. I proceed to the exit and have my license checked and the number on the inside of the dash verified against the paperwork, and as I pull away a small Avis bus is in front of me. On its other side is a small blue car shaped like a box. There was a line that said right turn only but this familiar looking older man driving the blue box decided to go left from the right side of the bus. As his front end peeked out just a bit, a speeding motorist came from the left in his lane and BAMMMMM! The oncoming car did two flips and landed upside down on the highway, then it slid about 50 feet on the roof with the wheels still spinning. The bus driver and about a half dozen people went to the rescue.

Two guys were dialing 911 and the service person that had just checked me out came running. I whispered a prayer. I had been so taken with the new rented truck, I didn't even know how or what to do to turn it off and leave it in place. Soon the sirens were blaring from all directions. I see the poor old man who was driving the little box in the wrong lane open his door and dizzily step out. His companion did the same. There was no fire, but scattered glass and fender debris were all over the road. Within a minute both passengers of the upside-down car crawled out and stood up, apparently unscathed from the accident. The driver and people who were on the bus returned to it and by now the police were directing traffic. It was late afternoon and there were plenty of cars and trucks wanting to get going again.

There I sat in this brand new Toyota Tacoma. I began to shake and breathe heavily. About a hundred yards away I spotted the Drury Inn, one of the chain owned by my good friend Charles Drury. I pulled in, parked, found what passed for the truck key and turned it off, then sat there until my nerves were back to normal. I wasn't even in the accident and it affected me. I had a short come-to-Jesus meeting with myself and with strong motivation vowed not to take any chances in the next three days while I was a Missouri trucker.

My longtime friend Jeff Wrench met me on time, having flown in from San Diego where he and his girlfriend moved several years ago. They are presently building a new home in Pismo Beach with a designated "Padre" room if I come to visit. He was my handball partner for a number of years and is the financial advisor to the God Squad. He is quite a bit younger and a very close friend. Jeff loved the country and we planned to do as much fishing in Missouri — Hermann and Cape Girardeau — as the weather allowed. We were hungry and decided to go to a barbeque place for some hand-rubbed ribs. It was called Bandana's and the meal was complete with Texas toast and beans. This was not good for Jeff, as he would be stuck with me for at least three long rides.

It was Thursday night football so we had a couple of beers and watched the first half of the Dolphins/Texans game. We finished stuffing ourselves and stopped by the BP mini-mart, where Jeff picked up a couple of guys, one from Kentucky and one from Tennessee, to join us for the trip. Jim and Jack didn't take up a lot of room in the truck and were there to help us relax after a hard days drive.

It began to sprinkle a bit, but was still daylight so we went to the Soulard area of St. Louis and dropped in at McGurk's. It had been a favorite of John Mahoney's, my late friend from our minor seminary days, when I used to go and visit with him in St. Louis after I was first ordained and living in Springfield. It was a genuine Irish pub with Irish food and Irish music and a bad bartender with a brogue. We made friends immediately. Jeff had never had this experience and he loved it. We paid our respects to both Jim and Jack who were making the rounds in the bar. We left before the music started, as you know how I love those Irish tearjerkers that go on and on into the night.

I mentioned there might be a casino or two around the area so Jeff got out the cell and googled the Queen. It was directly across the Mississippi River. We followed directions and found ourselves in East St. Louis, Illinois, at the door of the casino with an unusual sign on every door. It was a large black handgun with a red circle around it and a stripe through it indicating that firearms were not permitted. That was comforting. Jeff found a place at the bar while

I plopped down at a favorite machine that had eagles. I put in a ten spot and hit the button. Oh, oh! Bells and whistles! My first roll gave me $123. I rolled again and had $134. I pulled out and went to find Jeff, who was into the football game on the big screen. I showed him my winning ticket indicating to him how easy it was to win money.

We stayed another hour as I listened to the dings and pings of electronics and little things exploding, signaling that my winnings were growing. We left in the rain only too happy to know we hadn't seen any firearms and we'd been gifted by those generous people from the Queen, just another riverboat on the Mississippi handing out free money.

We were up at seven the next morning for the Drury Inn breakfast of sausage, biscuits and white gravy. Needless to say, it's a filling starter for the day and both Jack Daniels and Jim Beam from the night before appreciated the stick-to-the-ribs kind of compensation.

When we departed for Cape Girardeau, it was sprinkling and the Tacoma wipers were working overtime. The ride through the hills ablaze with the bright colors of the trees dotting each side of the highway kept us awake and fully cognizant of how lucky we were to have a day of fishing in front of us. My nephew Jimmy would be waiting for us.

I had a call from another nephew Ron and his wife, Pandora, that her brother-in-law Rick Geringer, who lived on a small farm outside of Cape, had gotten the news that he only had a couple of months to live. He had been fighting pancreatic cancer for over a year. The oncologists thought they had it under control, but when they opened him up they discovered that it had metastasized throughout. He was told to make the best of his time. I had his rural address on my cell phone so we gave him a call and I asked his wife, Patti, if it was okay to drop in and say a prayer with him. They were so pleased that "Monsignor", as she kept saying, was in their home and prayed over her Rick. My pal Jeff had never experienced anything like this and was so moved. I caught him out of the corner of my eye weeping for this sick man whose days were numbered. After the blessing, Rick was able to get up from his rocker and give me a big bear hug and tears flowed from his eyes as he tried to adjust his glasses. Here stood a once robust farmer who could lift much more than his own weight, who had worked the ground and made a good living for his family. Now he was thin and drawn and feeble, made so by this terrible disease. He was a man of about 60. And much too young to die.

There was a tearful goodbye followed by smiles and a sense of God in our midst reminding us once again of our gift of life and how precious it is. I was a bit tired and tossed the keys to Jeff to back the Tacoma out of the driveway. As we drove away, I looked at all the farm equipment, the fences and the livestock. I didn't know if it was his or not but realized he wouldn't be working the land he loved any longer.

As we drove down the Gordonville Road, I couldn't help but notice the Schabbing farm with acres and acres of cattle. Leo Schabbing, like Rick's older sister Judy, had been in my class at St. Mary's grammar school. These were families I'd known all my life. A couple of miles further down the road was the Kirchdoerfer farm. His fields were filled with his prize-winning brown cows that he had shown with the 4-H club when we were kids. I guess the continuous problem of spelling his name correctly convinced him to change it. On the big sign near the gravel road, it read: "JOE KIRK'S PRIZE WINNING CATTLE". I'll have to find out what they were. (The *Southeast Missourian* educated me. Joe started exhibiting jersey cattle at age 14 and had done so for 70 years.)

It was now near noon and nephew Jimmy was supposed to pick us up to go fishing in the Drury ponds south of Cape. We step out of the Drury Inn only to see a small vehicle being towed on a trailer by a much larger truck, bigger of course than my

Toyota. Sure enough, it's Jimmy! So off we go thinking we would spend most of the day in the rain. It was great fishing. There was teasing back and forth about who gets the first, the most and the biggest. It ends with me, of course, as I'm the first one out of the "mule" and have my hook in the water before Jimmy is able to assist my citified friend Jeff with the intricacies of catching pond fish. They are used to being fed automatically by a long pipe that extends over part of the water and shoots out little pellets. The fish are not able to order from the menu nor do they have much of a choice. It's what the farmer gives them. So, when they see shiny spinners with little feathers attached and colorful hooks with rubberized worms they, too, like most become curious and go after the vendors of these fine artificial foods casting from the bank to hook them. It took about four hours to catch as many as we did. We threw most of them back so they might see another day, or someone else's deep-fat fryer.

After a shower we met the entire Schlitt congregation at my cousin's restaurant. We were over 25 in number and had a full table of lively people, all excited for a meal on Uncle Harry. Would you believe, it's Italian ("Bella") and serves Italian food only. I had some of he best cannelloni I've ever had and that includes my four years in Italy. The irony of it is that my cousin's name is Dirnberger and he comes from a long line of Germans.

The family was a lot of fun. We joked and laughed and as Jeff had donned a baseball hat he asked, "Should I wear this, or not?" Of course! I know that at least two others in the family will have on hats and will not remove them for the meal. One said JOHN DEERE and the other one might have been a feed store emblem. Jeff's was a Jack Daniel's hat. You remember him and Jim Beam from the night before. They were still our steadfast companions.

Cape's biggest attraction on the Mississippi River is not a boat nor a barge nor the beautiful bridge that spans it but a casino complete with machines from Las Vegas. One of my nephews who landscapes for a living did the work there so we entered as guests of someone important. Jeff headed for the bar and lest I retell the story from the night before, I pulled out a ten and honest to God within two minutes had $230. I marched through the smoke and relatives to show him the ticket. He wasn't even surprised. So we visited a bit and headed back to the Drury Inn. It was going to be a two-and-a-half hour drive in the morning to get to the next fishing hole, which was along the Missouri River and a ways up the state.

We were up at 6:30 a.m. for more biscuits and gravy and sausage, with a Diet Pepsi for me. Jeff chews, a bad habit he got from playing baseball as a kid, but one that he has not been able to abandon. He is very discrete and almost secretive about it but for me I always know if he's carrying around a paper cup or a used beer can.

We pull in to the Grotewiel Farm about ten minutes late but we're there. The drive through the country hills in the fall is well worth slowing down and enjoying the view. The red maples and the yellow sycamores mixed in with a half dozen other kinds of trees showing off their turning leaves made a picturesque setting for a country road dotted with groomed farmland and the ever-present roadkill of squirrels, skunks and deer.

Our host, Mike Grotewiel, had his pick-up packed and ready to roll so we depart for the Valentine farm. Mrs. Valentine was a Busch. She had married an attorney. He passed away so she did not use the property nor the pond very much. Mike built their home and the docks and has been a friend of hers for a long time, so he has permission to fish there whenever he wants. We met my friend of nearly sixty years Leonard, who is miraculously recovering from brain cancer and is able to get around and sit in a chair to fish. He is handicapped in that he can't walk the banks like the rest of us to cast his plastic worm to this or that part of the pond. But he can have fun and listen once again to me bragging about how big the last one I caught was, and that mounting it as a wall trophy was inevitable.

Cleaning fish and sitting in a man-cave filled with antlers and bows and firearms on a farm can make a peacemaker like me a bit uneasy. However, knowing that we're going to be eating those fish in a couple of hours made it all worthwhile. Mike offered Jeff a deer tag and a bow and a stand in the trees to see if he could shoot a deer. He spent about an hour and a half at sunset, saw two does about 200 yards away and so never got a shot but it was a thrill for him. I returned to the cave to watch Notre Dame get beaten by Navy. Good team this year and I'm hoping they'll get a shot at the finals.

Did you ever have a meal with someone years ago and for many, many years you visit and they knew you liked this meal so they keep serving the same thing? This happens even though old bodies are different and eating habits change. Well this is our evening meal, almost to the exact slice of onion, fried potato, or filet of fish. It was delicious and I'm so grateful for having the privilege of dining with this family of friends.

It's Sunday morning and an early home Mass seeing the colorful trees and the sunshine shimmering off Lone Tree Lake makes for an inspirational and spiritual beginning of another day. I spoke about the remnant of people that God had designated all over the Holy Land and the giant quilt created in tribute to those lost to AIDS. It weighs 54 tons and each block represents an individual person. So, too, all of us are part of a people. But as Christian people we are one under God, indivisible and striving for liberty and justice for all. I followed up with the story of Bartimaeus son of Timaeus who was blind and wanted to see again. Our lesson is in the word "seeing", which means, "Oh, I understand, I see." We might be perfectly gifted with sight but blind to understanding one another, a culture, a problem.

After a quick toasted bagel with butter and some orange juice, we're off to Fayette to visit with "Peanut", or Linda, my great-niece who is quadriplegic. She is a living angel to me and a source of prayer and meditation. My niece is a country nurse and found her as a baby, abandoned in a barn. She was not supposed to live past one year and now is celebrating her 25th year on earth. Her thigh bone is pressing against her heart and she has struggled all these years to have a fruitful life. She can make sounds but has no speech and cannot lift her arms or legs or her head. But she is smart as whip and knows everything that happens around the home and her parents are able to communicate with her. We had a lovely visit and my niece baked a fresh apple pie from the tree in her backyard. She also had made a big batch of chili. After some pictures and a romp with her six dogs we returned to St. Louis.

On the way we had a phone call telling us that Charles Drury was very sick and that he and his wife, Shirley, would not be able to host us for dinner that evening. I phoned "Flickers", nicknamed for her long fluttering eyelashes, and told her how sorry we were but it's best for Charles to stay put. He had celebrated his birthday on Thursday. After living as long as he has, anyone would be tired.

Jeff and I watched football on TV and tried our best to finish off our two traveling companions, that is Jack Daniel's and Jim Beam. We didn't make it so the person who cleans that room might have a treat. Before bed we caught the end of the Red Sox/ Dodgers World Series. We enjoyed the win, as most of us from Northern California can't stand the Dodgers.

I got carried away writing on the plane, but this is what I needed to do.

CHAPTER 28

Has God Got Game?

YOU'VE WATCHED THEM just as I have, coming to bat but before stepping up to the plate they grab some dirt, toss it and then cross themselves as they look to the sky. This same scenario is repeated on basketball courts all over the world (minus the dirt). After the whistle blows and a foul is called, the offended player steps up to the foul line, looks to the heavens and crosses himself or herself. Again it's repeated while the receiver goes back into the end zone to wait on the kickoff to begin a game. He looks up and crosses himself.

I often wonder if God really cares or if he is present at every game in the world where his help is needed. When we used to pray before exams, I often thought if I had made better preparation for the test, I wouldn't need divine assistance. Superbowl and supernatural are very far apart and I suspect low on the priority list of the Almighty.

When I was coached in basketball by a wonderful man named Tony Rubich, he would gather us around and we placed our hands together as a sign of team and our unity and then offered a prayer that we would be able to perform at our best and, more importantly, that no one got injured. That's what I remember. Finishing the game healthy was always more important than whether we won or lost.

In the professional scene today, it seems like a selfish thing the way the eyes go to the sky and the quick crosses are made and often followed by a kiss from the lips. If the "big guy" on your team can do everything but shoot free throws, let him practice shooting free throws and save all the crossing for something else. I suspect this may sound a bit harsh for some, but I really think God has more important concerns than how our games turn out. Oh, and this doesn't have anything to do with the God you are acknowledging. For example at Duke University they have another brand of Christianity than, say, St. John's. Now, who is God going to favor once the ball is tossed and rather large men run up and down a hardwood floor in their underwear seeking to put a round ball in an iron hoop? Or, what about when the Chicago White Sox go against the Boston Red Sox? Is it gonna be a matter of the color of the socks that makes the difference?

If I saw 11 enormous men headed for my body at full speed as I caught a pass near the end zone, I would simply drop the ball and pray for good health or as Rubich always said, "that no one gets hurt."

***

How about those Giants? I love sports. I think sport has furthered my vocation to the priesthood and encouraged me to grow in grace over the years. It's always a topic of conversation for me, even in difficult situations where you have offered prayers and consolation and now you're in the waiting room expecting good news from the doctor about a child to be born or a person's leg repaired or open heart surgery. "Hey, how about those Giants?"

I feel extremely fortunate to have lived in a City where we have had multiple championships from our major sporting teams. The San Francisco 49ers were magnificent during their reign of glory. The City lived and breathed their activity. People planned their schedules around games, home and away. Times were penciled on calendars and anticipation of continued success was so great that, when there was a loss, it affected the general population. Many of us now live on those memories.

There was an elderly German in the parish where I lived during the heyday of the Niners. When he got sick, I visited him and took communion to him. When he passed, he left his season ticket to me in his will. It was a great seat. He had bought it in 1946 when the Niners played at the old Kezar Stadium. I used to take the bus from the cathedral and get to Candlestick Park just before kickoff. My seat was on the end and against the wall on the lower deck behind the team's bench. I could stand anytime I wanted and, the best part, it was 25 steps to the nearest men's room. That was important in the old Candlestick where places you could get to fast and not wait in line were at a premium.

I saw many great games in that venue. The most memorable moment in my viewing history as a fan was the famous "Catch" when Joe Montana threw to Dwight Clark in the end zone to defeat the Dallas Cowboys in the 1981 NFC championship game. Can't remember the date, but I recall how we all just stood in our seats and applauded, yelled and would have paid big money to see it again and again, but we had no instant replay nor a large screen (not that I recall). Now it's in every news story about unforgettable football games and especially those about the glory days of the team.

Just last Saturday I gave communion at Mass to Joe Montana and his wife Jennifer. They moved into the neighborhood and have been coming to Mass at St. Vincent de Paul. The Body of Christ, Joe! The warm and consoling memories that come to mind from the work he did here in this City as the quarterback of a winning team, it was just too much to imagine. He brought everyone's spirits up. It helped change our City to a more caring and loving place to live.

Baseball did the same thing. The San Francisco Giants won the World Series of baseball three out of five years. During those years (2010, 2012 and 2014) baseball was king. Batting averages and home runs and pitching duels were all part of the daily conversation for people who knew the sport and those willing and eager to learn because of the success of the team.

Frank Robinson died recently. He was one of the most memorable of all baseball players and, subsequently, managers in the history of the sport. He was here in San Francisco for a number of years and I had the privilege of interviewing him on my *Tell A Vision* program when it was coming to the end of its run. He was a strong believer in Christianity and followed a high moral standard both for himself and his players and coaches. I like baseball and I go to games, but I really don't know this sport like people who follow it fanatically and memorize statistics. (I had a most difficult time passing the statistic courses required for the master's degree in education.) Frank introduced me to Willie McCovey, who also passed recently.

Willie was kind enough to assist me with a dinner to raise funds for charity. I lived at Sacred Heart parish at that time. I recall him pulling up in his big Cadillac in front of the rectory at Fillmore and Fell. He asked if his car would be safe there. As he opened the trunk to get out a carton of new baseballs, the kids from the 'hood began gathering around. He signed a few and passed them out. I told him not to worry about his car. No one would touch it.

We went inside the rectory and he gave a signed ball to each of our guests, who all had put a bid on the dinner at an auction several weeks earlier. He left with the same beautiful smile that he had when he arrived. It was an outstanding evening. Later that year, I played golf in his charity tournament to benefit the March of Dimes. I'm not really a golfer and I recall the man who bought the foursome didn't say much and didn't seem to care. I shared a cart with him. As we trailed the other two with us, admiring their skills and ease, we knew they were good guys, as they patiently watched the two of us make golfing fools of ourselves. I asked the gentleman what he did for a living. He said he was a garbage collector. A what? "Garbage, I collect garbage," he repeated. "I have almost 150 trucks in the East Bay." The garbage business has grown since I was a kid. No wonder he could afford to pay for the three of us to participate in such a prestigious tournament. He, too, was a real gentleman.

***

That brings me to the third and final thrill of sports culture in the Bay Area, the Golden State Warriors. By the time you read this, they will have re-located to downtown San Francisco like the 49ers should have but for a stubborn and selfish mayor who is now governor of the state, who failed to reach an agreement with the team resulting in their move to Santa Clara . . . BOOOOOO! Boo hoo! (Too bad they didn't have the recall vote at that time. I would have been the first to sign the petition.) The Warriors have that magical mixture often referred to as team chemistry that makes them tick. But for me, more than anything, they are an unselfish group of young millionaire men who appreciate what they have and are willing to share their good fortune. It's the best of both worlds. Most young men who grow up with people fawning all over them from grade school because of their talent take on a certain air that the world owes them a living. This is not so with the entire group. I don't feel that any one or two can be given the credit, but to me it appears that they have all bought into it and will not fall apart even when they get long in the tooth and have to turn in their play/work clothes/uniforms.

It is too expensive for me to go the basketball games in person. Television has provided the ability to see every game whether here or away and nowadays all you have to do is tell it to turn on the game. We are re-living the '80s and '90s and the success of the 49ers and the beauty of the World Series with the Giants. It's a reason to get your work done in the day so you can watch the game at night.

I always dreamt about being a chaplain to a major sports team. There was a priest, a monsignor, in the San Francisco archdiocese named Armstrong. He was a good friend of the owners of the 49ers and sported five rings, one for each championship they'd won. It so happened that the pastor of the parish where Coach Harbaugh and his family attended got into some trouble. The archbishop asked me to go there and see if I could appease the people and bring the community back to normal. It took more than several months but the parish council was soon operating very efficiently and all seemed to be going smoothly. In fact, after one Sunday Mass a distinguished man offered me a major stock gift if I would remain as their pastor. Jokingly I said I could not accept the stocks but if he could get to Coach Harbaugh and bring me on as the chaplain of the 49ers, I would be happy to give it a try. I didn't expect it, but the gentleman told me he would look into it. After that season Harbaugh left the Niners and went to Michigan. Just another bucket that will never get filled, or a dream left at my doorstep.

I wish I knew how to conclude this experience with three major professional sports teams who have given me so much pleasure since the early '70s. God bless each and every one of them! I still have one jersey that a friend gave to me 40 years ago. It has the name "Hofer" on the back and now is too small for me to wear. That little halfback put more effort into carrying the ball and doing what he could to win than anyone I've ever known. He was a highlight film by himself. Unfortunately, the team was not very good and they were never successful while he was there. In his last year, he blew out his knee and could not play. However, that year was the Niners first Superbowl win and the team gave him a ring. Again, a generous gesture on their part. Paul Hofer, when last I heard, was working for Federal Express in his hometown, Memphis, Tennessee. I think he might also be coaching high school football. I've been wanting to have the jersey framed and in glass, but it lacks the personal autograph. Maybe if Paul reads this he'll send me one.

In some small way, it makes me feel better that I'm not the only one who didn't get the call from *Sports Illustrated* asking me to be on the cover.

CHAPTER 29

Winds of Change

I LIKE TO SUBSTITUTE at different parishes around the archdiocese and there are a few that I visit regularly. I've been helping for about ten years at St. Rita's in Fairfax, about 30 minutes north of the Golden Gate. Marin County and the Marina both have their charm and their differences. When I go to Rita's, I leave the City on Saturday afternoon so I can enjoy the small town atmosphere and the countryside. I usually go to the local market where everything is old and/or stale and I never seem to learn that their prices are better than anyone else's because of that. Inevitably, I'll buy a roast chicken that was probably done the day or night before and sat in the heater all day. There is such a crispness, or perhaps dryness, that it's impossible to eat without choking. Sushi is the same except the rice is kernel-like. There are plenty of places for me to shop for myself before I arrive, but I never seem to take the time to go elsewhere. I'm like a pigeon returning to the same bad food. Even the string cheese was old the last time I shopped there.

The people are few and far between at this now somewhat-rural parish. A few years ago, it was thought they might be closed by the archbishop because they were not "viable". That's a funny word when applied to a church, when it comes to faith and the expression of faith. Every group who meets to worship is viable. It's just that it's hard to keep up with the expenses when the numbers go down. A few years ago, they had to close the grade school at St. Rita's. The numbers were not there. Many could have given up on the parish and gone elsewhere but they didn't and, alas, they now have religious education classes. There are many positive elements to having a Catholic grade school, for example, you have children on the grounds, around the church. This makes it possible to have altar servers, a children's choir, regular Masses for them and a first-class introduction to advancing to a Catholic high school. Their school is rented to a charter group and looks to be successful. I guess they can charge more and deal with fewer students.

I supported the pastor when he had to close his school, but I also saw the future. The area has lots of ranches and is rural enough so that the possibility of a community that would grow children seemed very dim. I miss the boys and girls who used to serve Mass when they were in school there and, of course, the school Masses. They simply are gone.

* * *

St. Patrick's Seminary in Menlo Park, California, is over 100 years old. It's a majestic building in a beautiful part of California. It sits surrounded by beautiful trees and there is hardly a glimpse of the busy little burg of Menlo Park. It's kind of a spiritual paradise when you think about it. The grounds are gorgeous. The library is state of the art and houses the archives of the archdiocese. The Olympic-sized pool needs help, but the dining room and the food served by sisters from Mexico is the best. It's no wonder that it has done so well for so many years. Now there are all kinds of changes.

The Sulpician Fathers have been teaching at St. Patrick's Seminary for 117 years. Their "specialty" has been to instruct and form men for the Catholic priesthood. This last year, they decided they could no longer staff this facility. The departure of the Sulpician Fathers caused a great deal of angst among the local clergy who had been trained and educated there. They were more than upset. The one Sulpician Father I know well was devastated and didn't really appreciate the sudden departure of his brothers. But the archbishop had a different plan for "his" seminary and so waved bye-bye to the Fathers and hello to a new group, who, in my estimation, have yet to earn their stripes. When I was teaching homiletics at the seminary, my only degree was in counseling. It was easy to part with me. I looked over the qualifications at those coming in to teach there, and I wonder.

There is written in certain publications how this happened and what can be expected in the future. It's not my place to judge why or why not and I don't have the credible resources to say why, but it still shocks the system to know that this could happen in our day and age when things are supposed to be so transparent.

There are too few seminarians today to have fully staffed theologians and personnel to train these men. Rather than have a university for 50 or 60 men, why not just send them to a place with 150 or more? The Church is not that different, or is it? Some say that the Sulpicians withdrew because of an emphasis on the theology and the practice of both John Paul II and Benedict XVI. Pope Francis is quite a bit different than these two, saying: "I desire mercy not sacrifice." Even the Old Testament spoke the same words, when Moses was dealing with the complaints of the people as he led them out of Egypt to the Promised Land. Our God is a God of mercy!

My source for writing about any of this is based on my close relationship with Archbishop George Niederauer and our many conversations about the future of the seminary. I respect his honesty with me, so will not include him in my personal thoughts. I used to serve on the Seminary Board in my role as the vicar general of the archdiocese. I recall how much we once fought to protect a piece of land that the Menlo Park Fire Department was eager to acquire. Recently, I read that it had been sold. My heart sagged and I realized that they probably needed the money to keep the doors open and the faculty in place. It's no secret that whatever happens at St. Patrick's in the future has to be better than it is now. At least a couple of bishops pulled out their students to attend other seminaries. That speaks loud and clear to a need for a critical look at what's happening and why.

* * *

A wonderful retired priest related this tale to me. He said there was an altar server dispute at a particular parish where young ladies are no longer permitted to serve the Mass, like they have been for years. It happened to be a graduation Mass and the school arranged for some of their female students to participate. It so outraged one of the conservative parishioners that he went to the sanctuary and asked the young ladies to leave, as the parish did not allow female servers. Following his remarks, the father of one of the girls got up and the two almost came to fisticuffs over the matter. The police had to be summoned.

Can you believe it? A fight in the sanctuary of a famous San Francisco Catholic church over altar servers.

If you lived in the 1950s you would recognize the service. It's in Latin and the altar "boys" memorize the Latin and the altar is facing away from the people. Readings are from the altar, the epistle and Gospel books are switched one side to another, and there are a half dozen other things that should give the Vatican pause for thought. But they do have permission for the Latin Mass.

Now, you might ask, what is the Latin Mass? It's the way Catholics celebrated Mass before the Vatican Council in the first half of the 1960s. It's what the Church was trying to improve on, to make it easier for the faithful to participate with an understanding of the language by dropping Latin in favor of the local language. And yes <u>participate</u>, that is to say, feel part of what was going on, so the mystery of the Eucharist, the Mass, could at least be understood from a language point of view, and just a plain view, as you could now see the priest face to face and witness what was happening in front of you instead of looking at the back of the priest. I get many letters from viewers of the Mass I do on television each week, people who are so delighted to see my hands close up holding the bread and the chalice and saying the words of consecration. It's something many were denied for years because of the Latin Mass, which has now been restored in many conservative dioceses.

Don't misunderstand, I love the Latin language but it's not for everyone. Prior to Vatican II, it was routinely taught in American high schools. That changed in the '60s and French, Spanish and other commonly spoken languages were taught instead. During my four years in Rome, all our classes were in Latin. Our books were in Latin. After all, it was the most precise language to teach the mysteries of the Church. It was also elusive and out of date and there were hardly, if ever, real time examples given about cases of morality or Church teaching because there were no vocabulary words in Latin for situations like the practice of dating and engagement and pre-marital sex, and living together before marriage, and all the sins of violence against another or women or children.

I know Pope Francis has many more important fish to fry than to be concerned about the remaining Vatican II priests who felt like this would increase the quality of the faith and bring the cream to the top so to speak. Quality over quantity has been hard for me to stomach. I always look at the numbers, whether it's in the pews or my checkbook. It's hard to get away from it. But I've witnessed how wonderful the practice of the faith can be when there are people in church who want to be in church and understand fully that they ARE Church.

CHAPTER 30

The Mass

THERE ARE PRIESTS who are "bench players". They have been placed on the bench for any number of reasons, most of which should not have merited them this kind of "three strikes you're out" fate. Accusations without proof can bring a man to the bench where he sits until called to the pearly gates. His reputation is ruined. He loses his ability to wear the Roman collar, to say Mass, to hear confessions, bury the dead or do anything priestly that is public. It breaks my heart when a parent of one of these guys is called to heaven and their son, the Father, is not allowed to say the funeral Mass.

I remember a huge book, I would say two or three inches of pages, called *The Mass*. I thought to myself at the time that I'll never wade through this, much less pass a test on the contents. Little did I know that the book was only information. The Mass is so much more. It's the most important thing I do on a daily basis. It's where I get my energy to face each day. It's the alpha and omega of my life. Without the Mass, I would be nothing. That is just another reason why I hurt so much inside for men who have been denied the privilege of saying Mass publicly after they have been accused of misconduct. If they loved it as much as I do, it has to really hurt inside their souls.

I'll start with a basic understanding for the readers who don't know what I'm talking about. The Mass is a popular name among the English speaking to denote a spiritual exercise that is officially called Eucharist. Eucharist means thanksgiving. We celebrate the fact that God gave his only Son, Jesus, to be sacrificed for us, so that after his death and resurrection we might have the gift of eternal life. It's really very simple for a believer, that is, one who has faith and accepts the teaching and traditions of Christianity. For others, not so much.

Vaudeville used to have a skit about a non-believer (atheist) all dressed up, lying there in the coffin with no place to go.

Daily do we give thanks for the great gift of the Son of God, who redeems us for everlasting life, that is, life after death. We really have something to look forward to.

While these words roll off my tongue so easily, I can't imagine what others might be thinking who didn't grow up as I did.

The Catholic Church might be looked upon as a performing arts center. It has all the accoutrements of such: an entrance with double doors, seats, a raised area for the main attraction. There is an organ and a loft and several small alcoves with depictions of various people from various centuries who made a name for themselves in religious history and who are still venerated, not adored, but looked upon as special people with special gifts. We call them saints. This performing arts center has music and atmosphere for prayer, whether it be private, when the place lies dormant, or public, when the action begins. There is special lighting that brightens the space and a man with acolytes or ministers who appears from the back of the space parading down the middle aisle while all rise and sing.

The performance continues as the celebrant, with his arms extended, speaks to God. "Lord have mercy." Shortly thereafter God speaks to him and the rest of those gathered to see the artistic production, when the sacred scriptures are read from a book.

Following that, the man dressed in ancient garb makes comments and relates to the people what they have just heard from the "good book".

As I said, it's really very simple. Following more prayers for everyone, there is an offertory procession in which the gifts of bread and wine are presented to the celebrant. He makes the offering to God of these gifts that represent us and all our world.

Following the offering to God of our gifts, God offers himself to us through the consecrated bread and wine. We believe it's the real body and blood of Jesus Christ. Hang on! I'll go into that in a minute. We then pray the Lord's Prayer together (Our Father etc.) and commune with God and with each other, exchanging the Kiss of Peace, which is more often a handshake or sometimes just a nod. God then gives us his body and blood in the form of bread and wine.

As I said, it's really very simple. Let's review!

We talk to God.

God talks to us.

We offer to God.

God offers to us.

We commune with God by eating and drinking with God.

Now that wasn't too difficult, was it? Now comes the hard part. After you have gone to the sixth chapter of the Gospel of John, read it completely. I know it's a long chapter but worth your time. But it, too, is very simple.

In the first part, Jesus shows his power both by calming the seas and multiplying the bread for all to eat. Then he goes into a very repetitious dialogue about Himself and the Father. This is all to make sure that we get it.

It's a special relationship, father and son. After that it really gets more difficult. He asks us to believe that his body is real food and his blood is real drink. Then he asks us to do it. What? Yes, to do it. To eat and drink of his body and blood as real food and real drink. Don't worry, you weren't the only one who might not understand. Some of his close followers found this too much to stomach and they walked away. After all the other things that Jesus did in front of and for them, eating and drinking his body and blood was a little much.

But here's the clincher. Whoever does this, will live forever. Now, I believe it. That's why I do it. It's the Mass. It takes place in every church every day. For broadcast later on television, once a month I say six Masses in a day that are videotaped. It's a matter of economics for the most part, but it might not be when I cannot do it any longer. I'm not sure the priest who takes my place will be able to do six at a time. My lifelong experience in broadcasting gives me an advantage.

There is a prayer card in the sacristy of many churches. The sacristy is the place where the celebrant dresses himself and prepares to enter the stage. It could be called a dressing room, but sacristy gives it a special meaning as a holy place. On this prayer card in bold letters is printed:

"Father, say this Mass as if it were your first.
Father, pray this Mass as if it were your last."

The difference between saying and praying is huge. Saying means you are mouthing the words and not necessarily focusing on the meaning but being so careful not to upset those who might be watching the activity. Praying is a whole different ball game. It means you got it and you're hoping God is listening because, for you, it's the real thing and it might be the last time you have a chance to talk to God or God to you or offer something or commune with God. That's not so simple.

It becomes more complicated when you do it every day or multiple times during one day. It's not unlike the theatre where on weekends there is a matinee followed by an evening performance. All the same equipment and people are in place. The lights, the sound, the props (bread and wine), the talent all have to do again with the same script and the same mindset as they had the first time they did it.

It has to be prayed.

So here comes the challenge, as I look out over the people who have gathered. After all it's an assembly. The Greek word for church is *ekklisia* or gathering. The Latin renders it *ecclesia* from which we have the ecclesiastical which means "churchy". Anyway you peel it, it's the same onion with different layers. I can see those gathered and whether they are following what's going on. Most of the important action is on and around the altar. That's where the bread and wine in an unbloody sacrifice are changed into the body and blood of Christ. I'm wondering while I'm saying the words if the congregation believes what I believe.

I know they are struggling if they are new or if they are young with their parents who insist they go to Mass. "But Mom, I get nothing out of it." "I know, I know, but let's give it another try." I don't feel sorry for them. In fact, as I think about it, I don't feel much at all. Like a good actor, I'm trying to concentrate on my part, doing my best to make it sound real and seem real and be real. After all it is for me, and I want it to be for them. Because if it isn't real for many, we could question the script, the writers, the producers, the backers and the main character.

God is a mystery, so we're dealing with mystery. It's in the past, so we're dealing with history. But we're doing it now, in the present. It's supposed to be a gift from God, a present in the present, where we commune with God. Then how come I get these blank stares, or people fidgeting, or praying the rosary, or looking at their watches and calculating the time until they can get back into their vehicles and get home to turn on the telly and catch up on "real" life?

Remember the female pilot who aviated, navigated, and communicated? Well, that's me at the altar. I'm doing what I was taught and what I know will get me where I need to be and I'm telling you about it, as I pray to God that I won't crash and burn. Come to think of it, the pilot never mentioned prayer. But I would say 90% of the people in the seats behind her were calling upon whomever they do to see to it that they arrive safely on the ground. I know because I heard many of them being interviewed.

Crisis brings prayer to the forefront. It makes it easier when there is a faith aspect. I've always maintained in all my illnesses that without faith I would not know what to do. I am able to offer so much up for those worse off than myself. I really do feel for those who don't have that. You may call it a crutch or an opiate, as Lenin said about religion, but by golly, it works for me.

The Mass is the center of my universe as far as daily activity is concerned. I've said Mass in a car, on an airplane, on a boat, in a cabin, in a Vegas hotel, and a cathedral. From St. Peter's Basilica in Rome to a brush arbor in southern Missouri, it's the same for me. There may be whistles and bells or the chirping of birds and the wind hitting the branches above but it all comes down to communing with God. I was ordained on December 16, 1964, in Rome at St. Peter's Basilica. That was my first Mass. I was elated and inspired by what might be my future. I'm still saying the same Mass, praying my way and the way of others as best I can, so that we might meet with merriment in heaven.

Today, I pray the Mass at St. Vincent de Paul parish in San Francisco and assist at St. Rita's in Fairfax. But I try to concentrate on the Mass I offer each Sunday and on Christmas to my television congregation. They are my main ministry and perhaps why God has allowed me to live this long. I'm often reminded, "Harry, God is not through with you yet!"

CHAPTER 31

Politics

IF SOMEONE ASKED ME, I would have to say I don't like politics, but I know they are part of my everyday life. I'm a people person, so I can't deny politics are part of my life. The biggest joke going is that the Church and its leaders don't have a political forum nor political teeth to bite into issues and change minds, since they are really after hearts. Our God is one of love. So it's the heart that matters. I've had to laugh at those who suggest that we are not a political organization. We can claim Father, Son and Holy Spirit, but we're still a big bunch of people who have leaders who come to us not by election but by choice of someone who, somewhere, is playing politics.

My foray into writing about the political field is not yet concluded. My good friend Leonard Hall, who would have made an excellent politician in whatever state or field he entered, had only one — and I concluded with him — one drawback. He was toooo honest. He was unable to stretch the truth or make promises he couldn't keep. I admired him for that. As a young man right out of college working for the governor of Missouri, he was able to author the basic structure of the persons with disabilities law that mandates a sidewalk cut-out on every corner to allow wheelchairs access. It was his savvy that got that going. Looking back, one would say that man could really go places in the city, state, or world government. Not so, says I, he's still too honest. Why do politicians have to promise what they can't deliver? Right — to get elected. Then what? Right — they become less than honest and have to make up things to satisfy all those who voted for them. It's a vicious cycle and one that my friend was able to avoid — by having a successful career in educational software.

One politician, whom it irks me to have to mention or even write about, was the brash young Gavin Newsom. I don't even have to mention his public foibles. He still might be the governor of California when this is published but it won't be because of my vote.

I was asked to give the invocation on Saint Patrick's Day at a sold-out room in downtown San Francisco. Now why would they dare bring on a priest from a German background when the room was full of Irish born and bred priests and people? The sponsors of the luncheon were the Hibernian Society; they were supporting the Newman Center at San Francisco State University and I was the chaplain there. The money raised from the luncheon would support our ministry. So I said the prayer. We ate. An Irish comedian entertained and then through the back door comes then San Francisco Mayor Gavin Newsom. He was booed by the crowd as he stepped up on the dais. He tried desperately to rebuff his unwelcome but it simply did not work with the Roman Catholic partisan crowd who were against same sex marriage. He tried to speak about it but eventually had to step down. It was clear the votes were not there.

On another occasion where I accompanied Archbishop Niederauer to an ecumenical breakfast to honor the many organizations and individuals who fed the hungry and clothed the naked and many other corporal and spiritual works of mercy, there was Newsom, seated next to the archbishop. When it was time for him to honor and thank these many people publicly, he tossed his prepared remarks and began to rant and rave about same sex marriage. To me it was inappropriate and out of place, in light of his audience and the purpose of the breakfast. When he finished he took his seat next to the archbishop. There were no punches thrown nor stares of displeasure. It simply happened and life went on.

I write about this because of what I thought was wrong. But maybe I'm the fool. I could have easily risen from my seat in disgust and headed for the exit. I didn't. I sat there abused by this young man who, because he was the mayor of the City, could get away with this act of self-centered disregard for all those wonderful, giving people from charities around the Bay Area, who had come to be celebrated a day before the American holiday of Thanksgiving. All of us have done things we're not proud of, and some that were wrong and we're still proud of, but for me this took the cake. I suspect this man has made some changes in his life and has learned a lesson or two along the way, but I'll have to witness some real love and concern for the people of the state before I cast my ballot his way.

As long as I'm writing about politics and political figures, let's go to the national level and consider the Trump administration. Sorry, I just can't go there. I'm a chicken and there's too much to crow about.

Instead there are church politics. But it must be remembered that there are no politics without people. The late environmentalist David Ross Brower used to say, "Politicians are like weathervanes. Our job is to make the wind blow."

For ten years I lived with one of the best political churchmen I've ever known. Cardinal Levada had all the hallmarks of a successful politician. Most memorable was his ability to meet a person, get their name correctly and remember it. He was a master at this. We were looking at a piece of property, which we had to sell in the City. Both of us exited the car to be met by an Indian man, who with a strong accent introduced himself to us. It was something like Raahithya Ahluwalia. I could hardly pronounce it. Little did I know his name meant "wealthy man". He gave us the tour of the property and, upon leaving, Levada thanked him profusely and said his name better than the guy could himself. I was impressed, as I stumbled over something like sahib. I suspect that a sure way to get to a person's mind and heart is by knowing their name and using it in a way that's not sucking up or fake. Important people who meet people all the time have a knack for it and it sure makes an impression.

Cardinal Levada also demonstrated his ability to step into conflicting situations and come up with some common ground. I recall how contentious was the struggle for gay couples to obtain equal benefits from the government, unions, and employers in general that didn't recognize that their partner might be sick or unable to work. One of them then was the sole provider. Levada stepped into the public forum and finessed a compromise, by turning the discussion to health care and supporting benefits for legally designated members of the same household. He said, "I am in favor of increasing benefits, especially health coverage, for anyone." That satisfied everyone. Well, not everyone. There are still those who believe it's sinful and against the will of God to have a same sex partner. I'm not one of them.

Saint John Paul II also was a master church politician. The fact that he is a saint gives me pause, as who could fathom saint and politician in the same person. During the almost 30 years of his pontificate, he was able to bring about a change in Russia and the Communist world. The fall of the Berlin Wall is partially attributed to his intercession. These are no small matters. President Trump, should he become partially responsible for peace and tranquility between the two Koreas, would be right up there as a successful politician. Of course, if Iran or Syria blows up while this is happening, or the new capital of Israel in Jerusalem is destroyed, woe is him! On another level might be the Cardinal Archbishop of New York, Timothy Dolan. He has all the personality, intelligence and wit to be among the very best at capturing the attention of a crowd.

The real difference between the public politician and the church politician is the inner spirit and the time spent in prayer and supplication for the gifts that you need to do the job. I doubt that Trump and the myriads of people he has hired or appointed and who have left him had what it takes to meditate, to discern, to take the time to include God in their daily plan. If so, no one seems to be bragging about it or wearing it on their sleeve. This is not to deny that they pray.

In the parish where I now live, almost every Sunday when Congress is not in session, a huge Cadillac SUV pulls up and double parks in front of the church. If I'm on the altar, I can't miss it. Out comes a man about 16 feet tall with a little wire in his ear. He stands out among the usual group of smaller, older, Italian guys who take up the collection and usher people in and out of the church. A few paces in front of him walks a small, smartly dressed woman, Congresswoman Nancy Pelosi.

I never met her but from conversation and friends I was led to believe this lady practiced witchcraft and was herself very close to the cauldron. Her broomstick now was that big black SUV. I have not followed her career, but her accomplishments must be legion from the remarks I have not elicited but that have come from different sides.

Just like Cardinal Ratzinger before he became Pope Benedict XVI, I only despised him from what I read and heard. Then when he sat next to me in my living room and engaged me in a conversation about my German heritage, I had a change of heart, a genuine metamorphosis of what I feel and now know about the man.

So, with Nancy I see a woman who comes to worship, nothing more. She doesn't draw a lot of attention to herself and she is not usually bothered by other churchgoers who want to express their opinion so that she can return to D.C. and give the president a piece of their mind. Might be such a small piece that she makes the judgment before she boards the limo. After Mass she usually comes over and thanks me and asks for prayers for Congress. With a little raise in her brow, she says, "We really need it." She boards the big black SUV and returns to her husband and very large family in Pacific Heights for what I hope will be a peaceful and enjoyable Sunday dinner together. Anyone with that kind of pressure who has to travel back and forth across the country to be with their children deserves it.

CHAPTER 32

War

AS GENERAL PATTON once said, "Compared to war, all other forms of human endeavor are insignificant." I have often used that quote from the pulpit, as I recall vividly the war games we kids played, making mudballs and tossing them from ditches and hiding places as if they were real grenades. We used the names of Hitler, Mussolini and Tojo in our cries to defeat one another. The worst part of our games was to lose the coin toss and have to role play the enemy.

Michael Pritchard's record in working with young people is unequaled around the country, but recently a tragedy in Yountville, California, brought into focus his years of service to the military community and especially the veterans. Michael served in the military after he left the seminary and became even closer to the men and women who were subjected to war threats. He has been very outspoken about what they have done as guardians of our country and what they deserve, having put in the years and having faced the terrible notion of having to kill. The deaths of three talented, brilliant women, who were sacrificed in the sight of a gun barrel from one of their clients, point out the difficulty and the challenge in dealing with the mind and the body that faces death and is prepared to administer it.

Albert Wong was an Army infantryman in Afghanistan. He came home and never was able to shake the battle horror in his head. The Pathway Home at the Yountville Veterans Home was his first residential treatment for troubled veterans. In his case, it didn't work. He murdered three professional women there and then took his own life. All three of these women knew what they were dealing with and realized that troubled minds trained to kill can lead to deadly violence. And so it happened on March 9, 2018.

"These guys at Pathway are just trying to come home," said Michael, who has taught anger management and other skills at the program and knew two of the victims. "I was never afraid of the veterans being treated. Many of them had traumatic childhoods. Our job is to take care of each other, to love each other. We all need to do whatever we can, to do better for our young men and women who come home from war. They've suffered incredibly, and too often they were flawed and wounded even before they got there."

Michael has more stories than I and uses them to change the lives of many people. I'll only tell you one, as I often felt Robin Williams should have given him a bit part or two in one of his many movies. Mike didn't care much for Hollywood and I suspect the feeling was mutual, as he never did get a solid offer to have his own show. Almost daily I drive by the house on the corner of Steiner and Pacific, which was the home where *Mrs. Doubtfire* was filmed. People now leave mementos there and tour buses drive by slowly while the guide recalls the famous movie. At one point in those days, Mike was trying to calm down a couple of wild teenage boys at the Youth Guidance Center (fancy words for teenage jail). He was able to get two of the boys out for a day and took them to the set of *Mrs Doubtfire*. He told the boys there was an elderly lady there who wanted to talk to them. As the three of them entered the outdoor set in Berkeley, this old lady in full make up and costume approached the two boys shaking her finger and giving them "what for" about their mismanaged lives. She then became very calm and grandma-like and encouraged them to make some adjustments and see if they couldn't do better with what God gave them. She almost had them in tears when she pulled off her wig and introduced himself to them as Robin Williams. The surprise and complete shock in meeting an old woman had turned to admiration and pride. They had met the famous and one in a million Robin Williams.

Mike told me the ride back to the Guidance Center was quiet for a while and then animated to the point of euphoria as these two tough kids from a project neighborhood returned to their incarceration with wide eyes and big smiles to relate how they had met a great movie star.

I wrote about the comedy competition that was held some years ago when Michael won out over Robin Williams. They became lifetime friends and together made a promotional video for Pathway a few years ago. Michael probably has done more for young people and humanity than anyone I know. He is a well-known speaker around the country with law enforcement, addressing teen bullying, cancer and so many other things, like the sinister form of Parkinson's Disease known as Lewy body dementia. This is the horrific disease that beset comic genius Robin Williams, driving him to take his own life.

Recently, I attended a lecture by his widow turned activist Susan Williams that was opened by Michael to educate doctors and medical personnel about the disease. When it was publicized that Robin Williams had hanged himself, most people assumed that it was probably drugs and, like many other famous personalities, he was unable to handle the pressures of such success and simply overdosed and took his life. When you hear Susan tell her story and describe exactly what his disease was, it is very clear that he could not help his ups and downs and his unusual behavior. Susan is now travelling the country with the encouragement of the medical community to help discover a cure for Lewy body dementia. She herself is an accomplished artist and sells her paintings along the way. However, her full attention has been directed to this rare disease and she is using the hard-earned millions that Robin made in show business to pour back into a cure.

Those of us who lived during the Vietnam War and saw how our returning men and women were treated can see the difference in the attitude today. There are so many young people who have grown up with a sense of entitlement that it would seem impossible for them to go overseas to serve in a national conflict. So they very much appreciate those who have taken up the challenge, put on a uniform, subjected themselves to a very high standard of discipline and represented all of us for the sake of freedom. As the saying goes, "Freedom is not Free!"

CHAPTER 33

Power

MUSIC AND THE ARTS are love and, as Bishop Curry from the USA preached in St. George's Chapel at the marriage ceremony of Prince Harry and Meghan Markle, love is power.

I've watched his sermon a couple of times, and while I find it exceptional and moving, I didn't think the repetition of fire, and power, and love and redemption needed that kind of delivery, especially when it was supposed to be personal for a royal and an American beauty. He certainly moved many people. I can't recall the last time I delivered a message that anyone cared to repeat or offer to the media. Oh, I take that back, there was one . . . Now what was it? I remember. It's the bit about me going to the prison where the guard would ask me, even though he knew me, "Who are you? Why are you here? Where are you going?" It seemed pretty stupid to ask me the same questions every time I came to teach religion in the prison, but now I use the same three questions as kind of a mantra for personal reflection. It works.

Canadian pastor and author Carey Nieuwhof gave five reasons why the world took note of Bishop Curry's sermon. I pass them along so as to remind myself how important they all are. Then I'll add a couple of my own.

1. Was not a slave to his notes. That's why I always just go with an outline. A couple of words trigger a story or two with the lesson to follow.

2. He made eye contact with everyone. Hard to do but comes with years of preaching and the ability to not be sidetracked by a baby crying or someone getting up to leave while you're talking.

3. Passionate. This comes naturally with believing what you're talking about.

4. He knew his subject and his audience. None of this was off the cuff. He has lived a Gospel of love.

5. He used fresh language. Fire, power, love, redemption are not all that new, but when addressed to the Royal Family make a lot of sense. I use most of those words a lot and they don't seem so fresh to me.

I would add a spiritual life that demands the power of prayer and meditation and careful consideration of what you are going to say before you say it.

Bishop Curry didn't come up with his talk in a day nor did he wing it as some of the Hierarchy tends to do because they are Hierarchy. Maybe it's because they are expected to talk at every personal appearance. Some guys go to the opening of an envelope. Others would prefer to send someone in their place. Still others pick and choose. Much depends on the event, the crowd, the importance of the event. Take confirmations. Bishops have to do so many and they can't change their talk at each one; after all, it's the same sacrament, the same age kids. Bishops get a break because it's a different parish, a different group of people and a different locale. It's like the first time for everyone, except the priest who has to accompany him as the master of ceremonies. He puts on the bishop's hat (miter), he takes it off, he hands him the stick (crosier), he takes it back. This goes on and on throughout the ceremony, so that it gives pause to wonder what it all means. Again, it's simple. Both the crosier and miter are signs of his authority, and his sacramental ordination to the priesthood, and his advancement to full rights and powers by being appointed bishop. There is no sacrament for it and no big bump in the paycheck, just more responsibility and demand on the poor man's time.

In my opinion, bishops should be appointed during their last ten years of service so they have the basic skills of priesthood and pastoral experience, yet are not too old to move around their diocese and get to know the folks whom they shepherd. It's not an easy thing to do. So many of our bishops are appointed because they come up through the ranks working as secretaries and office jockeys. They study in the down time of the summer such subjects like canon law or moral theology and don't have the experience of knowing how a parish works. If so, they would understand the ups and downs of ordinary people, who still trust the priest to hear their confession, give them communion, visit their mother in the hospital or talk to their son who is about to be married. Despite having all the smarts in the world, and all the personal connections in Vatican diplomacy, and the secrets for coming safely out of the maze of the Vatican, when approached by a normal group of parishioners they back off like they've been threatened.

Of course, this is only a sampling of the guys I know. Many are able to hit the mark and enjoy what they're doing and it shows. Nothing better for the people of a parish than to have a happy pastor. It's a bit like family, "If mama's happy, we're all happy." If the bishop is enjoying himself as the shepherd of the diocese, it will show in the work being done by the priests and the laity.

I knew a couple of guys who made no bones about it that they were ordained to the Episcopacy much too early in life. They spent a lot of time running in circles trying to make the best of bad situations. They tried so hard to please everybody. Most of us learn in grammar school that we just can't. I really believe that the older we get, the more we understand how little we know.

The traditional role of a bishop, or more to the point a priest, "ain't what it used to be". The bishop is there mostly in an office and at the head of a table celebrating one thing or another, like confirmations. Kevin Starr, in the foreword of my memoir *I'll Never Tell*, wrote that with parish congregations dwindling the demand for their services is on the wane. I still see my pastor running to and fro from one thing to another and doing more and more dropping in, then discreetly checking out of a meeting, a marriage instruction, a parlor call, telephone calls and various and sundry activities where he is expected to be present, if not in charge. Frankly, some folks manage quite well and don't miss a priest. Others think it is not really "church" unless a priest is present. I could not write about these things 30 years ago. I didn't have time to think about them and then an offer an opinion. I was doing a lot of doing and not much personal introspection to be a discerning young man. I haven't made the circle that one might expect nor do I intend to. It's one of the reasons why I don't throw my entire body into this or that organization. The more involved, the more is expected.

PART III

The Other Side
of the Grass

"The souls of the just are in the hand of God
And no torment shall touch them
They seemed to be dead . . . but they are in peace"
(Wisdom 3:1)

* * *

"O, Death
Won't you spare me over til another year"
Ralph Stanley

CHAPTER 34

Men with Class

SINCE WE BEGIN with people who have recently died and the sacrament of the sick, perhaps a quote from Shakespeare would be in order.

> "The evil that men do doth live after them;
> the good is oft interred with their bones"
> *Julius Caesar*

I was at the tail end of a cold and my nose was leaking like a sieve. The sun was shining and it looked warm but the wind chill factor told the truth. It was cold.

It seemed like the coffin would never get to the hearse as some 30 bishops, a couple of cardinals and over a hundred priests had processed out of St. Mary's Cathedral following the funeral services of Archbishop Emeritus George H. Niederauer, eighth Archbishop of the Archdiocese of San Francisco.

I lived with him at his home for six years, in a converted convent adjacent to the cathedral known to the faithful as The Residence. He invited me to stay on when he succeeded Cardinal Archbishop William Levada, with whom I lived for ten years. George and I really enjoyed each other's company. We generally dined together in front of the TV in the evenings. We watched the news on public television. That way, I could make smart aleck remarks about the show and the way different people presented themselves, while he centered in on the content and educated me as much as was possible. Our taste for politics wasn't even opposite. He cared, I didn't. When a really boring talking head was on too long and we found ourselves more interested in finishing off our Brussels sprouts than the static figure on the screen, we called on our friend "mute" until it looked like Gwen Ifill was bringing the person being interviewed back to life.

There are so many expressions that kept us entertained and educated while we dined. "Harry, always hire the elderly," he would say. "They're fun to watch." Both of us, being old men at the time, knew how well this hit home.

George and I retired from our archdiocesan assignments at the same time; he left as Archbishop of San Francisco and I as his Vicar General. We often remarked over the following years how insignificant we had become, when we once thought the Catholic Church in San Francisco depended so much on us. Decisions were being made and people being hired who brought eye-rolling and a new wrinkle on the forehead. However, George was the first to say, "Harry, we had our time. It's now time for someone else to feel like they're totally in charge and also bear the burdens of the Church in Northern California." Like it or not, the pasture we enjoyed was on the other side of the fence. We could only look in and wonder. The gate we were watching seemed to have a new lock. Only a few had keys or the combination.

The aspergem (sprinkler) was passed among the hierarchy, who each took a turn shaking out a little holy water on the casket. Finally the body was rolled out on the bier and into the rear of the late model hearse. The Duggan Brothers were so careful with the clergy and especially those with staff and miter. All of the Duggans were always good to me and supported all the work I was doing in the ministry with the TV Mass, which I still broadcast each week. But I must add that some priests of the archdiocese would comment about their mother, Maureen, who often attended funerals of Catholic priests and as we processed out of the church she would eye each one of us from head to toe, seemingly measuring our heights and widths to see if she would have to do any special ordering for caskets. Of course, this was all poppycock as Maureen loved the priests, the Church, and a good old-fashioned funeral with pall bearers, incense, holy water and more flowers than were ever needed. Funny thing, flowers, a custom from the time when embalming did not take place and the odor of death abounded. They added some color alongside flesh that was finished and beginning to decay. The more to-do, the better.

So George is now safely in the limo waiting for his final ride and the cemetery, when my buddy Bert approaches and whispers in my ear that he just had a text that my handball friend Ed Dullea passed that morning. A flush came over my whole body and I felt my ears get red. It was another rend of my heart and I almost came to tears. There were others standing around wanting to talk and I had to turn my back to them so they wouldn't see my face. I just couldn't believe it.

Ed had an aggressive form of pancreatic cancer. After radiation and chemo, there was little hope for survival. I had visited him the previous Friday and, as I was leaving, asked his wife to call me for the sacrament of the sick and confession and Holy Communion. I could bring them anytime at their convenience. I told Ed I would bring my lunch because I knew his early years as a wild and crazy guy meant it would take more than a few minutes to clear his conscience. My last words to Ed were, "I'll come by when you call. Saint Peter will be waiting for you with a court reserved, a new pair of gloves and with a ball that you didn't have to heat before a game."

I never got a call. It was only a week later.

I had gone to visit in my shorts and sweats (from the gym) telling him how much we missed him on the courts. Sometimes when a priest visits a person with a terminal disease in full uniform, that is a black suit and a Roman collar, it can cause them to panic about their time on earth and thus be more nervous and anxious. I didn't want that to happen, as I was prepared to make Ed laugh and review some of the old stories we lived together. Jay Capell, another handball friend, was just leaving the living room as Ed's wife, Nana, let me in the front door. Jay and I had talked about my visit and both of us felt Ed would like the Sacrament of the Sick, as he was born and raised Catholic. He had two uncles who were Jesuit priests. He loved them both and always felt a twinge when I needled him about going back to church. His wife had found a home with a born again group and loved to worship and pray with them and he appreciated his wife and her form of prayer. It was all okay with Ed, as long as he didn't have to attend her services. He said they were always much longer than the Mass. I would say to him that he could use the extra time.

Ed was a retired San Francisco cop who had an unusual reputation for never shooting anyone. He always carried a ten-pound flashlight as he ran up stairs in the run-down flats and ghetto hotels chasing bad guys. He enjoyed the exercise and the challenge. He never walked away from a fight. Why should he? Every time I ran into him on the handball courts, I would simply bounce off. "How did you get so strong, Ed?" "I've lifted weights since I was 14 and I've never met a sport or an athletic contest that I didn't enjoy."

One time in the last three or four years, I turned suddenly and ran smack into him. We were playing at the courts at the famous South End Rowing Club down on the wharf. The courts were a bit larger than most double courts. I caught Ed off balance and he dropped like a fly. I tried to help him up and, when I saw he was fine, we had a good laugh. That didn't stop him from saying he was going to tell the boys that I bitch slapped him. I didn't know what that meant, but it got a round of applause from the locker room crowd as we were re-quenching our thirsts with cold beers.

Ed had quit drinking by this time, as he promised his wife that he was going to take a different route to heaven than the ones that many Irish cops had pursued. To his buddies he was "Harp" as he loved everything Irish including that fine lager that I tested more than once on the Emerald Isle and on Union Street.

Ed's last assignment with the police force was on the bomb squad. How fitting for such a brave man with a heart of gold wanting to do good for anyone he could. It was his duty to enter the unknown and find out if a simple package lying on the curb wrapped in brown paper with twine around it was just that or something deadly. He carried out his task in full bomb squad gear as easily as he approached the pimp in the Cadillac at 4:00 a.m. in San Francisco's seedy Tenderloin district. As the pimp rolled down his window to acknowledge two cops in a black and white, they inquired, "Hey, Brother, why the dark glasses before daybreak?"

"Officer, in my business, at 4:00 in the morning the sun is always shining and I'm cool." With a laugh and ten points for the right answer, the S.F.P.D. continued patrolling Golden Gate Park.

I can see Ed's black lab looking at me from the kennel in the living room knowing that something was not right, as his master was a loving man and would not have him penned up even with visitors in the room. Reminds me of a story I use about the man who was dying of cancer and the priest came to visit. The man was terminally ill and had just a short time to live. The priest said, "Your dog is sitting outside like he's waiting for you to come out and be with him." "Old Shep knows I love him," said the dying man, "And I will forever see that he is cared for, even though I'm in the bosom of Abraham." So it is with those who have faith in God. We don't always know or will never know what's going down in the afterlife, but we do trust that the master is there and he will continue to nourish and protect us as long as we're faithful, like Shep has been.

So as Ed on his white Harley and George in his black limo are off to meet God face to face for the first time, I returned to the beach in Half Moon Bay where I was still living at the time. In my memoir I wrote about my final trip and riding into the sunset there. Listening to the waves slap the sand and the rocks in unison and discord, you know of their power and your own personal weakness. But when I told God my plans for my earthly exit, he laughed.

* * *

The more I thought about George dying the more upset I became. I really didn't get to see him off like I wanted. He had told his classmate and best friend about his terminal illness but never mentioned it to me whenever I visited him at Nazareth House. I always tried to be funny and uplifting, but it doesn't come so easily when you see someone you love suffering. He was on full time oxygen and found it very difficult to breathe. He did say to me that he would not be returning home to Menlo Park. I missed his meaning.

Archbishop Niederauer and Cardinal Levada had celebrated their 55th year of ordination at the residence they shared near St. Patrick's Seminary. There were a dozen guests, almost all bishops except for Monsignor Warren Holleran, a guy I didn't know, and me. Warren had been my homiletics teacher at North American College and still served as a teacher and mentor to me. Before we sat down for the luncheon, all were gathered in the living room. George asked if any of them had read my memoir that recently had been released. Not a whimper, not a nod, not a stare. This was the basic *tabula rasa* response. Finally his successor and my current archbishop, Salvatore Cordileone, admitted that he had seen a copy and sniggered as he pointed out, "Oh yes, the rock and roll priest."

George broke the stifling silence that followed with the announcement that he was buying a copy of my book for every prospective seminarian who was interested in the priesthood. They were coming for a weekend of discernment, arranged by vocation directors to have young men spend some time in the seminary talking to students and having a basic orientation of what they could expect if they wanted to pursue the Catholic priesthood. George was going to speak to them and felt that my book would give them a realistic view of what they might expect both in the short and long terms. Having served as a seminary rector for more than 20 years, he knew the pitfalls and the platitudes that one might encounter if pursuing a vocation to the priesthood. He said he would suggest *I'll Never Tell: Odyssey of a Rock & Roll Priest* to them as a good read, to see what one man had done in the pursuit of his life as a priest. Needless to say, I was thrilled to hear his praise of my book and especially his recommendation to men looking for some answers to the mysterious calling they were experiencing.

I think he expected a smaller group than 47 but that's how many books I mailed out to guys shopping the idea of priesthood. I wonder whether it will influence any of them? I did receive thank you notes from two. That says something.

It reminded me of when a young Tim Dolan was ready to drop out of our alma mater Cardinal Glennon Seminary until he heard me speak at a retreat. I asked the young men there to let me know if they decided to pursue the priesthood. Of the dozens of seminarians in attendance, the future Cardinal of New York was the only one to write when he chose to be ordained, thanking me for the words of encouragement.

No one told me anything when I was thinking about priesthood. I knew there was a Holy Spirit and I relied on a big shove. San Francisco Archbishop John Quinn used to say, "Harry, when you think it's bad, it can only get worse. And don't worry about it, the Holy Spirit is in charge and no matter how much we flop and flounder, success or failure will not be ours alone."

Looks like John Quinn will follow George soon and go before even Warren Holleran, who is 90. The Archbishop emeritus picked up an illness in Rome from which he will not recover.

Archbishop George was the second learned man who complimented me on the work I had done. Both he and the late Kevin Starr, who wrote the foreword to my memoir, were two gentlemen of superior learning and literary sense. Both saw something lasting in what I had done. It won't matter much to me if what I write gets panned. I have the opinion of these two icons, intellects and thinkers who were good men as well.

In George's last days on one of my visits, I was a bit jealous of the attention he was getting from others. One woman even tried to stop me from going into his room. I had lived with him for six years and felt we shared an affinity that no one else had. When I entered the room it was like I had ascended Calvary and was gazing at the cross. His face was sunken and wore suffering. The breathing from the tortured chest was shallow and came in gasps. It felt like he would be called to eternity at any moment. Yet there was no darkness covering the earth and the rocks were not split nor the temple shaken. There was no sour wine offered on a sponge or a soldier with a spear waiting to pierce his side. Instead the little room was filled with machines and tubes and flickering lights with bouncing green dashes on a monitor extending mocking succor. I remarked to a number of friends that I didn't want that to be me, should I be given the grace to die slowly and with foreknowledge that the end was coming.

There always seemed to be a gaggle of women at the watch. It didn't bother me at first but then I felt it was so obtrusive. I remember the scripture where it names the women waiting in agony for Jesus to give up the ghost.

"There were also women looking on from a distance.
Among them were Mary Magdalene, Mary the mother
of the younger James and of Joses, and Salome."
(Mark: 15:40)

It wasn't until after he died that I discovered from one of the women that George had requested their presence, so as not to die alone. His only living relative was his cousin Ann who had already come and gone a few weeks before as she could not endure his last days.

That become the second wrong judgment that I made during this process. I was also very jealous and envious of the two bishops who were chosen to do the vigil, the homily, and the memories of George. After all, I knew him better than they did, I thought. But alas it's still a hierarchical church and the miter matters. Besides I'll never know that he didn't request each of them before he died. Maybe I wasn't as close to him as I thought?

It happens. All kinds of relationships go south when one or the other of the two parts ways. The one left behind can never know for certain about the closeness of the relationship. Remember this one? "It's me, not you. I just don't love you anymore." So there!

I had a few bad days of remorse and soul-searching following the deaths of Archbishop Niederauer and Ed Dullea. About the other stuff, I'll never know.

CHAPTER 35

Life: Not Ended, Changed

SO WHEN AM I going to get off the death march of friends? I guess age has a bit to do with it, but more importantly what friends leave behind as example and discipline is worth continued consideration into three more fun people who helped make the world a better place to live and me a better human being.

I'd known Louise Molinari since she worked for me in the 1970s. She recently passed in her sleep and when her daughter telephoned to let me know she added that *I'll Never Tell* was at her bedside. Louise did not linger nor did she have any idea that God was calling her home. The family, a son and a daughter and their children, boarded the Neptune Society boat at Pier 39 and we scattered Louise's ashes near the Golden Gate Bridge. I could hear her piercing voice saying: "Hang in there, Boss. You don't have to start a fight to win one."

She was Armenian and I learned of the sad plight of the genocide that took place in their homeland from her father, George Krouzian, who was a survivor. Once, as a guest on my TV show *Tell A Vision*, he mesmerized me with the terror of crawling under cover of bushes in the daytime and running in the dark of the night to escape the genocide brought on by the Turks. He nearly starved but managed to make it to the border and eventually to the United States where he married and became a very successful pharmacist and philanthropist.

His father was a married priest of the Armenian rite. George often spoke of him and how important it was to the children to have a holy priest for a father. Of course, it gave me speculative thoughts about the kind of father I would make if we were permitted to marry in the Roman rite. I know I loved children and I loved women. When last I thought about it, that was the general formula for family. I know from statistics that the rate of mortality for human beings is about 100%. That's pretty close to the chances I'll have of raising a family before mortality arrives.

* * *

Michael Clark never married and perhaps that was why he never left his zip code. It was emblazoned on his baseball cap: 94123. That's where he lived and he ventured out of it only a few times.

Like the time he woke up in Florida with the Stork, a good friend and former football player with the old Oakland Raiders. The nickname was inspired by his long gangling arms, used to grab runners trying to gain yardage by coming around his end. The Stork was big and strong and popular. Michael was short with long eyebrows and a personality that attracted all kinds of people (who drank). The two of them had left the Bus Stop bar on Union Street and in lieu of having one more cocktail they went to the airport and caught a flight to Florida. "What am I doing here?" Michael mumbled as he opened his eyes to bright sunshine and 80 degree heat. "You tell me and we'll both know," replied the Stork.

At his funeral outside the little Episcopal church on the corner of Union and Steiner, someone said that you couldn't get a drink in San Francisco between eleven and one because every bartender in town was at Mike's memorial.

I shared the honor of presiding with a female priest from that parish. She was delightful and very accommodating. It was my very first official service with a female priest. I joked with close friends that there wasn't much difference in the way we celebrated the Eucharist nor our prayer. However, in the sacristy, once the robes had been retired, it was pretty obvious we were male and female.

Michael was the kind of guy who had been ridden hard and put away wet. His penchant for the drink was going to eventually consume him. He enjoyed what he called a "trapline" that ran from Fillmore to Chestnut back up Fillmore to Union and then returning through Buchannan Street. His stops, mostly for Dewars and water, included Mulherns, Horseshoe, Marina Lounge, Chestnut Bar & Grill, Perry's, Bus Stop and Brazenhead. Don't let the "grill" fool you, they were all watering holes.

Some titled him the mayor of Chestnut Street but he was far from a political figure in the neighborhood. Of course, he always had an opinion and was quick to defend the poor and the downtrodden and eager to chop up the people in office who could not tell the truth or be straight with their constituents.

We celebrated the same year of birth with his best friend, Eddie Keane, who also walked the planks of keeper of the booze closet at the Marina Lounge. The three of us got together from ages 55 to 77 to celebrate June 1939. We were last hosted by Jim Martin at the Brazenhead. I recall our 55th birthday when a pal brought a sign from the freeway that read "SPEED LIMIT 55". The double nickel on the freeway has gone the way of our fifties and now, as Michael was about to see 78, the lucky 77 was going, going gone.

As Michael trailed off on his Harley leaving New York for San Francisco, a man of the towel (cloth is for priests, towel is for bartenders) accompanied him to the curb and remarked how losing his tips from Michael would take away his chance to summer with the family somewhere on the shore.

Michael had earned a few bucks back East and didn't need to work. He knew how to work his money. I often teased him about not having a job for so many years and he took it well, only to let me know that his money was working for him. He had plenty to live on and plenty to live for. San Francisco and his trapline were quite exciting.

While he rarely left his zip code, I was able to persuade him to go to Hawaii, New York, and Washington D.C.. They were all memorable trips and we re-lived them years later accompanied by his deep grunts, as he now sported an artificial throat from his many years of smoking. It was a major inconvenience for him. He refused to go out to dinner and if invited to a function, he would hold a glass until food was served and then disappear. I saw him a number of times as the center of attention and then, like Jesus with the 12 apostles after the resurrection, "Now you see me, now you don't."

In Honolulu, we had spent the day with our old friend Arnold "Kelly" Kaliszewski, riding around in his little red Volkswagen convertible. Rain or shine wherever he went he assured us that our clothes would be dry in a matter of minutes, as the clouds would part and a warm sunshine would return to burn or bronze us. I would get brown, Michael would get red. Kelly was white and red. His six-foot-eight frame occupied the front and back seats of his little red Beetle. He had the chair way back on the driver's side so only one human being could fit in the back behind the passenger. It had to be Mikey. (By the way, a perfect hand of dice in San Francisco bars was called a "mikey".)

When Michael got in the car you couldn't tell where his white Wigwam sweat socks ended and his legs began. He was what we used to call "white Irish". I told him that Don Nelson was a pitchman for Wigwam when I was a guest on *Regis Philbin's Saturday Night in St. Louis,* a TV talk show that aired in the 1970s. I was on his shows at least three times and he always repeated the same question. "How can you be a disc jockey and a Catholic priest?" Don had just retired from the Boston Celtics and Regis launched another talk show in Los Angeles and was climbing the ladder to stardom, eventually becoming the host of *Who Wants to be a Millionaire?* I liked Regis and told him this personally when I met him after a football game in South Bend. He was also a great supporter of Notre Dame and I'm sure has buildings named after him, as does Eddie DeBartolo, one time owner of the San Francisco 49ers. (As a matter of fact, the Philbin Studio Theatre is in the DeBartolo Performing Arts Center.)

Back to Mike's white legs, he really couldn't take the sun especially on an island of it. Later that evening I walked home and left Mike and Kelly at a local pub. Kelly was very popular in Hawaii, as he once was an All American basketball player who went on to play professional ball for the Washington Generals. They were an exhibition team and the whipping boys for the Harlem Globetrotters for many years.

Kelly was a wonderful man and years later I had his funeral at St. Dominic's in San Francisco. It was the same situation. You couldn't get a drink in the zip code because all the bartenders were saying farewell to Kelly. I said the Mass and the church was packed. Just as people give to people in fundraising, so they show up at funerals when they appreciated the person who passed.

I was not the kind of guy who could close a place whether it was 2:00 a.m. or midnight, even though Honolulu was five hours earlier than San Francisco, so I said my goodbyes to Mike and Kelly, ambled home and had a good night's sleep. Next morning I put a cross around Mike's neck while he was sleeping. Startled as he awoke he said, "What's this? What happened last night?" "Not to worry about the hereafter, Mike. I baptized you a Catholic,"

I said with a straight face. "Oh, by the way, you'll have to go to church every Sunday from this day on or you're doomed." It was Sunday and I was going to Mass on the island. "Put on your Wigwams and let's go!" Not obscene but low-toned grumblings came forth as to what he was doing when he accepted this cross. "Oh, you were sleeping. Not to worry!"

After Mass I looked for him, not on the beach but in the bar. The 'keep said "Oh, you mean Vodka Cranberry. He said he was going for a long walk in the shade." I knew he wouldn't be far off as Hawaii doesn't have that much shade at the beach and you have to be indoors to get a vodka cranberry.

Our next foray into the unknown was our nation's capital, Washington, D.C.. I was a speaker at a meeting and I knew I would have a double room for three days and invited Mike to tag along. He loved his country, his government and history. I knew the prospect of a couple of days in the museums would entice him into enduring a long flight. Our first night we took a walk around Georgetown and were looking for a suitable place to dine.

Out of nowhere came shots, very close by, from a bad guy being pursued by what seemed like a regiment of officers of the law, both on foot and in cars. Mike and I ducked into the doorway of a store, which was closed. We curled up into fetal positions waiting for the war to end. It did shortly and we saw a man in cuffs about a block away being hustled into a black and white. I looked at my buddy who was a "peacenik" inside and out. He brushed himself off and shaking from the experience and responded like the Irishman he was, "You have dinner, I'm having drinks."

All the years I knew Michael, and all the altercations that can happen in adult beverage places, I never saw him get into yelling, name calling, nor fisticuffs. I never saw him as much as lift a finger, unless it was around a glass to toast or wish someone the best. He was always protective of women and particularly redheads. I can still see him patting their hands and expressing his sincere care and concern for them.

Michael loved animals and trees. He would often on his way home hug a tree or smell its leaves, especially in the spring. He used to tease about scent and how he could smell a beautiful woman miles away. Thus, he often used the expression "sniffen". There was a small enclosed alley between ten former stables on 36th at Third Avenue in New York City. Its name: Sniffen Court. I guess that's where he got it.

Next day was spent in the Smithsonian Space Museum. His feet hurt and so we were off to the hotel. But first things first with Michael; lubrication was in order. Washington has lots of monuments and the next day we planned to visit the Vietnam Memorial because both of us knew names that were in the stone.

Michael could best be titled "a character". Every neighborhood has one. When I walk Chestnut Street today, I keep thinking I'll run into him and he'll force me off the street into one of his favorite spots along the trapline for liquid nourishment and friendly conversation. It's the Irish way! Mike was English with an Irish soul.

* * *

I'll never know why good people die young. It seems such a waste. This is especially true after people have worked and toiled their whole lives to be educated, make a living, raise a family and hope that one day they'll see their grandchildren. I have some experience with such families, but would like to tell you only about one.

I guess you could say he was my best friend. After a number of years on earth there are best friends who come and go and even after they've gone, can still be referred to as best friends. Patrick was an attorney, but not the kind who elicits questions. I would say right off the bat that he was a frumpy dresser. His tie was never over the button of his shirt and even with expensive suits, you felt they were just hanging there for a good impression, which he really didn't care about. Pat and I became good friends at St. Gabriel parish in the 1990s when I was the pastor. He was president of the parish council and did loads of pro bono work for friends and foes alike. We fished wherever we could but mostly on the Pacific Ocean. He was the one guy who could persuade me to rise at 4:30 in the morning and be on the boat by 5:30 a.m. for a long ride out to sea knowing that *mal de mer* was part of my DNA. I never really got used to it. I can still hear him in my ear, "Flat calm today, Padre. It's gonna be a beauty!" Catching fish took away most of the pain, but I was always ready for some fried chicken or anything greasy when I got off the boat and arrived back in San Francisco.

Pat and I also traveled a bit but mostly for fishing. He was with me when we received our first major gift for the God Squad. When we retired from the dinner, I told him I had been given a check. "Guess?" I teased. "$500," he said. "No, a thousand dollars!" I threw the check on the bed and his jaw dropped when he saw $35,000. ("For every year of your priestly ministry," the donor had said.) 2019 will mark 55 years. I should return to the same people. Even though the check was made out to Father Harry, he knew I would give it to my favorite charity, God Squad Productions, in order to support the Catholic TV Mass.

I was at Safeway in the vegetable section trying to decide if I was going to eat cauliflower or broccoli, when my cell buzzed. Pat asked if I could come over and visit with his family. He had just received some bad news and wanted to have our opinion on what he should do next. I no longer cared what I was going to eat and raced over to his home to meet with his wife and two daughters. They were all in the living room in tears. Patrick was such a matter of fact guy and as an attorney was almost devoid of outward expression. It helped tremendously that his oldest daughter was in medical school and had completed her internship and so was familiar with the nature of his tumor and what the test results meant.

There really isn't a lot of choice when doctors are forced to put things in percentages and tell you what might be and what might not happen. In his case, the cancer in his brain meant it was a choice to either lose his capacity to remember, and maybe his sight, and perhaps go into a vegetative state, that is if he had the brain surgery. Or not have the surgery and begin radiation treatments and simply make the best of the few months he might have to live. It came down to that old adage about what you would choose, memory or sight. What would you prefer? Losing sight would completely debilitate a man in his mid-60s and losing memory would surely make it hard on his family.

After a couple of hours of back and forth with all of us in tears, we came to the conclusion that he would not burden his family with lack of sight or memory or both and simply make the best of the time he had. It turned out to be about six months. I remember when we had a dinner for him at his favorite restaurant on Nob Hill, the Big Four. He had lost so much weight that when he stood up his pants fell down. His daughter was the only one who was embarrassed — not Patrick. Like the trooper he was, he simply bent over, pulled them up, smiled and made his way through the restaurant to the front door.

I'll never know why God chose this man to be with him in heaven before so many others. Perhaps, he needed a good lawyer. Or maybe Saint Peter just needed a fisherman he could count on.

CHAPTER 36

What Lasts

I HAVE A SMALL brass shoehorn next to my bed that I use almost daily. It's a little thing. That's exactly what I thought almost 30 years ago when I went to a friend's home in Greenwich, Connecticut, for a Christmas party. He gave these little gems out as a present so that if anyone came with or without a gift, there would be something for them. While I thought it was an idea that had some merit, I stared at the little piece of brass and wondered if I would ever use it or not. Now, almost every day when I slip on my shoes and pick up the simple device, I think of this guy and his family and wonder whatever happened to him. I know his shoehorn made a lasting impression and was such a pragmatic gift.

It struck me that so many of the people I've talked about in this work have come and gone. I have no idea what or where they might be today, but they have made a lasting impression on me and here I am writing about them.

I visited a lady at the request of her caregiver and executor of her estate. He said she was feeling down and needed some cheering up. He also said that she asked for me, as I had had the funeral of her best friend and her husband. Freddie said, "Don't wear your black suit, you'll scare her to death." Not much chance of that; when I saw her she looked pretty good.

We sat at the kitchen table and when Freddie left the room she said she wanted to die. "No," I said, "You'll be 100 next week. You're too old to die. We all love you and want you to see that day." "No," she persisted, "I want to die." "Why?" I finally asked. With a wry smile on her face and as if she knew I would bust out laughing, she said, "All my friends are dead and I'm sure they think I went to hell."

I wonder how many older people are eager to join their loved ones and friends who have gone before them marked with the sign of Christ and enjoying everlasting life. More than one husband and wife have experienced this when they are advanced in age and one goes before the other. It's almost like, "Come and join me. I lived all those years with you and we just can't be broken up because of death."

Freddie heard me laughing from the other room and came back into the kitchen. "It must have been a good confession," he said. "You two are having too much fun." She lived past her hundredth birthday and I hope she continues to laugh with me for telling the story and making others laugh.

I frequent the Marina Lounge on Chestnut Street because my good friend Eddie still tends bar there. As I mentioned, we're the same age and celebrate our birthdays together. Of course he doesn't look like an octogenarian and is able to move back and forth on the boards with ease. He serves mostly an older clientele, as his daylight hours do not include the young and the restless looking for Mr. or Ms. Goodbar. A number of the patrons attend the local parish where I am in residence. They are always friendly and warm and in some cases, warm is the operative word. I told Eddie that it looks like a geriatric asylum waiting for the grim reaper. And you keep pumping up their spirits with spirits and the will to laugh, share old stories, and suggest that the weather might be different tomorrow.

"Who knows if I'll be here tomorrow," pipes one old gent.

But that can be said for all of us. I try to walk late afternoons with tunes in my ears in order to get my 8,000 steps and daily exercise. When I hit the lounge, I'm about 700 steps short of my goal. A quick beer or a stemmer and I'm out the door. A stemmer, you ask? A martini glass with a yellow mermaid swimming on top (that would be a lemon twist). Eddie gets off at 6:30 p.m. and more often than not he'll join me at the rail and we'll have one together. In case I've got my steps in, there is always the 22 Fillmore bus that stops just a block away and then will transport me to the door of the parish. I never have to get behind the wheel. It also reminds me to say "thank you" to the bus drivers. Since I've been using public transportation I'm amazed at the people who take the time to thank the driver. When I lived in Manhattan I never had that experience. It also seems very genuine. Last week when I boarded, I saw a broken beer bottle in the aisle. It was rolling around and it was a fresh bottle because you could smell the beer rolling up and down. I had a plastic bag with me from the gym and asked the driver when he next comes to a stop to pause and I would clean it up and put the glass in the bag I had. I did.

He was equally grateful for just a little thing that made his day easier. He didn't have to call into HQ and have them delay his schedule while a person assigned to clean up could board the bus and do the job.

With retirement there is more time and you don't need to rush here and there or ignore a broken beer bottle on a bus. Courtesy as you get older seems only natural.

CHAPTER 37

Old Guys

I'M A REGULAR READER of *Sports Illustrated* and I've frequently imagined myself on the cover for my ability to play any sport. The only one I still work at is handball. It's the apex of my social life. There have been so many close friends over the years whom I have met playing handball and that closeness continues. It's not a very popular sport, but it certainly is all one needs for a workout. I'm playing regularly with guys in their 80s. While it's not much to see from the outside of the glass, it's a picnic inside for the energy and competition that comes from old bodies whose minds tell them to do something and the bodies respond with a grunt or a groan accompanied by the unspoken words, "Are you kidding me?"

Retirement is good except for weekends when you have to do the same things you did all week. There is no looking forward to Friday and Saturday nights. As my pal Don used to say, "Worst thing about retirement is you don't get a day off." As a cancer survivor I count my blessings whenever I start up my car to go any place, walk to the altar when the music is bad, go to the gym when I feel like I could be more productive at the bar. But I do it all with a smile. It's not for myself but for all the guys who've worked harder than I and who have put more years into following

God's plan. Some are sick, old, worn out, nervous or with heart problems, where their keys have been taken away and now they are prisoners of their problems or caretakers of their challenges. I have been so blessed to live through the cancer to be able to do this work and have an avenue of expression for what means most to me . . . as I was told, tear up your notes and tell people how you feel about God.

Whoever said age is all in your mind, never had to try and get up fast without wobbling, nor read the sign of the next exit, nor the numbers on the board as you are asked to open your hymnals to sing number 101. Hey kid, can you read that? What number is it? What? I can't hear you. Shout it in my good ear! Parts start to go at a certain age. I first noticed it a couple of years ago when I couldn't keep my balance when trying to put on my pants. I had to lean against something or hold on to a chair. I could no longer put on my socks without sitting down. You might not think this is much but, when it happens to you, the idea of someone taking away your car keys looms larger.

There are so many old jokes about it, I'll spare you. However, for those who might be flirting with 80, here's a bit that someone sent me. It was written by my friend Warren Halloran at his 80th birthday and I use it here with his permission. I call it "Eightieth Birthday Ode":

> "Sociological studies have recently shown
> What we who are seniors had long ago known
> We're the happiest people of all, it appears
> And five percent happier every ten years.
> If we live to two hundred, that means there will be
> Not a person on earth more contented than we.
> Still, whatever the future we favor or fancy,
> The prospects of living that long are quite chancy.

As it is, we spend half the time paying our bills
For doctors and dentists and dozens of pills
For every conceivable human affliction
There's a test and a treatment, another prescription.
We take pills for our allergies, nose drip and sneeze,
Or our gastrointestinal reflux disease
Coumadin for thin blood, Celebrex for back pain
Boniva for bone strength, fish oil for the brain.
Prilosec or Imodium, each new panacea
For hiccups for heartburn or plain diarrhea
With shots for pneumonia, tetanus, flu,
Or TB and typhoid, to name but a few.
The kidneys are failing, the bladder's no better
The prostate is ailing, and life seems much wetter.
How the bowels will behave is increasingly dubious;
Will they jam like a log or erupt like Vesuvius?
We plan to move into the bathroom this year
With the TV, the laptop and all of our gear.
It's a fairly large room, with a handy alcove
For the dining room table, the fridge and the stove.
If there's not enough space for the couch or the bed,
We'll upholster the bathtub and toilet instead.
Our memory is flagging, our eyesight grows dimmer,
Our shoulders are sagging, the future looks grimmer.
With scarcely opposable arthritic thumbs,
And nightly disposable teeth for our gums
We will stand and feel dizzy, sit down and feel sore,
Take a nap on the couch and wake up on the floor.
There'll be walkers and wheelchairs and handicapped ramps,
Which we struggle to climb without muscular cramps.
The drivers will swear at us crossing the street
And accuse us of willfully dragging our feet
We will pay no attention to what they have said;

They can shout all they like, but our batteries are dead.
Our membership card in the intelligentia
Will expire with the onset of early dementia.
We will deal with depression in psychoanalysis
And spend three days a week doing kidney dialysis.
But hope springs eternal, the old saying goes
That's at least what our doctors would have us suppose.
Technological marvels will shortly abound
To assure our survival and keep us around.
With transplanted livers and kidneys and hearts,
Titanium knees, and a host of new parts,
With prostheses and implanted pacers and pumps,
And computerized chips from our brains to our rumps,
With stents in our arteries, aids in our ears,
We will no longer need to keep track of the years.
We can live on forever, or so it will seem,
Smoke our Cuban cigars, and enjoy our Jim Beam,
Or our single malt scotch and our Sapphire gin,
And the finest of wines from the rare vintage bin.
Let us eat, let us drink and be merry today,
For tomorrow we live in some bionic way.
Where there's life, love and family and friends near and dear,
There will always be laughter and hearty good cheer!
So a toast to us seniors and long may we live,
To enjoy all the future can promise or give!
Cheers!

CHAPTER 38

But For the Grace of God

MY SPIRITUAL DIRECTOR by way of talks, tapes and his writing is the Father Ron Rolheiser, an Oblate of Mary Immaculate, which simply means he is a priest of a religious order and not a parish priest in a diocese. I have been an admirer of his for years and I like to listen and then take time to contemplate what he has to say.

He is Canadian by birth but has spent most of his life in the States. I served on the Oblate Board of Communications for 25 years and that is where I discovered him and the way he relates to God, the Church and people. He has an understanding of "moral loneliness" that I believe is part of us all, but it becomes a focus and a highlight for people who live the celibate life. The Book of Genesis says pretty clearly in the creation story that God said (not me) that it is NOT good for man to be alone. And so he does the rib thing and Eve comes upon the scene.

Saint Augustine said our hearts are restless until they rest in God. I think I wrote about being the happiest guy in the world in 1961 right before I left for Rome. And as I sat on the swing in the breezeway enjoying a cold drink after a wonderful meal and knowing how proud my family was for me, the squeak in the swing annoyed me. A little squeak, nothing major, but it took its toll and negated a magic moment.

I'll have to look it up, but it has been said that if you want to avoid loneliness, plant a tree, write a book, or have a child. All three will assure you of a certain amount of legacy on earth. None of these can be erased and yet they don't fill the bill for total satisfaction. So this moral loneliness is not just for guys like me who have chosen to live alone, to be alone.

About once a month I visit an elder care center where my good friend Father Wilton Smith resides. Like me, he is a retired priest and I have known him since 1973. When I drive to Nazareth House I think a lot about the priests who are "put away" with no or little family to visit. After 50 or more years of service to a parish community, they now sit in the straight back chair staring at the walls just a few feet from them. Their quarters are called cells for good reason.

Father Wilt retired many years ago, not because he wanted to but because Parkinson's disease would not allow him to continue to drive or offer Mass publicly. I see him often. Wilt is confined most of the day and night in his small room with a small desk, a bed, a dresser and oh, a bathroom which has a door. His room is not much larger than my bathroom. There is a closet but since he doesn't go anywhere there is no reason to have a large wardrobe. There are too few occasions.

I on the other hand live in a suite of rooms with about four doors. It has been a bad habit of mine to measure one's success by the number of doors you have. For example, when I lived in an apartment in New York, I had two doors. One was to get in and out of the place and the other was for the WC, that is, the water closet. Where I now live at St. Vincent de Paul parish, I have a door to the apartment and two doors, one to the bedroom and one to the study and then there is yet another to the bathroom. Only one has a lock but they are still doors. What luxury! A friend of mine often remarks that she has a difficult time staying at her in-laws because they have so many doors in the house and she's afraid that they are not all locked when they go to bed and someone might enter.

I've been in homes where there are only three doors, one in the front, one in the back and the one to the privy. Everyone in the family sleeps, eats, lives in the confines of these three doors. There is no slamming of the bedroom door when one wants to get away and have a good cry. There is no escape to the basement and the cellar, not the upstairs or the attic. Poor people who are subject to this kind of living usually spend more time on the streets and that can often lead to problems.

I bought a small TV for Wilt and he can also listen to music with it. He sits in a wheelchair most of his day waiting for the next meal. I promised myself, that if all possible, I was not going to spend my last days like that. But then who knows? It might be the Lord's will that I be taken care of in such a manner. Oh to age! Every time I sit in the guest chair and look around Wilt's room, I say to myself, "I hope this isn't me in a few years, or a month, or whenever the Lord takes away my ability to serve, to work, to be on the go." I visit however not to feel sorry for him or myself but because it's a corporal work of mercy and a means of grace.

Wilt is my confessor and seasonally I go to confession to him and renew my promise to sin no more and avoid the approximate occasion of sin. We talk and laugh and after ten minutes he usually falls asleep. Yep, I'm that interesting to be around. No he just gets really tired. He is 87 and doing very well. He has to have a nurse to go to the bathroom or dining room or anywhere for that matter. He has to wear a bib when he eats. He wears a little padded helmet to prevent injury if he fell. He was a great tennis player in his time. It's hard to look at his gnarled fingers now, which used to grip a racket and ace a serve. When we've dined together, he has a fork that is bent in a right angle so he is able to feed himself. Someone has to cut his food if it's meat, or tough, or unable to be eaten with a fork. You all know people like this and perhaps you live with one. It's a joy to be able to spend even a small unit of the day with Father Wilt.

Remember when I said I would not like to retire in such a small place? I did something about it. With the help of a close friend I invested in a small condo north of San Francisco. It's the first time I've owned anything more than a car in my 80 years of life. It is going to be my home when I can no longer work or say Mass publicly or get around like I want to. It has no steps in case I have a wheelchair and there is an extra bedroom for someone who might take care of me. That, too, is planned.

Did you ever have to ask for a big chunk of change from a friend to buy something? I wrote letters, I did the homework and I planned my strategy to a T. So I walk in his office and he says, "Oh, you need how much?" I give the figure and he says, "Let me call my attorney." Five minutes later he says, "The money is yours, go in peace." The ask is over! It brought tears to my eyes.

No it wasn't a gift. I'll have to pay him back and am now paying on the loan for ten years. Should I die before then, there is a plan for him to recover his loan. Hey! I own something. At my age, it's about the only thing I've ever owned that I have a key to that no one else does.

I am now renting my condo to a friend so that I can pay the taxes and the homeowners' fee, as well as many other little things that crop up for an owner. Don't priests make a vow of poverty? Yes, some of them do, those who make solemn vows of poverty, chastity, and obedience. For a priest of a diocese and under a local bishop, it's a promise and not a solemn vow. So, if you give me money or I sell a book or two, it's mine, I don't have to divvy up with anyone nor do I have to turn it over to some higher power who will look after me. This, of course, doesn't apply to the IRS. They are looking after me and want their fair share, every year. You know how that goes.

CHAPTER 39

Francis, Vigano, Sal

I SAID I WOULDN'T but I feel like I have to now; that is, write something about Pope Francis and the present dilemma. By the time you read this it might all be over and I will say that I should have kept my musings to myself.

It all began with a letter from Archbishop Salvatore Cordileone. It arrived by email and that's usually what I get to first in the morning, after I say my prayers. A woman in his office sent it and I didn't pay much attention until I saw another archbishop's name, Carlo Maria Vigano. I had seen a short story on the news the night before, so I began reading with great interest. My face soon saddened, as I got deeper and deeper into the innuendos about the problem of turning a blind eye to clergy abuse and how it might go all the way to the top, thus, Pope Francis. The letter from our San Francisco archbishop about abuse was devastating. He was challenging the pope. Once I completed the two-pager, I was tempted to hit the little arrow that points back to the sender with one simple word, SAD.

I spent the entire day mulling over a reply and wondering whether it was worth it. After all, Sal said he knew Vigano personally and that Vigano's self-proclaimed "testimony" had been written "with absolutely no consideration given to furthering his 'career', all of which speaks to his integrity and sincere love of the Church". Cordileone, therefore, concluded that Vigano's statements must be taken seriously.

In his letter, Archbishop Cordileone recalls his first exposure to abusive clergy shortly after he was made a bishop. He remarked to a friend that this was not a good time to become a bishop. The response was, "It is a good time to become a great bishop." In light of his years here in San Francisco, it might have been better to skip that anecdote.

Apparently, I was not the only one who found the letter difficult to digest and, even worse, understand why our archbishop would want to take on the pope. About a week later Sal asked for a meeting with all the priests, where he might have a chance to explain himself and do away with any and all rumors that he was calling for the resignation of Pope Francis. That meeting was held and if he'd 'fessed up, said he'd made a mistake, "if I disturbed priest and people", if there would have been an apology . . . but he did not back down. I will be happy to report any return to sound ground, but it appears that for now the burial of his idea has taken place. We all say and do things we would like to reverse and sometimes we have the chance to reverse them. However, it's like eating something you don't like. It leaves a bad taste in your mouth. It's a bit of what I'm feeling today.

More than one Catholic has expressed to me this simple question, "How come the hierarchy of the Church is asking us to do penance, to give up meat on Friday, to say the rosary, to make holy hours in their parish churches, when clearly, these are not our sins?" They are not to blame for any of these abusing priests or bishops. The answer to this is from the writing of Saint Paul. We are all the body of Christ. All the members have a part in what the body is and does.

"One body but many parts. There is one body but it
has many parts. But all its many parts make up one
body. It is the same with Christ. We are all one."
(Corinthians 12:12-27)

I listen carefully but not with ease as my friends, almost all educated people, tell me about going through Catholic grade school and high school and never even hearing of pedophile priests. Although there is one attorney, who, without hesitation, points out that there was in his parish a guy they called "queer" who definitely had the problem. He was discovered, defrocked and I believe moved to Mexico. Needless to say, it's now been proven that there were a number of young men who were his victims.

I don't buy the concept being furthered by the right wing of the Church that most of this is part and parcel of homosexual priests, that it's all part of the agenda to change the culture from the inside and cover up abuse. I recently heard a recorded homily given in a parish in Minnesota about the cause of the whole problem. To this preacher, it was part of a Communist plot to conquer the world. Since it could not be done using arms and the technology of warfare, it would have to be done in the minds and in the culture — thus the infiltration of people who now are part of the fiber of society and fit in nicely with the common man. The homilist was clear and distinct in his delivery but nowhere near the mark as to his conclusions about gay people. Personal experience in working with both men and women who are gay leaves no room for doubt that this is not the problem, even though we keep hearing of the 86% of clergy abuse is by homosexual men. I could cite a number of Catholic priests who have admitted being gay and yet are pastorally and professionally far more effective than many of the rest of us who minister in the Church.

I've been trying in my own mind to make a comparison with alcoholism. It, too, is a disease that a number of the clergy have that ruins their ministry or at least curtails it until they can make an adjustment. Pedophilia, on the other hand, is quite different, as it leads to criminal activity. It may also be a serious sickness that was thought to be curable by a number of psychologists and psychiatrists, who had under their care at the request of their bishops many clergymen who were pronounced "fine" after six months in a home or hospital, only to return to their diocese and eventually to criminal activity.

It was a sad interview I heard with one priest who, with tears flowing, admitted his downfall and said he only loved the boys that he had abused. They were all special to him and there was no way he had any intention of hurting anyone. It's a problem for me to try and figure out from my own perspective how this kind of activity could ever be justified because of love. It's absurd to think that it could be. And yet some evil spirit, okay, the devil, has found a way to twist even love and use it to his evil advantage.

Love is the most powerful emotion and the first and most important gift from God. Why tinker with it when you know how important it is to humankind?

"Let us love one another, for love comes from God.
Everyone who loves has been born of God and knows God."
(1 John: 4:7)

Conservative author and political analyst George Weigel, in a recent article in the *Wall Street Journal*, called the problem, "a crisis but not of faith." His writing on the subject is to the point and, without tampering with his words and idea, let me just say how much I agree with him and have posited the same idea in another way. The Holy Spirit is still in charge and no matter how much we priests, bishops and popes try to decide what is right and wrong, it's Jesus Christ who allows us to commune with God in the many different forms of prayer and meditation that we use. This is from the Hymn of Jubilation:

> "I and the Father are one, no one comes to
> me unless through the Father."
> (Matthew 11:27)

It's like not going to church any longer because you don't like the priest or his homilies or how he conducts himself. God is bigger and the Eucharist is available in more than one place. We practice our faith because of scripture, tradition and the many good people who have passed along their belief, their culture to us. The Second Vatican Council made it quite clear by definition that the people of God are the Church. It is now part of our dogma and should not be put aside or forgotten. Thank you, Mr. Weigel, for the gentle reminder that these happenings in our church are not a crisis of faith.

His Excellency Carlo Maria Vigano

The letter of Sal Cordileone championing Carlo Vigano and making his personal expression of solidarity resulted from Vigano's 11-page exposé of Cardinal McCarrick and a number of others, which left me feeling soiled and wanting after reading it. It read like something from the *National Enquirer*, which began with a sleazy diatribe of the many doors that were closed on him when he began his exposure of American prelates. He describes two meetings with Pope Francis and both are unsatisfying, either from the content or the way Vigano went about it. He left both encounters thinking that the world around him was going to change. He above all should know how the Church works, when it comes to making decisions about faith and morals. Vigano's "testimony" said that McCarrick had "shared his bed with seminarians". His letter was a translation and perhaps he expects us to understand what this means in English. I'm not naïve enough to think that there was just sleeping going on. There must have been some sexual activity that he does not mention. Now, if someone came to me with this story and tip-toed around a direct accusation by saying "sharing a bed" as immoral and unbecoming of a bishop, I would agree with the unbecoming part. There has got to be *materia gravior,* graver material, but it's not mentioned in his letter.

As Vigano does say in the letter, there are so many others whose names are mentioned as part of the collaboration. Those of you who are fans of the blog "Whispers In The Loggia" will find this exposé sufficient fodder for dismantling the Church as it is today and starting over.

Roger Karban, my scripture-professor classmate from Bellville, Illinois, who keeps me informed, mused on Facebook why there are twice as many law professors and teachers in the Catholic Church than scripture scholars. Sure makes sense to me that we see the "law" as much more important than the word of God. I never hear much about legal departments in the offices of our non-Catholic Christian churches.

Of course, we would have to find another savior and he or she would have to find apostles and they would have to go out over the whole world baptizing in the name of the new father, the new son, and the new Holy Spirit, and making everyone aware of everlasting life. But somehow I don't see this happening.

I'm not fond of the word agenda, but I have felt it afoot in our church here in Northern California. I have seen it with the appointment of bishops in the environs and points beyond. I see it in the changes in our St. Patrick's Seminary, where the Sulpician order of teachers was summarily dismissed after 117 years; in our weekly Catholic newspaper; and in the meetings and presentations that come to us from the outside. According to Catholic theology, marriage still has a twofold purpose that is mutual love for one another and the potential of making babies. But then there were columns and columns of gibberish about *Humanae Vitae*, a document reiterating the seriousness of using birth control and suggesting that the ONLY option is the rhythm method, which many of us see as just another form of birth control. Let's just call it what it is and not put married couples through the ringer when they're trying to raise a family. Obviously, from empirical data, Roman Catholic couples did not accept the document and its consequences. We don't have parents with five, six, seven or 14 kids around the table anymore.

I continue to hear about the advancements of these plotters and the success they're having. We're going to be a smaller church but one of quality and perhaps more Caucasian than most and in some way being helped by President Putin of Russia and on and on and blah, blah, blah. In my part of the world there are more brown-skinned people filling our churches and practicing what's been preached than ever before. It's just a matter of time before they will be the majority of our worshipping communities.

Like a lioness with her cubs, we humans who love and care for one another begin to show our claws when our kind is threatened. I was a close personal friend of Cardinal William Levada and we lived together for almost ten years. Cardinal Don Wuerl was a class below me in Rome at the North American College. These two men are included in the housecleaning that Carlo Vigano suggests to Pope Francis. Of course, Pope Francis is also included. If I were either one of the first two mentioned, I would be happy to be in the company of this Pope of Mercy, who has proven himself to be a dedicated and faithful servant of God. I sincerely believe that all this abuse and criminal activity can be handled in another way.

So, you say, in what way?

I'm not sure of the year but it was at Cardinal Glennon College in St. Louis, the minor seminary that I attended from age 14 to 21. I was probably in high school. We had a liturgical celebration by a Greek Catholic priest who came with his family and his choir. His articulate form of prayer along with his display of piety deeply impressed me. He swung the incense burner back and forth until there was so much smoke the entire chapel looked like it was on fire. The sweet smelling aroma rising to the heavens gave me such a euphoric feeling that if I'd ever had a serious thought of switching my faith commitment, that day would have been a sure fire way of knowing that my vocation to become a priest was in the bag.

After Mass, he took time to introduce his wife and children and I thought to myself, "There but for the grace of God go I." But it wasn't to be. Perhaps that is why I left father and mother, sister and brothers, and dedicated my life to serving the Roman Church — the same one that is now being threatened by right-wing groups who feel that homosexuality and its irrefutable offspring, pedophilia, will bring down the whole kit and caboodle. This is when I point out, as did Pope Benedict to others, that it's not a matter of us bringing it down, it's a matter of us following the nudging of the Holy Spirit to build it up.

Now, back to names, even my good friend Bob McElroy, who preceded me as Vicar General and is now the bishop of San Diego, made his person felt in the Vigano letter. "The appointment of McElroy in San Diego was also orchestrated from above, with an encrypted peremptory order to me as Nuncio, by Cardinal Parolin: Reserve the See of San Diego for McElroy. McElroy was also well aware of McCarrick's abuses, as can be seen from a letter sent to him by Richard Sipe on July 28, 2016." (Sipe is an ex-Maryknoll priest who had written to Pope Benedict in 2008 about clergy abuse.)

As Vicar General, Bob McElroy helped guide the ship from hell as abuse cases came pouring in to the San Francisco archdiocese. He knew full well their import and consequences. I succeeded him as the Vicar General, when he was appointed pastor upon the arrival of Cardinal Levada to the City of Saint Francis. He told me more than once how difficult it was to read the reports from depositions about certain priests who had committed crimes against children. He made no bones about how they should be drummed out of the corps. At that time, I still did not fully grasp the justice in "one strike and you're out" except for criminal cases. It didn't matter, one simple phone call from a disgruntled person and you, too, could be sitting on the bench wondering what happened and how do I get back in the game. There are more than a few guys on the bench right now who are wondering just that.

* * *

December 16, 1964, was cold and dank in St. Peter's at the Vatican. It had been raining for a few days and the chill of the rain hitting the marble and then the marble finding a way to suck it all in made for an unpleasant environment. However it didn't seem to bother the 62 candidates, who lay on the marble floor in front of the window of the Holy Spirit, listening to the Litany of the Saints being chanted by the Sistine Choir. "Saint Peter, pray for us. Saint Paul, pray for us. All you holy men and women, pray for us."

At one point in the ceremony each candidate approaches the ordaining bishop and kneels before him. He places his hands within the hands of the bishop and as these words are read: Do you promise obedience to me and my successors? *"Promitto,"* I promise, affirms the candidate and by that promise you are bound for the rest of your life to the commands and orders of your bishop. It's a no win for anyone who does not get along with or respect his bishop. One could always say to himself that he was ordained in Rome by Bishop Francis Reh and at that time, the most reverend bishop of his diocese might just be graduating from high school. But then the catchall is the phrase "to my successors". They got you there. As a priest, you'll always have a bishop boss. You can't escape it.

But a *promitto* is different than a vow. A vow is a solemn promise made under oath. Religious order priests like Jesuits (who also were not spared by Carlo Maria Vigano's letter of implication and conclusion), Dominicans, Oblates, Franciscans and others take solemn vows. Most religious women orders do the same. In those cases it means (according to Canon Law) that a solemn vow broken by a priest or religious is a serious sin. He or she must confess it as such. The promise made by diocesan priests is less serious and deals with poverty, chastity, and obedience.

A priest could choose NOT to follow the orders of his bishop, for example, by not following his instructions about saying Mass. Would that be breaking a promise made to the bishop and his successors? I think not. A classmate of mine in the Midwest was suspended by his Bishop for not following the liturgical norms for saying Mass that had been changed in the previous few years. There were different translations and he refused to change and stuck with the old. His bishop suspended him from his priestly duties of ministering to his parish. He was basically fired. He was asked to change and would not. This is hardly hellfire material. The priest I'm speaking of is a very holy and faithful man who has put in 55 years of service. He lives a life of poverty and humility and now it's come to this. In the early '60s we studied together and we both loved to play soccer. Believe me, I feel for him.

One of my favorite stories that I often use in homilies and talks that I give has to do with a mother watching her six-year-old son scrape the last bit of peanut butter out of the jar. "Mom, do you think it's true what the teacher said about God today in school?" "I don't know, Johnny. What did she say?" "She said," as he rises to his feet and moves nervously back and forth, "that God is everywhere." "Well, yes, Johnny, that is true." He then slowly puts down the knife and picks up the jar, then clamping one hand over the opening of the jar yells, "GOTCHA!"

Too often we want God all to ourselves and we make the mistake of capturing him so that only we can experience his presence. It's time we take the hand off the jar and let God be wherever God wants to be and to be with whomever God chooses to be with and to love whomever God chooses to love. That's worth a celebration, a promise, a vow, a whatever you want to call it that makes you the kind of person that God will take a slap on the back for and whisper to Himself, "I did that?"

CHAPTER 40

The 80s Reunion

I DON'T BUY that stuff about 80 being the new 60. While it might seem that way to some, the reality of the age is quite the contrary. I just returned from a class reunion of my brothers who studied in Rome from 1961 to 1965. It seemed more like a geriatric convention than a class reunion. All of us were 80+ and it was evident.

First some statistics (never perfect): there were 72 of us who left New York in early October 1961 on the Italian liner *SS Cristoforo Colombo*. From that lot, we were 62 who were ordained on December 16, 1964. This present meeting we ascertained that there were 30 of the group who had died, another five who were MIA and the rest of us muddling through, though most could not attend because of age or ailment.

We were 15 strong. Three of that number brought their wives. Yes, they had left the active ministry some time ago but still felt that strong connection to both the class and the college. It's hard to live close together for four years and not feel an affinity for each other. In some cases, like mine, there was built a bond that draws me to the people even though it's been 55 years.

Some of you who read *I'll Never Tell* might recall the tale of my brother monsignor Wayne Ressler. He is in an elder care center in

Iowa and doing quite well. After various strokes and a multitude of pills (23 each day), he has been able to walk with a cane and pretty much take care of himself. His brother knew how important this reunion was to him and drove him from Dubuque to Chicago and after three days came to pick him up. During that time I shared a room with Wayne and was asked to be sure that he took all his pills at the right time. To me, he was very alert and able to converse just like anyone else. Naturally, age has affected memory but not any more than mine. Wayne was able to enjoy the witty exchanges of a group of octogenarians and contributed himself to the conversation and stories of bygone days on the Janiculum Hill in Rome.

He reminded us of "seven, seventeen, seven". Those were the numbers of steps in the back of the building where we lived. On racing to return to the college after an afternoon away having *panini* and *birra Peroni*, we would run underground through the tunnel to the rear and try to tackle the back stairs. There were no lights and we had nothing to guide us except the count — seven being the first flight, 17 being the next and finally a short turn to the right for seven more steps before we hit the exit door, which would lead us back to the security of a long marble corridor with each room numbered in brass numerals. No keys, still no lights for fear of alerting others to our tardiness. We slipped out of black long robes and into our house cassocks with the blue trimming and the red sash that identified us as young men from the North American College and, at that time, "Yanks" to those who knew the various colors worn by the men studying for the priesthood in Rome. One by one we slithered into the back pews of the chapel just in time to rise with the rest of the men and hear the opening words, "In the name of the Father and of the Son and of the Holy Spirit." Ahh, once again by the hairs of our chinny chin chins we made vespers with seconds to spare. Wayne was wheelchair-bound and could not walk at the reunion nor manage steps of any number, but he could still relate with great clarity the adventure of the seven, seventeen, seven.

We arrived in the Windy City in time to gather with the guys and gals and experience the deep-dish pizza so famous in Chicago. My own tastes run to thin crust and the almost cracker like quality of the pizza we had in Italy those many years ago. It's good to try new things especially when you are a guest in another village. When in Rome . . . That evening both of us tired from the journey retired to our room just in time to witness another play-off victory of the Golden State Warriors basketball team against the Houston Rockets. It was close and exciting. Both Wayne and I love sports and it gave us a chance to continue our dialogue. He fell asleep but with every basket from the Splash Brothers I would shriek with joy only to see his eyes flutter and his lips move, "What happened?"

Looking around the room during the reunion and seeing Parkinson's and dementia exhibited by guys you knew were just short of brilliant during their student days made me feel how fortunate I was to still have my faculties and my wit and wits about me. I never thought I would be part of a real discussion about Depends. Sure there were jokes but every morning in the bathroom waste paper basket undeniable evidence of Wayne's reality was there. Eighty is no 60.

As we prepared for a celebration of the Eucharist in the presidential suite of the hotel, one of our group, an archbishop, made the announcement that he had been diagnosed with the early stages of Parkinson's. I had been told by another priest who knows this archbishop that he would never have come to our meeting unless he had a travelling companion. It would be even more evident as he began the Mass. He mixed up several prayers and stumbled through the liturgy even though a priest next to him presented it to him in the book. Rather than feel sorry or begin a pity party for him, most of us admired his admission to his illness and accepted his status as it was before us. Walking to dinner, the archbishop asked me the same question about three times. It was then that I knew something terribly unusual was going on in the mind of this accomplished and holy man who had been so successful in his 55 years as a priest and bishop. No one knows how difficult it might be for him, if he was aware what was happening at the time. One of our other classmates died from another neurodegenerative disease, ALS, and I always felt it was such a blessing to go to heaven rather than be here in such a vulnerable state.

There were three Musketeers plus d'Artagnan, there are four Horsemen and numerous other foursomes from playing golf to cards. Jim Kogler, Wayne Ressler, Roy Riedy and myself bonded during our first days on the transatlantic voyage from New York to Naples. We sang, we laughed, we drank, we swam, we ate at the same table almost every evening. We forged a bond that lasted all our lives. I'm the last one standing.

If you look up the word religion, you'll discover that the derivation of it comes from the Latin *religare* (to bind). I still have people come to me who say they are spiritual but not religious. It's a difficult explanation that usually falls on deaf ears, but I try to convince them that both are helpful and one does not cancel out the other. We all have various cultures and concepts that come to us from family and our homeland. It's best served if we bring in the word faith because that really tightens up the meaning of a spiritual person who uses religion as the "bond" that holds them together with something beyond themselves and knots them with others who are following the same plan of life.

Jim Kogler passed first. His story is in my memoir, *I'll Never Tell*. In summary, he was the brightest and most gifted of the four of us. He became a theology professor but was dismissed from his position because he failed to teach *Humanae Vitae* (On Human Life). This was the document that drove so many of the faithful from their Catholic commitment because it upheld the Church teaching on contraception. That's another story. But Jim ended up with a strange disease that he likely got while visiting his sister, who was a nun working in the African missions. I believe it was the Congo. He left behind his wife (high school sweetheart) and two beautiful children. Wayne and I had baptized both of Jim's children and also assisted at the daughter's marriage. Of course, you will read in these pages about Wayne and our relationship as the last two of the four.

Roy Riedy passed just two weeks after Wayne and I had visited him at his home in Florida. He had ALS and was spared a lengthy illness, which can be so debilitating and frustrating. We uncorked a bottle of our long-standing favorite Orvieto Classico Bigi Abboccato and toasted Roy as he lay dying.

The final day of our reunion we went by bus to the beautiful Holy Name Cathedral in downtown Chicago. As I walked in I noted the first pew about ten feet from the pulpit. In 1973, I had sat there one weekday morning waiting for Mass to begin. A tall priest came out of the sacristy and I thought to myself, "I know that guy." But it wasn't until he was directly in front of me that I realized it was Father Ed Egan (now deceased, former Cardinal Archbishop of New York City). He had been my Homiletics teacher in Rome. I looked directly in his eyes and could almost hear him thinking to himself that this young man was grading him on his sermon. I smiled as broadly as I could. After Mass, I made my way to the sacristy and without me saying a word he knew who I was and why I was in town.

"I saw you on TV this morning on *Kennedy and Company* subbing for Mr. Kennedy. How in the world did you get to Chicago from southern Missouri?" I explained that I was based in San Francisco and working as a priest full time in communications. I'd been appearing as a guest on Bob Kennedy's talk show for over a year and he asked me to fill in as host while he went on vacation.

What a privilege and what a responsibility. Father Egan said, "I know. I wondered what you would say to your guest from the Playboy Mansion with the life-size figure of the perfect Playboy bunny." What could I say? She was latex and couldn't respond. I did get invited to dinner that evening in the restaurant at the Playboy Tower. It was a good meal. I was in a booth by myself and got more attention than I deserved or expected.

"Father Ed, do you recall one time years ago when you were critiquing my homily and you felt that I was taking chances with my stories? I believe you called it 'walking on eggs'." "No," he said without cracking a smile, "I don't remember, but you must have stepped on a few in these years since your ordination in order to draw such an assignment as hosting a very popular TV show."

"Kennedy is a wonderful man and a devout Catholic," I responded. "He trusted me with his reputation he built up over the years and has counted on me to keep his ratings going while he's away. I've been able to do that and I look forward to much more television exposure in my priestly ministry."

As I left the sacristy and shook hands with the good monsignor I said, "Oh by the way, your homily was excellent at the Mass, but I think you should take a risk or two and let the people know how you really feel." I recalled another priest giving me the advice that I should chuck all my notes and let the people know how I feel personally about God. Speak from your heart and not your homework! That's easier said than done. I've tried it a couple of times but I tend to go on and on without an organized plan. After the rapture, feeling subsides and it just becomes monotonous, or worse, boring. I don't want to be accused of such an adverb? Adjective? Wish I could!

Back to the reunion. One of our other classmates mounted the altar as the main celebrant. He too had to be helped along the way. He had just been released from the hospital two days earlier in order to participate. He coordinated the reunion and had to manage all of us coming from all over the country. One would think after these many years of saying Mass that the words would come automatically. Not so. He too had difficulty with the liturgy book and his memory faded and he forgot to say the Lord's Prayer. There was present a second grade class who that Sunday had received first holy communion in their parish church. Even these little ones noticed, "Father forgot to say the Our Father." But the celebrant was savvy enough at the end to compliment them and repeated how much Jesus loved little children and how much he encouraged his followers to be more like them.

We boarded the bus for our traditional "bum run". It was a custom in Rome during our student days to have an occasional day trip somewhere to foster our education and broaden our minds. Our 55th reunion bus headed to Old Orchard and the Skokie area outside of Chicago to the Holocaust Museum.

I have a T-shirt given to me at a winery that said: "YOU HAD ME AT MERLOT". I'm not sure if that came from a movie or is just a popular saying but it was apropos for me, as we entered the building and the lady in charge began explaining why this museum was built and why it was in this particular area and how it has served the public. There were a number of Jews who had settled there. I had been to the holocaust museum in Israel and also to the second largest one in Washington D.C.. This was now my third experience. As student in Europe for four years, I recall spending a full day at both Dachau and Auschwitz. My mind was full of the horror of both camps. As she continued, I said to myself, "YOU HAD ME AT HOLOCAUST."

Studies have shown that 20% of our population does not believe there was a holocaust. I've heard people on television claim that it's all a Jewish hoax for us to feel sorry for the Jewish nation. Pictures and survivors don't exaggerate the horror of this event in the history of humankind. We listened to a survivor who was our age recall that as a teenager he had been in one of the camps. He was a Polish Jew and his whole family save one had been exterminated. He and his younger sister were able to survive. But his tale to us and two classes of high school students brought to reality what those deniers will never know. He spoke of a piece of bread every other day and watery soup and no shoes and rags to wear left by those who had died in the train cars that took them to the camps. The museum had one of the train cars in it and we could only imagine the horror or the holiness of those who were sacrificed. I'm sure some took advantage and others took care and were kind to the sick and dying. To stand inside the car and let your mind wander is a worthwhile meditation for the future and why humankind must never sink this low again.

On the bus home, we exchanged old tales from our youth and experiences as we returned from Europe to take up our first assignments as priests. Some of you might remember from my memoir that in 1965 I was appointed the Dean of Discipline at a minor seminary known as the House of Studies in Springfield, Missouri. But a more memorable story was of our classmate named Bob who was assigned to an older pastor who enjoyed hunting. The two of them could not get along so Father Bob went to another priest and asked what he could do to get along or at least to have some kind of relationship with the guy. After all, they shared a home, dined together and saw each other every day. His kind mentor suggested to Bob that he might buy a shotgun and take up hunting. So he went to the library and sat down with *Field and Stream* and then went to the local gun shop to buy a firearm. This was in the southern part of the country and so was not difficult in a rural area where almost everyone had a gun and hunted, some of them for necessary food.

Young Father Bob was proud to show off his new 12 gauge to the pastor and after using some new lingo he acquired from the library suggested that the older priest might invite him to go hunting. "Great," said the white-haired pastor. "This Monday, after we count the collection, we'll head out to a farmer friend of mine and see if we can't scare up a covey or two of quail. I'm so glad you have considered this Father Bob and I know you won't be sorry."

Monday morning rolled around and after a quick count of the weekend offerings and a deposit in the local bank, they headed off to the country. I'm sure many of you recall the scene in *Vice* where the Vice President of the United States accidentally shoots another politician, and the real life counterpart. Father Bob's story is worse. The hunting dog, a love in the life of the pastor, was coming over a small knoll in the field when a covey of quail was spooked. Bob raised his gun but not high enough or fast enough to hit the birds and miss the dog.

Sometimes they say the longest journey is from the head to the heart. Father Bob's longest journey was from the farm back to the parish with the body of the pastor's favorite and only hunting dog lying on a towel on the back seat of his Ford. No words were spoken and tears were rolling down the pastor's cheeks as he turned sharply into the driveway and into the garage. His beloved dog would not be going back to the kennel nor would the young Father Bob be much longer at that parish. His transfer came within the month. He tried to fit in, but it didn't happen. I remember when Bob had told me how he became a convert to Catholicism after he and his mother watched *The Story of Fatima*. He had a great devotion to Mary, the mother of God. He needed every bit of favor and grace that she could offer him. He is among those who left the priesthood and married. No one knows where he might be today. Maybe he'll read this and contact me.

The lady in charge of this gathering of geezers was so kind and dutiful. She suggested that I bring copies of *I'll Never Tell* to the meeting and sign a copy for everyone. I was happy to do so and was complimented by several of them. I gave a copy to both husband and wife of the three couples who were there and espoused. It made a difference with them, as it was another sign of acceptance by many of us who felt that the rules would be changed shortly after our ordination in 1964. Lo and behold, 55 years have passed and it still is not a serious topic in the Vatican. After the Church's recent experience with pedophilia, I'm sure it will make the lists of many who feel that having a woman involved with a man who ministers will help the situation and in some cases might put an end to it. It would certainly be worth a try. One of the men is having to raise his daughter's child. He said she was nine. "Oh my!" said I. "How do you do it?" "Mostly with the help of my dear wife who is younger and knows what she's doing," he replied. I just can't imagine at this age having to be a father to a small child. Grandparents always smile when they give their grandchildren back to the parents and then recall how challenging it was to raise them. They know the burden. This particular fellow is a scholar and a social justice activist. He really has his hands full with a nine-year old who must be very active and social at the same time in the same house with Father Grandfather. I'll never know.

I saw a number of examples of the wives being caretakers of the former Fathers. It rang true with me, as when I can no longer work I plan to spend time in a home where I know someone will take care of me and assist me to the pearly gates.

When I returned home from my college reunion, I sat across from Father Wilt in the hospital and he was barely breathing with numerous tubes attached to his body. He smiled as I tried to cheer him up. "This is about your third time with a stroke," I said. "Do you feel like you can beat it?" He murmured weakly that it might be God calling. I said without thinking that you better pick up the phone, because you're not looking to good from where I sit. After a light chuckle, he asked me to pray over him. We spent a few minutes in petition to God about his will for Wilt and two days later he was back in his own room at the elder care center where he lived. I'm glad you didn't answer the phone Wilt. We're not ready to lose such a devoted and holy servant like you to the other side. And there but for the grace of God . . .

CHAPTER 41

Once and for All

I TRIED TO LEARN to meditate at the age of 14. I never really got it until I was in my 20s. I tried for so many years to force prayer instead of just letting it happen. There were always books and guides and gurus to tell you how, but meditation is a form of prayer unique to each individual. When it's not happening for you, time imitates the turtle. When it works, you wonder where the time went. Too often we were asked to read long passages from the Bible or stories from people's lives and then formulate our mental prayer. I never really was successful until I began just taking a small phrase or a few words. Oh and by the way, they were mostly in Latin as that was the language of silent prayer when I came to know it in the seminary.

So, from the Letter to the Hebrews in the New Testament there is this phrase *Semel et pro semper*. This simple expression, which means "once and for all", has changed my thinking and I dare say my life in appreciating what it means. Saint Paul was given credit for writing this, but biblical scholars now disagree and feel that it came after Paul and was written by one of his disciples. Here is the full quote:

First he says,

"Sacrifices and offerings, holocausts and sin
offerings, you neither desired nor delighted in.
These are offered according to the law."

Then he says,

"Behold, I come to do your will. He takes away
the first to establish the second. By this 'will',
we have been consecrated through the offering
of the body of Jesus Christ once for all."
(Hebrews 10:8-10)

The next time you feel guilty about what you have done or not done and the pangs of hunger for forgiveness dominate your spiritual mentality, think about Jesus dying for us ONCE AND FOR ALL. It can be a sobering and sensible answer to so many who are hung up on recurring sin and subsequent guilt. "Once" means one time and only one time and God is not going to ask nor require a savior for generations to come. Redemption has happened.

The "for all" takes away all that comparative religious nonsense. We are all eager to make comparisons about almost anything. My religion is better than yours. My church makes sense, yours doesn't. Back in 1956, a priest from Boston was preaching that only Roman Catholics could be saved, that is, go to heaven. He was quickly reprimanded by the Vatican and asked to stop preaching this false doctrine. Jesus died on the cross "for all of us" and that means ALL. It is no secret that Father Feeney's preaching still exists in the narrow minds of some Catholics who might have been taught this in their early catechism classes. But it's as false as some of the news is today, with one cable channel or reporter trying to outdo others and make a name for themselves. Religion and faith are not in competition. Both are welcomed and needed.

Faith of course is a gift from God. Religion is of our own choosing and practice. There is a big difference. Some people work so hard at their religion and still lack the gift of faith. On the other hand, some don't even practice a specific religion and have faith.

When I go deep into meditative prayer, it almost brings me to tears that I cannot fully appreciate what a magnificent gift from God this has been. I can never seem to fully grasp the depth of it. Too often I can go for long periods of time without the realization of what God has done for the human race. *Semel et pro semper*, once and for all. I beg you to give it a whirl and see how it fits into your life. You don't have to be the least bit concerned about the Latin.

CHAPTER 42

Wayne Ressler Funeral

THE LAST OF MY three best friends from my early 20s, with whom I shared so much in this life, has now gone to eternal life. I hope that even bringing it up doesn't seem so self-serving. I hope it will bring to mind your close friends and give you the opportunity to enjoy them while they are still with you and to appreciate how much richer your life has been because of them.

I got the call mid-morning from Wayne's brother in Iowa letting me know that he had taken a turn for the worse with heart and kidney failure. It wasn't even nightfall when I got the word he had passed. I waited for information about the services then made my reservations for Dubuque, Iowa. I had to fly to Chicago and arrived at 11:30 p.m.. I rented a car and by quarter past midnight I was whizzing out of O'Hare airport without really being sure where I was going. The flight had tired me and nine o'clock is bedtime. I had the GPS, but there is always doubt when you're my age. The voice of this sweet young lady is not really that convincing when you're alone in the dark in a strange place and don't know the roads or the route. The rain didn't help as I made my way to Rockford and I just couldn't stay awake. After a scary neck-jerk moment, I pulled into a Best Western and went fast asleep.

Up at six to make the last two hours of the journey. It was late August and I passed endless farmhouses and corn and soybean fields but eventually crossed the Mississippi from Wisconsin and found myself in downtown Dubuque. It was a wonderful meditative drive through the Midwest and I had a chance to marvel at the richness of the land and the stewards of it who are rightly so proud of the crops they produce that feed the world. I stopped to check the GPS to make sure I could find Wayne's parish church where the funeral was set to start at 10:30 a.m.. Murphy's Law assured me that it was not going to be easy as there were two St. Josephs in Dubuque. I went to the wrong one. But eventually with a couple of calls I made it to the right one and entered the church.

There he was, laid out, adorned in his priestly garb. On the lid of the lower half of the coffin sat his Notre Dame hat, his very favorite golf club (an old wood that never failed him from 100 yards from the pin) and the glass-encased basketball given to him by the state of Iowa when he was inducted into the High School Sports Basketball Hall of Fame, an honor he received a couple of years ago. He looked peaceful and real. He was always real, from the minute I met him on board the SS Colombo en route to the seminary in Rome.

The church was full. It holds over 800. There were so many people who, after the viewing, stopped to see me in the second pew. Many of them knew me from the book that Wayne had given them a couple of years ago. I'll Never Tell was a big seller in Dubuque because of him. Wayne's brother, Mark, also a priest, gave the homily and the archbishop of the diocese celebrated the Mass. There were dozens of priests present. Father Mark told the people how Wayne had suffered his first heart attack while vacationing with me in Florida. His second attack came after he and I were on a golf outing with two other guys during a trip to Ireland. His third and final problem occurred in June of 2019 when we attended our North American College class reunion in Chicago. When his archbishop spoke at the end of the service, he thanked all for coming and warned them not to go on vacation with Monsignor Harry Schlitt.

His casket was motored some 30 minutes away from the church to his hometown of Cascade and the Calvary Cemetery. Father Mark invited me to do the commendation at the gravesite. Wayne grew up there and both he and his brother have plots in the St. Martin's parish cemetery. It was pointed out to me that he was so proud of his high school that on the stone was engraved:

"Graduate of St. Martin's HS 1957
Ordained a priest in Rome, Italy 1964
Priest, Archdiocese of Dubuque"

His brother said, "Who in the world puts their high school on their tombstone?" Wayne did, that's the kind of guy he was.

I was so happy that I could make the trip even though the GPS lady told me at one point that night in the rain, "In 500 feet turn left off the freeway." Fortunately, I looked first and there was a huge tractor-trailer on my left. I hit the brakes and thanked Wayne for seeing me safely to and from his funeral. I sure miss the guy, especially during football season as he could usually predict the wins and losses of the Fighting Irish of Notre Dame University. The two of us made a point to travel to South Bend almost every fall for a game. He was my best friend.

Of the four of us who became lifelong pals in college — Jim Kogler, Roy Riedy, Wayne and me — here I am left to tell the story and reap the benefits of three gifted men who saw fit to pass along to me what they knew and lived for. All three loved the Church, but Jim and Roy passed early on and only Wayne and I have had the privilege of serving so many people into our 80s. The sacramental life of the Church cannot be outdone when it comes to giving graces. We must be open, welcoming and do what we can to make sure that Jesus Christ did not die in vain but rather "once and for all of us".

CHAPTER 43

Lord Have Mercy

EARLIER IN THIS BOOK I wrote about having had the privilege of blessing the ashes of a dear friend and then going out to sea with her family and a few close friends to scatter her to the wind and the water. Louise and I had worked together for a number of years in the 1970s and she was very generous to the God Squad in her later years. One night not long ago, I received a desperate call from Louise's daughter imploring me to go to a hospital in Santa Rosa and administer the sacrament of the sick to her son and baby grandson. Their story was all over the evening news and it seemed very unusual and contorted. It was late and Santa Rosa would have been a long drive. I asked her to call St. Eugene parish nearby and they would be able to have a priest there in less than 15 minutes. They did and it worked out for the best.

A day or two later, Lisa, whom I'd known since she was a young girl, called to arrange the funeral service for her child and grandchild. The story is still not complete, but it appears that the son had been a drug addict most of his life and just recently had found peace and sobriety with the baby's mother after they had the little boy. The baby was just over a year old and the father had been sober for over a hundred days. Life seemed to have made a turn for the good for this little family. Then whatever occurred drove him back to the darkness of drugs and fentanyl took his life and that of his little baby boy, too. From reports it appears the baby ingested the drugs after his father overdosed. So you can imagine the grief of a mother who loses a son and a grandson in this way.

The service was arranged for a parish where I used to live and where Lisa and her family had worshipped and prayed. The day before the funerals were supposed to take place I got another call and Lisa told me that the service had been canceled because of the chance of some gang activity among friends and possibly relatives of the deceased. The police had suggested that they might postpone or have some kind of private service after the investigations were complete. Can you imagine with all the tragedy of losing two loved ones and now you can't lay them to rest because others who have also been hurt are prepared to add another dose of violence to what has already been a tragic departure from life? While it angers me, I am just a friend and a priest and not part of the misery that has to be engulfing both the mother of the son and the mother of the baby. It's just not right. When I stepped up to say I wanted to be a priest, I had no idea that such situations as this were included. Again, what do you say? I'll never know.

I suspect my readers by this time are wondering if I'm consumed with death and the death process. I suppose it comes with the territory of being a priest and an 80-year old. No, I'm quite sure it's part and parcel of ministry. Vulnerable can mean wounded as it is derived from the Latin word for wound (*vulnus, vulneris*). Those who lose people in their lives can be weakened and even made sick by the loss. Too often we learn of older people who have been married for years and one of them passes. It's not long thereafter that their partner will succumb.

***

As you are aware, I lived and worked with Cardinal William J. Levada for a full ten years. I moved into the Archbishop's Residence at St. Mary's Cathedral while it was still being renovated. He arrived on July 4, 1996, just in time to say, "Harry, let's go get a barbecue grill and have some ribs and corn on the cob." So we did. Even before most things worked in the house and there was still sawdust and plywood on horses, we were basting some ribs and sipping something light. We had known each other since our seminary days in Rome and the ease of that relationship still remained.

Bill passed away in his sleep on September 26, 2019. He had just returned to Rome from Germany and went to bed without having dinner, telling his housekeepers that he didn't feel well and please don't wake him in the morning. He was in the comfort of his own bed in Rome. It was fitting, as he was more than enamored by his residence just outside the boundaries of Citta del Vaticano. He had spent a good deal of his adult life working at the Vatican, advancing to the highest position of any American churchman as Secretary for the Congregation for the Doctrine of the Faith. I recall when he told me about this appointment. It is so clear in my mind. I told the story in *I'll Never Tell* so I'll simply repeat that he was shocked and surprised as he left Pope Benedict's chambers and began a walk through the Piazza San Pietro and down the Via Conciliazione wondering what just happened.

The announcement of his death seemed such a "ho hum" response from the present administration of the Archdiocese of San Francisco. I don't know who is at fault or who is to blame, but I was appalled and hurt by the way it was handled. There was an announcement in the chancery office to the employees. There was absolutely nothing in the *San Francisco Chronicle* until about two weeks after his death. There was a photo posted on Facebook by Angela Alioto, whose connections in Rome passed it along. It showed Pope Francis blessing the body lying in state in front of the altar of the Holy Spirit, where Cardinal Levada had been ordained in 1961 by Archbishop O'Connor. He was lying on the floor on that day, reciting the Litany of the Saints. Before the ordination of a priest right at the beginning, the candidate prostrates himself on the floor for about two or three minutes of silent preparation for the ceremony that follows. It is both an outward sign of humility and an inward sign of prayerful preparation for what is about to happen. When he was presented as a candidate who was worthy for the priesthood, he answered *adsum* or "present". I was there. Now lying in the same spot was his lifeless body.

His life and ministry answered to God through all that he was able to accomplish in the Catholic Church. His journey after ordination from Rome to Los Angeles, to Rome, to Portland, to San Francisco and back to Rome spanned more than 50 years. He accepted every change without any apparent surprise. Everything was a challenge even when he came to San Francisco, where he was referred to by the media as "Darth Vader". He proved to be the enemy of all evil and brought his many gifts to the City of Saint Francis.

Bishop Stephen Lopes, his one time secretary in Rome, remarked at the vigil service that when the cardinal's body was carried down the six or seven floors from his apartment to a waiting hearse, there was a gathering in the alley at the main door to his home of street people who mourned and wailed at his passing. It was an honor guard of the poor who let it be known that they loved him and would miss him. This would make for a gentle yet remarkable epitaph for his worldwide work and his commitment to the poor of the church.

"Blessed are the poor in spirit"
(Matthew 5:3)

PART IV

Valley of the Shadow

"He guides me along right paths
for the sake of his name."
(Psalm 23:3)

***

"Well the top brass don't like him talking so much
And he won't play what they say to play
And he don't want to change what don't need to change
And there goes the last deejay."
Tom Petty

CHAPTER 44

Privilege

MANY OF YOU who know me and know what I've been exposed to as a priest probably will find it hard to believe that I was so closely tied to the Chinese branch of the Junior Chamber of Commerce and was coaxed into emceeing a fundraising dinner they had in Oakland for bone marrow transplants. It was a very worthy cause and my mentor felt would serve the public well.

What he didn't tell me until a few days before was that the entertainment for that evening was going to be a fashion show sponsored by Victoria's Secret. You may have seen one or more of their TV shows. It's underwear and mostly for women.

"Jon, I'm sorry, but you know I can't do that," I protested.

"It's for people who can't afford to have bone marrow transplants, Harry," responded my Chamber friend. "You don't have to comment. Just introduce them and say goodbye."

How could I say no? I tried again. "People will talk; it will be in the news." (Or worse, I thought, Herb Caen's column.)

"Not to worry," he said. "I've spoken to the Victoria's Secret people and there will be no exposure, nothing you wouldn't see in a swimming pool or at the beach."

I finally blurted the obvious out loud. "Yeah, but this is in a Chinese restaurant!"

Dismissing my concerns he said, "They have them there all the time. The patrons are used to it."

I'll do it. I did it. It was wonderful and very nicely done.

The same group took me to a Junior Chamber of Commerce convention where I gave the opening prayer. From there I was invited to Terminal Island in Long Beach, California, to deliver an after-dinner talk to the inmates. It was a white-collar prison for non-violent men, who are not a danger to themselves nor society but who have broken the law. It includes many famous people who are spared the "hard time" that a general population prison would bring.

The tables were covered with red-and-white checkered cloths and a fine Italian spaghetti and meatball dinner was served. No wine of course. During the dinner there was music that I could not believe. It was fantastic! I sat next to the warden and commented about how professional sounding the music was and how he might want to market them in some way.

"Oh, they've been marketed. Have you ever heard of Crosby, Stills and Nash? Well the guy on the end is one of them and he's in charge of the music."

No wonder.

Following the prayer after meals, a number of the inmates came up to shake my hand none more notable than this guy who told me how much he loved my messages on KFRC radio in San Francisco and how much I meant to the formation of his young life. He went on and on until I finally had to interrupt and say, "If I meant so much to your growth and development what are you doing in jail?"

"Oh," he said, "I drove a Brinks truck for years and got tired of hauling other people's money around, so one day I loaded up with more than a million, drove to the airport and bought a ticket for a faraway place. I spent almost a year before I returned, only to be caught because I went to some of my old hangouts. I had a pretty good year and lots of fun."

But he was still in jail. Never heard from him since that day. Not sure how much good I did for him while listening to me on the radio.

People will let you into their lives without asking or prodding. Fifty-five years after my first day as a priest, it's still true.

* * *

Not sure where this came from, but I use it:

Humpty Dumpty sat on the wall
Humpty Dumpty had a great fall
All the king's horses and all the king's men
Couldn't put Humpty together again.

When you're heart is broken by what has transpired, it's the glue of God that I call grace that seeps into the nooks and crannies of your heart and puts it back together.

This Dumpty guy was obviously hurt and wanted to be consoled. "I don't know Father Harry, I just don't seem to be as close to God as I used to . . ." "I wonder who moved," said I. The experience of the dark side of life is part of our human condition. Even Saint Mother Teresa wrote about it and it was made known after she died how so much of her time was spent on the dark side where she had little or no hope that her work was effective.

A priest is supposed to live a virtuous life and in fact be someone to be imitated. When I read Saint Mother Teresa's book about the "darkness of her soul" it made me dig deeper into my own conscience. She was so holy and so far above most of us and yet here she is talking about how she didn't have a lot of confidence about being who people said and thought she was.

The antidote for such feelings was made known to me when I read somewhere that dark times are the times when we are in God's pocket. He is looking after us and will reach in and pull us out when it's the right time for us to be exposed. Makes sense to me.

CHAPTER 45

Upon Being Tested

DID YOU EVER think that God could be tested or tempted? I don't think so, that's why in the scriptures there is a story of Jesus, fasting for 40 days and then coming down from the mountain only to be met by the Devil. This evil character arranges a shootout with the Son of God by offering three Bible bullets to dodge.

The first was his hunger and Jesus replies, "We do not live on bread alone."

The second is power and Jesus replies, "God alone shall you adore."

The third is to be the only God and Jesus replies, "Don't test God."

My favorite line from the Devil is, "Throw yourself down from here and your angels will rescue you, lest you dash your foot against a stone." That's very interesting language and worth the challenge of digging deeper into the etymology of the words.

Numerous questions come to the fore, like all the WHYS from so many, especially parents who have lost children. The temptation is to simply drop God, leave Jesus hanging out to dry and give up on all your spiritual growth over the years. To witness a funeral of a young person is probably the most challenging of my priestly functions. In one family, I had the burial of both a son and a daughter who each had families of their own. The neighbors of the bereaved planted two trees outside their home in the country. The mother told me she often has coffee outside in the summer and converses with them as if they are still with the family. She has never told me but I'll bet she asks herself over and over again, "WHY? Why my kids? Why not me?" Kirk and Paula, as I gazed on them covered with snow this past winter, were the inspiration for me to continue to examine temptation and how it affects each one of us. Of course, it's different as we are different. It's also timely, as the word itself comes from *tempus, temporis* meaning time. I don't know if I've used this expression before but here it is. Carl Rahner's reference to our humanity and all of us, when commenting on our human condition, is that we are an "unfinished symphony". I have to admit that temptations for an 80-year old are less of a real threat than when I was 30.

I like to use the example of a construction site. When a family is building a home and the builder takes them out to see the foundation and perhaps some of the lumber being raised to the sky, they step out of the pick-up truck into the mud and mess of the site. They are asked to imagine what it will look like, as they walk up a makeshift ramp to see "the living room" and the view from it. The hope is there that this will be an outstanding way to see the lay of the land and all that it embraces. They are cautioned to watch their step as they proceed to see "the kitchen, the bedroom, the bathroom" and the stairs that will take them either up or down into a whole new world that they have not experienced where they presently live. Once the house is completed, they sigh, move in and next is a checklist of all the things that are not right. A window leaks, a door is not flush, the heater goes on by itself at odd times and so on. They ask themselves, "Will it ever be right, perfect?" The answer is no.

It's only an example and it might limp but it's close. We are always under construction. We follow checklists all the time. We can go for a few years and not be bothered, then all of a sudden a friend might say, "How you feeling? You've got raccoon circles under your eyes. Stay out too late? Tired? Maybe you should see a doctor? Why do you look so bad?"

Why my kids? Why not me?

I have had this question so many times during my 55 years as a priest. My answer is from the Book of Job. He simply says after all he's been through, the Lord gives and the Lord takes away, blessed be the name of the Lord. It's as good as I can do.

Not sure where I read this but there was a sign on an old dirt road on the backside of farmland in southern Missouri. It read: Choose your RUT well. You'll be in it for the next three miles.

So why did God do this or that? I love the option of choosing. That's exactly what we do. We choose. Even if it's a rut and we feel stuck. It's our rut and in order to get where we're going, we have to follow it. Once we're through it, it's another story. We don't have to repeat ourselves. We might also check to see if there is another way so we don't get stuck with the choice of one way, which has a rut. Be glad you're not on a motorcycle!

SPEAKING OF SIN

I'm not quite through with temptation. Many of us say the Lord's Prayer every day. Next time you do, note the words, "Lead us not into temptation." Many of us are already there. It comes with life in the big city. It's not so present in convents or monasteries where people devote themselves to prayer and a closer relationship with God, but wherever ordinary people are around ordinary people there really and truly is temptation.

Sin is a bad word for sin, which is a bad word. Many of us have changed the word "problem" to "challenge". It makes it a lot easier to deal with. So the Greek word for sin, *hamartia*, means to miss the mark. That seems a lot more plausible than sin. "Hey

Joe, I saw you last night with that floozy, what's her name. I'll bet you were tempted to sin." Try this. "Hey Joe, I saw you last night with that floozy, what's her name. I'll bet you missed the mark." What? What mark? Are you nuts? We just kissed. Do I get a mark for that?

There is no right way to do a wrong thing. I believe it's very difficult to commit a serious sin, one that merits the eternal fires of hell. I heard a confession recently where the man didn't really know what to say. He said, "I haven't been to confession in 30 years, but I've been very fortunate. I have a wonderful wife and family. I've had a good job and now I'm told my cancer has returned and maybe I should see a priest. Well, here I am. I don't know of any sins that I have." I concurred. He was an outstanding person and an example to many.

That might be the case with many of us. But we still go through this exercise of examining our conscience. There are a number of folks who count temptations as sins. It's so far from the truth. By the way, truth brings up the opposite. The "father of lies" just happens to be the opposite of good and the purveyor of evil. Sin has many tools. A lie is the handle that fits them all. All the reality shows these days demonstrate that the proof of the pudding is in the eating. Be real! Be yourself! Quit trying to be someone else or someone that you're not! Denial raises its ugly head. Losing your identity is usually brought on by someone or something that draws you away from who you really are and what you're striving to be. "He's just not himself."

Sin is not a STOP sign. When you're driving and come upon one, you stop, look both ways and move on. You don't get out of your car because the sign says STOP and go to the curb and wait until it says go. You have to live with the stops and pauses that come with life.

Some people come to a part of their life that is not good, that is sinful, that is wrong, and they stop and give up. I'm a bad person and it looks like that's going to be my lot in life. Well, if it's a lot, maybe you ought to build something on it and begin getting out of yourself and doing something for others. I like the triune expression of how to handle sin or temptation:

NAME IT

CLAIM IT

TAME IT

Discover for yourself and your culture or mores if it's right or wrong. Then, if it is wrong, admit it, own up to it. Then do something about it. Seek help!

Remember that awful word that gets most of us in trouble: denial. If you ever worked in prison ministry or worked at all in or around places of incarceration, you will hear the most famous mantra, "I didn't do it!"

Ash Wednesday in 2018 was on Valentine's Day, the first time that had happened since 1945. I recall viewing the TV news of the terrible tragedy in Parkland, Florida. It was similar to Columbine in Colorado but worse. Seventeen were wounded and another 17 killed. It was a school setting, which we all used to believe is among the safest places to be in our society. However, on this day, it wasn't. The TV camera panned the scene beyond the police yellow tape and focused in on two women, probably mothers of the children. They had to be concerned about their own. As the images became sharper and sharper, I noticed the black ashes on the forehead of one of the women in the sign of the cross. That about summed up the scene for me. The fragility of life cannot be taken for granted.

"Remember man/woman, you are dust and unto dust you shall return."

When I lived in New York in the early '80s I helped out at a parish on Park Avenue. It was near Grand Central Station. One of the biggest days was Ash Wednesday. People got off the train and went directly to the church for ashes. The pastor gave me instructions for the three Masses that I offered: I must conclude in exactly 20 minutes or less. That would give several priests and lay people time to sign the working people of New York with ashes and remind them of the uncertainty of life. Twenty minutes with a two-minute homily can be done but not with a lot of reverence. I did it. It was justified by the ashes, physical signs of the reality of the shortness of our lives here on earth and our appreciation of how we should make the most of it.

If I was going to include a photo in this publication, it would be of the Rembrandt painting of the prodigal son returning home to his father. You know the story and this might be a good time to re-read it. Archbishop Niederauer went to Russia on vacation and visited the museum of Catherine the Great. There you will find the original. Henri Nowuen wrote a book about it, in which he began to notice the hands of the father as he is blessing his wandering son, who had just returned to ask forgiveness and be reconciled. Nowuen notes that one hand is masculine and another feminine. It refers to our God who is neither masculine nor feminine but God. In our human way and because of our culture and history, we have referred to God as masculine. Even the father of the prodigal is sporting a long beard and is obviously very masculine, but the hands tell a different story. If you happen to be in Russia, have a look for yourself. Or, if you come by to see me one day, I'll take my Rembrandt copy off the wall and we can study it for a spell.

A good way to end this segment is to copy a letter from a "lifer" in San Quentin. He sent me this several years ago and I have followed his wish of extending to his mother on television an open apology for what he did that has merited a life sentence of which he has served 24 years. Read it and weep!

"Dear Monsignor Harry,

Hello to you and the God Squad who I hear so much about. My Mom is an avid fan and watches your Catholic Mass, religiously. She always tells me that you say prayers for me. I thank you for giving my Mom some peace of mind. She's a great Mom and worries about me a lot. I've been in prison for 24 years. I don't know when I may if ever be released. I committed a horrible crime and to this moment my actions have been a constant weight and painful memory that I carry. I cannot let go of the thoughts of all the pain I caused my victim's family. Most of all I struggle with taking his life, although I wasn't a willing participant or the orchestrator of the crime. I did not make the right decision that night and trusted the furthest person from God. I could have chosen another way.

I've tried to find a way to allow myself to get past the depression. I have read numerous books of the Bible and just can't forgive myself. I know how much pain I've caused my family and especially my MOM. I've tried so many different things to get past my issues. I don't know what else to try. I know you would like me to open up to God and trust in Him. I believe and trust without pause. I pray and talk to Him daily. My temporary relief is to help a new and younger inmate. I need your help Father. I need to do all I can for my Mom's spirit. If she knows I'm making an effort, it will be good for her. I'm thinking maybe at one of your televised Masses you could take a minute to address her and convey how much I love and appreciate her. Let her know that she shouldn't carry the blame for anything I've done. She was the best Mom a son could have.

Could you do this for me?

I shall bring my plea to a close. I apologize if I've asked too much or taken you for granted. I appreciate you even reading this letter. And thank you for my Mom.

May God bless you!"

CHAPTER 46

Sin, Satan, Sickness

I GUESS I WAS eight or nine. I was running from the kid who had his eyes covered, leaning against the tree counting to 50. The rest of us were scurrying about trying to find the perfect place to hide. It didn't take me long to run from the backyard to the front and see my Dad's old barrel blue pickup truck parked in front of the house. I stepped on the running board and heaved my little being into the back and quickly ducked down on the floor. It wasn't long before I heard "Here I come, ready or not." I crouched even lower on the bed with my head against the cab of the vehicle. I didn't hear another thing until I saw a man staring at me over the sides of the truck. He asked me my name and what I was doing hiding.

I don't remember what I said as he grabbed my arm and touched me between the legs and asked what kind of underwear I was wearing. Fortunately, I had sense enough to stand up and yell for the other kids playing the game. It was enough to startle him as he turned and ran off down Hanover Street. He crossed the tracks on Independence and disappeared. I never saw him again. I went in the house and told my two older brothers what happened and they both jumped up and dashed off the porch and down the street.

My mother asked if I had known the man or had ever seen him around the neighborhood. "Never. Mom, I'm scared."

John and Charlie returned soon after and said they didn't see anyone nor could they find anyone who shouldn't be in our neighborhood. It was frightening for me as a little boy but an experience that I never forgot. At the time I didn't realize just how desperate a person, a man, could be that he would prey upon a small boy. And yet I read about ancient Rome and even in the history of the Church how Saint Peter Damian proclaimed: "The befouling cancer of sodomy is, in fact, spreading so through the clergy, or rather like a savage beast, is raging with such shameless abandon through the flock of Christ." (*Letter to a Suffering Church* by Bishop Robert Barron)

I still can feel the queasiness in my stomach the first time I stepped into the office of the secretary to Cardinal Levada. Father Tom Merson had the *San Francisco Chronicle* on his desk. He looked up at me and said, "That's the end of the priestly life of Monsignor Patrick O'Shea." I couldn't believe what I had read. Both of us sat there in silence and my stomach moaned in sadness.

It still makes me sick to think that after all these years the same topic captures the headlines and the lead on the evening news. I would have guessed that even the media would be worn out by the same old stories. I guess they'll keep on coming until the pope himself is brought down or one or another of the popes of the past. Oh, and you know there is plenty to write about if one goes to medieval history and looks at the Borgias and their clerical clan. As a priest, even though the subject has been overdone, there still remains the emotional pull that stretches my stomach all out of order.

I have been asked if I could help the faithful and the fallen away understand how for centuries the powerful in the Church have abused or turned a blind eye to sexual abuse of minors. If I COULD do this, my writing would be a bestseller and I would be doing talk shows all over America. That doesn't mean that I won't take a stab at it.

The idea of pedophilia turns my stomach and challenges my wits as to how and why it is done. There are other abuses like alcohol and drugs that I "get" but this one, along with beating women and little kids, is beyond me. Most of us have suffered some kind of abuse in our lives but not to the extent that pedophilia and priestly pedophilia have reached.

My simple explanation is sickness. Although I know a little bit about alcoholism, drug abuse and pedophilia, none has been my personal problem. I've had alcoholics and drug abusers in my family, but the closest I've come to pedophiles is knowing a few of them before they were discovered and jailed. I've had close relatives abused by a priest friend and had no idea it had occurred until many years later when the media and the whole world began to pay attention to what was happening and the victims started speaking up.

Sickness of the mind or brain chemistry, which both frazzle what your will and your brain encourage you to say and do, is only a guess on my part. I wouldn't be surprised to learn that pedophiles are born with DNA that says one day you will abuse a child. I also don't think it's a learned trait that happens from knowing that someone else has been a abuser and you are like them and so you can do as they do. With that said, how is it possible to go through the same seminary training that I did and find yourself desiring a child? With all the young men and old men I studied with over the years, I simply can't imagine that they would want to pursue a spiritual vocation if they were out of tune with common and sensible mores. It doesn't appear to be in the same category as the rapist who performs his or her act to show power over the victim. It might be that a clergyman has access to children who can be so loving, so cute, so unaware that anyone would want to take advantage of them, as I was at eight or nine. DON'T TAKE CANDY FROM ANYONE!

A priest I do know was trying to excuse his actions and said that he loved little children and the scripture and even Jesus had encouraged his followers to become like children. The wires got crossed somewhere — he wasn't able to make all the right connections — to see what he was doing. It had nothing to do with love but perhaps to satisfy his own weird and unique mindset that made him think that way. I suspect there are a number of homes and asylums filled with men with minds like that.

One of my close friends used to chalk up every church scandal as "stupid". It was almost as if he was giving approval for what happened and blaming them for getting caught. I used to debate him but always with the warning that something deeper was at play and stupidity followed only when the act transpired. Many of us fall to temptation because of our own views of what lies before us. If we act on it, we might be stupid, as in the Tom Hanks line from the famous movie *Forest Gump*, "Stupid is as stupid does." I've seen it on T-shirts. But there is still something deeper and more intrinsic than simply making a bad choice.

Several years ago in the Archdiocese of San Francisco, Archbishop John Quinn was advised and acted, upon counsel, to close 11 churches. He was then subjected to terrible scrutiny and name-calling, as well as a loud and subjective call for his early retirement. As wise and holy as he was, he did eventually step down and faded into the woodwork. He wrote a couple of books and did some counseling, but he was essentially out of the ecclesial picture.

I often sought his advice on different problems and challenges that I faced. His standard answer usually involved the Holy Spirit. "Harry, you and I, no matter who we are or whether we think we have control, are still under the guidance of the Holy Spirit. God is in charge and we're not. We make our decisions based on our prayer and the confidence we have in those who know more and have had more experience in a particular field."

His experience with pedophilia and mine in those early '80s was practically nil. He told me that he couldn't find the word pedophilia in the Webster's dictionary in his study. It didn't take long to know exactly what it is and how it's done. But here we are these many years later having suffered through our ignorance and not knowing what to do, and making the mistake of following the advice of psychiatrists and psychologists who would examine Father so-and-so and say he's okay to minister. "Of course you can return him to a parish. He has been with us for six months and knows his problem and has reconciled." Any of you who have dealt with alcohol in your family know that you can't return a person to a home filled with a built-in bar, well stocked and easily accessible. It's just too much temptation.

What to do . . .

I take my lead from an Oblate priest who wrote a brief article to his fellow Oblate brothers about how sick they all must be after hearing old and new reports of clerical sexual abuse and cover up. He encouraged them to look at three things that might help the stomach ache.

1. Whatever negativity and pain we're suffering is nothing compared to the abused who put their trust in the companionship and authority of a priest.

2. The trust on which priestly ministry is based needs to be rebuilt by us, even if we are not the ones who broke the trust.

3. This is a long, long process of healing. It will work, and we are not alone in this work. The Holy Spirit is still in charge.

I think Father sums it up pretty well for me. One thing for sure, it's not going away during my lifetime and the O'Shea type of abuse will be repeated somewhere in our world and will go unheeded for many years or perhaps forever.

There goes my stomach again.

Back to the Holy Spirit . . . all of us who have been ordained priests believe that through the mystery of God's grace we have been given the gift of the Spirit. We pray about how the Spirit works through us and how we are able to do things that we couldn't ordinarily do, but they happen because of this unique gift. It comes with the sacrament of Holy Orders just as it comes with the blessing of baptism. How then do priests who are pedophiles reconcile the Spirit working through them? I'll never know. But I suspect like anything evil, it overcomes the power of the Spirit, for a time, and then goes away.

I saw a film *Usual Suspects*. There was a line that I took the trouble to write down later. It concerns the spirit of evil.

"The greatest trick ever pulled by the devil was to convince the world that he (the devil) didn't exist." I suppose I'm among those who have a hard time believing in Satan and his power over good. But it must be true in light of all the darkness we encounter each day.

CHAPTER 47

Internet Mass

I'M SURE MANY of you can't sleep at night and after awhile find yourself into a major project that seems to grow and grow until you just have to get up and jot it all down. That's what happened to me with the internet Mass.

For more than 20 years I have been celebrating Mass on television for those who are unable to go to their parish churches. Admittedly the audience is older but they are growing in number.

I have been doing research on my audience for most of that time and, through letters and anecdotes and from priests who hear from their people, I have some solid factual information that has encouraged me to take the TV Mass to the internet, in a big way. I have hired an advertising agency to do some research and see if what we've experienced here in Northern California might be true in other parts of the country.

Here are just a few of the facts:

• 28-minute Mass, no more, no less; it's television. The attention span for something that is not filled with car chases, gunfights, screaming, terror or natural disasters is very limited, especially with shut-ins.

- When people are sick or bedridden or not feeling well, they don't want a choir, a long sermon or bells and whistles.

- Many viewers have written to tell me that they appreciate the close-ups, the low-key delivery, the short homily, the shots of the bread and wine and, more important than anything, the scriptures proclaimed in a straightforward manner by lectors who speak up and speak clearly. I have always been a firm believer in a short homily and the constraints of television force me to follow my convictions. Don't repeat the scriptures, don't speak them in your own words, but allow the Word to penetrate the heart of the listener. Use a story or an everyday event that will drive the lesson home, so that the viewers can be inspired to appreciate what God has given to us in the Bible.

Even the late Cardinal Levada once remarked when he was in the hospital for back surgery, "Harry, at St. Mary's they played your Mass over and over again this morning. I liked your homily but after the second time I turned a deaf ear." He should have turned it off. But what was more telling is that he confirmed my point about not feeling well and that in the throes of recovery a person did not need a dog and pony show with long drawn out liturgical rites that only forced him to stay awake. I quote the cardinal because he was a close friend and never hesitated to let me know if he thought I was doing anything that was not a positive approach to Church ministry.

There are at least ten pieces of mail for me to answer every week. I only reply to the ones with individual requests or challenges and also those with a sizeable donation. My producer, Jan, sorts through them all. There are many more letters and cards but then I ask for mail. I take time, if I have it at the end of the broadcast, to read a few. It helps with the viewer connection and makes their experience more real. I have included a few here for your perusal.

Dear Father Harry

I am 90 years and always love to hear a good sermon. In my life I have heard a lot of boring sermons, but yours are wonderful and can make us laugh and make us feel good.

Thank you so much
Cecilia and daughter Nellie

Thank you for TV Mass
I am blind and can
not write well. I
watch TV Mass every
Sunday.
Eileen

Dear Fr. Harry,

I am a condemn inmate at san quentin state prison. i just needed to write you and let you know how much myself ~ and many other inmates, appreciate Catholic t.v. Mass.

Blessings to you dear Father, the God Squad, and all who work each week to make the broadcasts possible.

with love and respect,
Todd

Dear Father Harry,

It is always nice to watch the Catholic TV Mass on Sunday morning at 6:00am. We have two children, Nicholas (5 years old) and Gianna (2 years old), and watching your service on TV, allows my wife and I to get a lot out of the mass with minimal distraction from the kids. It is interesting how they are a captive audience when they watch you on TV, versus when we are at our local Catholic Church in our town, and they can't sit still for the duration of the mass. They always look forward to seeing you, Father Harry!

We sincerely appreciate your dedication, to making this all possible for not just us, but the many others who don't have a way to get to church, or are incarcerated, or have health ailments that keep them housebound. It is truly a blessing, to have you come into our home weekly, to share the great teachings of Jesus Christ, our savoir and the word of God. God bless you always.

The Leone Family

Good God Almighty,
The God Squad
is
ALRIGHTY!
Tom-n-Pam

Dear Father Harry,

Due to a forth heart surgery and complications, I was recently released from the hospital after 20 months. I am recovering well.

I wanted to thank you for your Sunday weekly masses. They gave me great solace while I was in the hospital and since my release.

Keep up the good work and I have enclosed a check for $100.00.

Thanks Again,
Harry

Dear Father Harry,

We are sending this donation as a way of saying thank you for offering the TV mass each week. You have such a special gift for making us feel as if we are actually there in the chapel with you. Your positive outlook and inspiring sermons stay with us throughout the week.

Alda and Perry

Dear Father Harry,

Please accept our small donation to help keep the TV Mass going. I watch every Sunday and do so enjoy the service and your homily's. The fact that the Mass comes on a 5:30 AM is a blessing as it is during the quiet time for me and I am able to pay closer attention. It is a little difficult sometimes as we had to have our son and his wife and family move in with us. He lost his job and we have room, so we help as we are able. With two beautiful granddaughters (2 and 3) you can imagine the din becomes a little overpowering at times. I love our children and our grandchildren very much, but at 71 I tend to be set in my ways a little and it has been a bit of an adjustment for my wife and me. Please pray for us to maintain our sanity . . .

In the Love of Christ,
Bill

In the decades I've been doing the TV Mass, I have only had one negative letter. It had to do with one of the teenage lectors from a local high school and the complaint was that her uniform skirt was too short. I had to agree with the viewer and we corrected the situation.

Back to the newly hatched idea when I could not sleep. By the way, scripture is full of references to significant dreams. You remember when Saint Joseph was forewarned by the angel to return to his home by a different route because King Herod was out to kill all boys two years old or younger. He was also told to take Mary as his wife even though he knew that she was with child and it wasn't his. That took some super kind of courage, especially in those days. My dream of expanding the fatherharry.org website is endorsed by the huge number of people who now watch the Sunday Mass online and have not even been encouraged or coaxed to try it.

If you have an internet connection, whether on an iPhone, iPad or computer, just type fatherharry.org in your browser. You'll see me on the screen and a few words letting you know who I am, then directing your attention to a red box that says "CLICK HERE TO WATCH THIS WEEK'S TV MASS". Click the box and you have the Mass for that Sunday from beginning to end in 28 minutes. You can watch it day or night, any day of the year, wherever you might be. It's a great convenience. I have people tell me that they use it when they travel. I have a couple of families who said they cannot make it to Mass on Sunday because of the distance and they gather around the dining table and celebrate Mass in cyberspace. I have letters from caregivers telling me they play this virtual Mass at home with sick parents who are housebound. It is my hope and dream (which is why it got off the ground) that by the time this work is published you will have checked out fatherharry.org.

Due to the deadly Covid-19 pandemic, the Catholic TV Mass has been a great help to the many who have been ordered to stay home. Our churches are closed, there are no Sunday Masses. Even the sacred Triduum and Easter Sunday are off limits for the people of God in California. In the first two weeks of people being at home there was a huge spike in viewership. Normally, I would receive about three to five gifts through Paypal. I have counted over 60 in the last ten days. People have stepped up to support the ministry and by the end of this terrible onslaught, I'm sure there will be a fair number who are old and sick and unable to get out of their homes who will continue to visit our parish in cyberspace and on the airwaves. I have had so many personal messages from viewers who are now praying the Mass with me each week. It's not what is desired either by the Church or myself, but it has served a people who want to pray and have plenty to pray for during this intense time of recovery.

One would think that the Archdiocese of San Francisco would be so pleased to have this ministerial tool at such a time when the need is so evident. It's been pretty quiet from the office and even at the archdiocesan newspaper, which could be touting this Mass as something to be substituted for all our closed churches.

I've had a couple of letters and emails that gently informed me I should not have been giving the cup to my lectors, nor should I be so close to them when celebrating Mass. We actually tape far in advance, in order to serve the hearing impaired with closed captioning, and there is little we can do to correct it except place a banner at the beginning and the end of each Mass informing the people of the pre-recording.

This reminds me of when Pope John Paul II died. There were several Sundays when I was praying for him as if he were still alive. Some of my followers even sent me pictures and newspaper clippings to let me know that he had passed and we had a new pope. There was little I could do about it during the time after the pope's death and the election of Pope Francis. You do your best. Angels can't do better. I guess it's a compliment that people see the Mass as live.

The TV Mass is an alternate way to pray. We all need as much help as we can get, don't you agree? Father Harry, pray this Mass with your mind, as if it were your first, and pray this Mass with your heart, as if it were your last.

CHAPTER 48

Celibacy

THE HEADLINE IN the *National Catholic Reporter* read: "Priesthood Crucified on the Cross of Celibacy". It was an article by Father Peter Daly, a retired priest from the Archdiocese of Washington, who also happens to be a lawyer. Those of you who know me or who have read my memoir, *I'll Never Tell*, understand that I have a keen interest in this subject and admittedly for selfish reasons. I truly believed that in due time, celibacy would be a choice and not a mandate for the Roman Catholic priesthood. I felt that way immediately after ordination at age 25 and with the changes made at the Second Vatican Council in 1965, I was certain it was just a matter of time. In my 56 years of practicing celibacy, I never quite had all my ducks in a row to write down what might be a reasonable answer as to why I followed that priestly promise. Father Daly opened the windows of my mind a bit wider in his beautiful article to further my thinking on the subject.

I'm feeling guilty about writing what I've learned from this man, so I will try to point out two major concerns.

He says that the Church is harmed because it restricts the pool of candidates who might consider the priesthood. Over the years, I have known so many wonderful candidates who have come forward and then retreated because they wanted a wife and children and grandchildren. I was ordained a priest with 72 classmates. I'm not certain of those who are still active, but it can't be more than a handful or two. I recall Bishop Louis Jadot from Rome, who was the Apostolic Delegate to the United States and a talk he gave in Missouri around 1967. There were about 60 priests present for a retreat. He told us in 20 years it would be a whole different scenario. Men like us would be overworked and would find ourselves ill and unable to handle the load of running a parish. It would just be too much work. He puffed on a cigar and added, "Some of you will leave and marry, mark my word." I marked it but never married. It's a joy I'll never know.

Daly offers a second barrage of statements with which I concur when he says that celibacy is not normal. I just have to quote him lest I lose some of the flavor in paraphrasing:

"Celibacy is not healthy for many people.

Celibacy fosters a culture of mendacity and secrecy, which contributes to sexual cover-ups.

Celibacy is not essential to holiness or to priesthood.

Celibacy is not mandated by the Gospels.

Celibacy contributes to a culture of clericalism."

Now that you see what he has written, let me take a stab at these from my own experience.

NOT HEALTHY FOR MANY PEOPLE

I'm not exactly sure what Daly means by this, but I suppose it has to do with all the emotions and feelings, as well as growth and development. Denial is a big word and whether one wants to or not, when it comes to a natural urge, like sex, how can it just go away? That urge was always strong as I was growing up and I was told it was natural and I bought that, but then I never really got the point about going to hell if you touched yourself impurely (whatever that meant). It didn't seem fair to an adolescent boy much less a young man looking around at what was to be seen, known and loved.

We have a sports announcer in San Francisco who continues to use the words "eye candy" when he describes a running back breaking through the line and only facing a much smaller defensive back. Eye candy has also been used to describe beautiful women. Most of us have had those kinds of desires and wants all our lives. When you're in your 80s, satisfying physical needs doesn't seem as important or even as possible as it did years ago.

CELIBACY FOSTERS A CULTURE OF MENDACITY AND SECRECY, WHICH CONTRIBUTES TO SEXUAL COVER UP

My experience has been that this is right on the money. I have lied (mendacity) about where I was or who I was going to see or ignored reasonable questions about my personal life simply because I felt it would lessen my commitment as a priest by answering. Going back to my seminary days, after summer vacation there was always the chance that you might get a letter or two scented with perfume wanting to know if you were going to stick with it. It might also thank you for time shared in flirting conversation on a hot summer night when you might find yourself alone with a young lady who found you attractive. It would make me sit up and bark as I thought it might be the end of my vocation if the seminary authorities knew. In those days secrecy and cover-ups were essential to protecting your privacy and your assurance of sticking with the program.

CELIBACY IS NOT ESSENTIAL TO HOLINESS OR TO PRIESTHOOD

This one really gets me. Married men who follow their relationship with God have always been a great example to me. It never gets old to see a man patiently correcting his kids and giving them the right way to do things by his personal example. You all know how important and how precious are the parents who have led their children into the kingdom of heaven by what they say and do. Spirituality is so close to the human heart and so connected with the individual soul that it is no wonder that it cannot be hidden or put under a bushel basket. It is to be used, as it was meant to be, for the betterment of everyone. We all know priests (or for that matter, other Catholics) who live the letter of the law and follow the rules but have little or no faith. Sure, they do what is asked and not much more. The priesthood is supposed to make you holy just by reason of doing ministerial work (priestly duties). Celebrating Mass, hearing confessions, baptizing new Catholics, can all be tasks at times and barely connected to the spiritual heart of the matter. Centuries of people and priests who have prayed, and have not always reaped the benefits of being holy or even spiritual, are still functioning in the system that permits them to simply do a job and not be truly connected with Almighty God.

CELIBACY IS NOT MANDATED BY THE GOSPELS

There is the famous story in Matthew's gospel of Jesus curing the mother-in-law of Saint Peter meaning, of course, that our first pope was married. Throughout history celibacy came and went and then came back again. Upon its return at the Council of Nicaea, 325 years after Jesus died, it became mandatory mainly for economic reasons. Too many bishops were giving away land and property to nephews whom they were ordaining priests just to keep it all in the family. I often wonder if the boys with the beanies don't feel the same today. Would that they could live a little longer among the people of God instead of being kept up in old and eerie tight quarters waiting to make more rules and admonishing and punishing those seeking change. I wonder how eager a bishop would be to send a pedophile to another parish or another part of the diocese if he had his own children attending that parish school.

CELIBACY CONTRIBUTES TO
A CULTURE OF CLERICALISM

This has certainly been my experience. It separates the priest from the people more than anything I know. While there may be good results because, as a single man, he has more time to spend with people, a priest certainly is branded or brands himself a "better man" for what he has sacrificed.

This is corroborated mostly when there are lay people (non-clerical) who agree that we're different. They want you to dance with their wives. They hope you'll come to their homes and have a meal with their children. When they hear you talk about laundry, or what you eat or how you spend your free time, they will know and appreciate the likenesses more than the differences. They won't worry about you drinking alone or going on luxurious vacations, or hanging out at a gay bar, or heaven forbid, doing something inappropriate with an underage child.

Clericalism is like most other "isms". It corrodes and calls to itself that there is something special about me that you are not and will not be. The gift of the Holy Spirit that is intended to enlighten a newbie priest can more often estrange him to a community of regular folks who are looking for a spiritual leader, one who will look you in the eye and won't run off to his brother priests for consolation and encouragement. People expect from any priest that his depth of commitment and his tenacity to his calling will allow him to have the right answer for most questions about the challenges of family life. What God has joined together man must not divide. When two people join hands in holy matrimony, their individuality is sliced in half. They are now a family unit, even though two. It's like the sound of one piano key. It's not music, it's just a note but, if you put it together with more sounds and organize them, it becomes a tune. The same is true with motion. One movement does not make a dance. One step is simply one step but, when followed by a rhythm and other steps, it becomes an art. Husband and wife become one in marriage, while the newly ordained is called to be alone in the clerical state, where he dare not form a relationship based on love and commitment like the married couple lest he overstep his celibate calling.

So, Harry, how can you write this stuff? You've been a priest for 56 years. You drank the Kool-Aid. You've promised obedience to your bishop. You've sacrificed the privilege of children and grandchildren. Why moan and groan? You're right. I have no rights. It's too late for me, boys and girls. But I'm out to make it better for the Church of the future, if there is one without priests. I would like to see major changes now just as this last synod, which met in Rome in 2019, considered the Amazon and the problems they are having because there are no priests. Well, dammit, ordain some married men or allow young men to be priests and be married.

We have a prototype of this centered in Houston and headed by a bishop friend of mine whose diocese is the entire country. Its purpose is to serve men of other faiths who are married and then accepted, if they ask, by the Catholic Church to practice their sacerdotal promises even though they have a wife and children. It's sour grapes to think this is not fair. It's my opine to say, who cares? The end of it all is to spread the Gospel, to do and live what Jesus left us to do. It means we have to unload a lot of historical baggage and see our Church, our faith, as a garden to be worked and cultivated rather than a museum simply to be guarded and protected. It's a big request. I'll admit, I haven't really made it part of my prayer life. I suppose it's like most other retired priests: we ran the race, we fought the good fight and now we hope to be accepted into eternal life for what has been gifted to us to do. Amen.

CELIBACY FOSTERS OBEDIENCE, OR DOES IT?

Daly doesn't talk about the labor factor when he goes after celibacy. I recall in the middle 1960s Catholic education was threatened because we were no longer getting religious vocations. Women religious (nuns) were no longer entering orders dedicated to teaching. Woe is the Catholic education system. They can never afford to pay lay teachers and administrators to take over, run and teach. I was one of those who thought that way. I was wrong. People got together and said how much they wanted Catholic schools. They spoke up with their pocketbooks and their donations. Lay men and women worked for less and lo and behold, Catholic schools survived. I didn't give it a chance. When the Sisters of Loreto left St. Agnes High School where I had taught alongside them in the '60s and early '70s, I thought it was only a matter of time before the doors closed for good. I underestimated the power of the people, the people of God, the Church. They loved their religion, they lived their faith, they paid for their children to be in a Catholic school. My bad.

I could be all wrong again. There might be a whole new batch of boys who are waiting to be brewed into the next phase of Roman Catholicism that will be offered. They might discover that this celibacy thing is good, profitable and good for you. If that is the case, the Holy Spirit continues to work in mysterious ways that I'll never know.

Bishops who are responsible for the Church in their neck of the woods will find it difficult to come up with the cash to support a married priest and his family, but then we'll once again see the power of the people. If they could do it for their schools, they will certainly step up to support their parish church. I would bet on it. And also make a hefty donation to keep things going.

CHAPTER 49

Alleluia People

ONE OF THE GREAT privileges of being a priest is to take a baby into your arms after you've poured water (usually cold) over his or her head, made the infant cry and then have all present applaud the new Roman Catholic. It usually pleases the baby to see smiling faces and hear voices saying their name and clapping. In all these years it has yet to fail. Sometimes it makes me cry. Babies are a sign that, no matter what, God still loves us.

Recently, I baptized a little boy, Michael, at the chapel where I presently celebrate Mass every Sunday. The chapel sits on the campus of St. Vincent's School for Boys in Marin County and Sunday Mass serves the students there, but the public is welcome to attend. The baby's father was a mentor to Whitney Houston and co-writer on much of her music. The godparents were Carlos Santana and his wife Cindy Blackman Santana. She's the drummer for his band. The next night they performed at the Chase Center, new home of the Golden State Warriors, to a sold-out crowd. I had never met Santana before despite my decades as a broadcaster in San Francisco, but I recall his great initiation to the worldwide scene when he performed at Woodstock in August of 1969. His music was new and his ability to command thousands to stand and dance in the mud on a huge hill out in the country made him an instant success. Half a century later, his star still shines brightly, especially here in the West. He held the candle for little Michael and seemed impressed by the whole ceremony. I asked him a couple of dumb questions that someone else had prompted me to do. "Mr. Santana, do you know so and so?" they had asked me to inquire. "No, not really, should I?" "Not sure, sorry about that . . ." At the end of the baptism, Carlos mentioned to Michael Pritchard, my old friend and his longtime acquaintance, that they would like to do a benefit concert for the Boys Home that would include the God Squad. It was going to be a thank you beyond my imagination. Well, we'll see what happens.

About six months ago a monsignor from Seton Hall, the former president of that university, asked if I would be open to taking up his role as the Sunday celebrant at St. Vincent's. He said he had to return to the Hall, as requested by his bishop. I had heard of his Marin County community that has been built up for a number of years. They were ALLELUIA PEOPLE. They came to Mass early; they sat in the front pews. There was standing room only most weekends, a stark contrast to other Catholic churches in the archdiocese. They prayed aloud. They sang. They smiled. They laughed at your humor. They are believers. Needless to say it was a wonderful privilege for me to follow in the footsteps of Monsignor Robert Sheeran.

For almost 25 years, I have been celebrating Mass for television in the presence of two cameramen and two lectors. The camera people take the pictures and the lectors read the scriptures and respond to the prayers. There are few other distractions except an occasional bug flying around the chalice on the altar. We videotape the programs inside a mausoleum in the All Saints chapel at Holy Cross Cemetery in Colma. Famous people like Joe DiMaggio and Manson clan murder victim and coffee heiress Abigail Folger are buried at Holy Cross. I have my plot secured right across from Joltin' Joe. That's probably as close to fame (and the cover of

Sports Illustrated) as I will ever get. Too bad I'll be dead. I'll have to look into forwarding my subscription.

The cemetery people assure me that these bugs are normal in most burial grounds and that they are perfectly harmless. When I see them, I recall a childhood tune that went like this:

> "The bugs crawl in
> The bugs crawl out
> The bugs play pinochle
> On your snout
> They eat your eyes
> They eat your nose
> They eat the goodies between your toes"

From this, you realize my childhood was simple and jaded.

The main reason we tape at Holy Cross is because it's quiet, the chapel is beautiful, and no one bothers us. Equipment can be moved in and out easily and we don't bother a soul, living or dead.

So you get the idea. Compared to Colma, Marin is a dream. What a wonderful experience it is for me each week to preach in front of real live human beings who want to be there. They want to pray. They want to listen. They want to be inspired. More than all of this, they are proud to be Catholic and have the opportunity to participate in the Sunday Mass. It's like what I've heard many say, "I feel like I've been to church."

So this privilege of mine is greatly appreciated and I have no idea how long it will last, so I'll take advantage of the way it is right now. St. Vincent's Home for Boys has been around for more than 165 years. Today there are about 65 kids in small residential homes. At one time there were over 500 boys there. They were mostly kids whose families could not feed nor care for them. Many of them lost their fathers in the Gold Rush. The place kept growing and growing. Today there are so many restrictions on this kind of service. Most of the kids are sent there as wards of the court. Catholic Charities of San Francisco is in charge. It takes a great deal of money to keep it going. You might remember the old black and white flicks that featured Mickey Rooney at Boys Town. Kids could come off the streets and go into places without doctors, counselors, volunteer parents and professional organizations to be responsible. Today, everything that involves the care of a teen brings with it the possibility of a lawsuit. Crazy but true.

So here sits this beautiful chapel, almost a mile off the 101 freeway down a winding road with eucalyptus trees on each side and wild turkeys running around. This St. Vincent's couldn't be more different from St. Vincent's in the City, where I still reside. Back farther on the property sits a large barn and stables for 16 horses that are used by the boys so that they can focus on something besides their problems and the challenges of growing up in a broken home or no home. We recently named the stables after a man who has worked with these kids for 53 years. In fact, he instituted the use of horses for therapy. He donated six of his own at the beginning. He is older now with grandchildren and they were all there to celebrate his retirement. Several of the former residents, now adults, took to the stage to testify to his work and the success of the home. I couldn't help notice a table of old timers, all gray or bald, with plastic cups and a quart of Irish whiskey on the table. They had all graduated from the home and had become successful citizens and came to pay their respects to a man who had helped so many become men.

I blessed the sign at the road going to the stables and felt blessed myself by the parade of horses led by these little boys and with help from the trainer. You could see the connection between the animals and the kids. Would that so many other boys who are going astray in the world might have the privilege of becoming "Wranglers" and proclaiming it with great pride on their T-shirts.

I hope God gives me good health to continue to pursue my own happiness by being a part of a home for boys and a church full of ALLELUIA PEOPLE.

CHAPTER 50

Missouri Mule

I HAD DINNER with the Drurys tonight. Charles finished his book. It's 600 pages. His secretary said he was going to present a copy of it to me this evening. That will be my airplane reading for the rest of the trip.

Charles handed me the book, all 600 pages, complete with multiple photos and charts of building plans that I would not be able to decipher. The pages were all slick and the book was heavy. "I was going to send it to you in the mail, but you said you might be able to read it on the plane." That's what I thought, until he handed it to me. It was going to cost me extra to carry it on. I'm going to weigh it when I get a chance. Charles told me two years ago that it was going to be around 600 pages and I told him he needed an editor whom he could trust and who would be honest with him. *Don't Get Kicked by the Same Mule Twice and Other Lessons from Kelso University* is a down home rendition of his life and family from the early beginnings of the "boys" on the farm to the billionaire company that is now the Drury Hotels corporation.

I came in from the cold with only my black suit and a sweater vest to join Shirley and Charles for a quick dinner, as they were on their way home from a board meeting where they had just learned Drury Hotels was now a billion dollar corporation. Charles was in a wheelchair and "Mommy", as he so affectionately calls Shirley, was pushing him through the restaurant that I think they own. Well, I know they built it. It was 12 above zero in St. Louis and 67 when I boarded the plane earlier that morning in San Francisco. Shirley and I did most of the talking during dinner as "Daddy" had the hiccups. He said they were part of his life for several days and he just didn't feel well. He ate all of his dinner and we had a glass of red wine for a finish. I finished the green beans that Shirley passed along and she bragged about the fried catfish served at her request that wasn't even on the menu. We spent three hours remembering the early days when my brother and his nine children were never invited out to anyone's home for dinner. So they would join the Drury family of six children. Each family would host every other Sunday. Everyone got fed and a genuine friendship developed. My brother Charlie and his wife, Mary, both passed early in life so the Drury/Schlitt dinners came to an end and the kids grew and scattered. None of them stayed close over the years. I'm the one who had maintained the relationship since they came to my ordination in Rome in 1964 and have kept up since that time.

They have been very generous to the God Squad and have made it possible for me to build an investment account, so that the TV Mass and the God Squad might continue after my demise. Charles is 92 and Shirley is 85 and still able to drive him and put the wheelchair in and out of the trunk of the car. As we were leaving the restaurant, I asked about a ramp. Charles then 'fessed up that when they built this place it was not part of the code. The manager and one of the waiters gave a hand and I waved goodbye. I thought as I watched my breath turn to white steam that I might not see Charles again before he goes to meet his Maker. (And six months later, he was dead.) What he has left for his children and their children is a masterpiece of memories that the entire Drury clan can pass along from generation to generation and know about who they are and where they come from and how they ever got to where they are.

CHAPTER 51

St. Vincent de Paul

COVID-19 HAS drawn many unusual bedfellows together for sheltering in place. I have been so fortunate to have spent the last few months with three men who love both God and their neighbors as themselves. I'm not sure whether they would give their lives for such, but I do know how four men living in the same house (rectory) can not only get along but also see each other as a blessing to one another. I spoke to a priest friend on the phone this week who has been by himself in a rural parish for the same amount of time with only the computer and the telephone. He has all his meals in quiet or with the television on, waiting to hear the next outpouring of bad news or the preposterous vision of our current president (Trump). It could be downright painful.

I'm so lucky to have Father Roy, who just celebrated his 49th birthday in full Niner regalia gifted to him by his American friends and Filipino fans of the football team. He is the newest member of our household and a canon lawyer who is working from home on his computer.

Father Michael is three months older than me and loves music, especially the opera. Symphonies flow from his room most of the day and far into the night. He has been in this parish the longest and knows everyone, so when someone dies he is the first to be called. He was a professor at St. Patrick's Seminary for many years, as well as a missionary in Africa. There is no shortage of tales at the table each evening.

Father Ken Westray I've known since he lived with me at Sacred Heart parish in the 1970s. As a pastor, he's the best. He served in the Merchant Marines for a number of years before going into the seminary. As an African American who comes from Washington D.C., he brings a unique view to almost any topic we choose to discuss. I could not have asked to be holed up with three finer men than these. What a blessing! I often pray for those families who are having domestic squabbles and possible abuse and have nowhere to go for ease or comfort. They're stuck. Of course, statistics show an increased number of violent incidents in the home since Covid. The police are registering more and more calls to homes to break up potential crimes that might be committed if the residents were left alone. I thank God everyday at prayer for the gift of living with these men I've been lucky enough to be with every day.

When Father Roy said to me that he finished reading my memoir and was very impressed by all the adventures I've been able to have, he did not use the word odyssey. I was waiting for the other shoe to drop. His face lit up as though he were conversing with a famous celebrity and was eager to ask questions and find out more about who I was. Naturally, I ate it up. His presence at the parish was a matter of assignment to fulfill both his calling to work as a canon lawyer in the archdiocesan Tribunal Office (where annulments are determined) and his energetic age, which could be a great asset to the pastor.

The Catholic Church uses Canon Law for its internal administration. Roy spends a couple of days a week working on marriage cases and the rest of the week doing the normal parish work of saying Mass, visiting the sick, chairing meetings and offering his services to the elementary school. It can be exhausting and very fulfilling at the same time. But when you're young it's life-giving and exciting.

All of us who live together are so grateful to have each other during these Covid-19 times. With the shortage of priests these days, there are only a few parishes that can afford to have a younger man. Father Roy is able to fulfill all his obligations both here at the parish and at the chancery office. He works on marriage cases the way an attorney would if he were hired to counsel during divorce proceedings. The difference is that the Church is trying to put back together the bond that has been broken. It can be very pastoral or very ugly depending on the lawyer and the procedure that the office follows. It's a mixed bag and one that either is to be applauded or booed depending on who is doing the case. Some canon lawyers are sticklers for keeping the letter of the law and find it difficult to bend in any direction when a case comes to them. Others, with a pastoral sense, are open to listening and discovering what might have happened to sour or ruin a marriage and then are ready and able to try to either patch it up or look for grounds for an annulment, so that one or other of the couple might be able to enter a new relationship that would allow them to return to the fold and practice their faith. As I said, it's too often left in the hands of men and women who are hard-nosed and have not had the opportunity to work in a parish or feel the needs of families who are broken and looking to be fixed. It takes a great deal of courage on the part of people to admit they didn't make the best choice for a life partner and to go to the trouble of treating it all like a court case, complete with the personal exposure which they might not be very willing to undergo. It takes grace. Usually, people are so in love with the person they intend to re-marry that they are eager to jump through all the hoops and mend whatever fences with their ex in order to pursue a different road to happiness. By the way, Father Roy is one of the good guys.

Now that we're having dinner together five or six nights a week, it's easy to follow each other's life and times. We're not that interesting to the general public and could never provide the proper fodder for a talk show or a roundtable discussion. We are not "E" network material. For example, Father Mike listens to opera most of the day and watches all the classical music stations on TV, while I report on the latest episode of this or that adventure which Netflix is showing. *Outlander* is a 67-part series (so far) and I am only five seasons away from finishing it. It's been a learning experience for me as I'm not that keen on history (I was a solid B-student) and even less concerned about the evolution of Scotland. What can I say? I got hooked early on and now look forward to a couple of hours every night before I go to bed.

Father Ken continues to worry how we're going to be able to re-start the engine of the parish without disappointing many people. We can only get so many in the church with social distancing and it would be very unpleasant to have to turn people down on Sunday. Me, I think I'll wait another month before I open up the mission chapel where I offer Mass each week at St. Vincent's School for Boys in Marin. I'm in no hurry for more people to become ill just because they feel the obligation of Sunday Mass. It's no sin to avoid getting sick. But if you had some idea that you might have the Covid-19 virus, and you go to church because of personal commitment and your conscience, the sin would be in passing along the virus.

CHAPTER 52

Hugh and Evangeline

DURING THIS COVID-19 period while I'm sheltered away like most of you, it has given me more time than I want to turn on the telly and learn what I can about how we're doing. I discovered Governor Andrew Cuomo offering clear and succinct analysis to the world and especially to the City and State of New York. It spurred me on to call a dear friend who has been mentioned before in my writings, Jim Normile.

I asked Jim about the governor and what he thought of him and how he was doing with this whole infectious mess. Jim knows him from his business affairs as an attorney in New York. Here are a couple of personal points about the man.

It is apparent that he works very hard and doesn't have much time for hobnobbing nor making friends outside of work. He loves his daughters and makes sure that we all know that he hasn't spent enough time with family and friends. Maybe he needs more, or at least some, friends to help him lighten up.

I've noticed that our California guv seems to be aping him in some areas. Believe me, it's all good. It's been a long time since government has had the opportunity to weigh in on the people and their plight. I'm also pleased to see that it seems to be working.

The general populace appears to understand the challenge we all face.

When I lived in New York in the early '80s, I was fortunate to have met and established a friendship with then Governor Hugh Carey, who was succeeded by Mario Cuomo, Andrew's father. After his term in office, he turned into the toast of the town of New York. Whether he was being led out to public events or private cocktail parties by his firm, or simply having a beer with a friend, Hugh Carey was impressive. The lights went on when he entered the venue. He sang, danced, told stories and generally entertained wherever he might be. It could be late at night where he had a table almost anywhere and knew by name the people you need to know in NYC in order to be classified as a major celebrity. Many politicians, like old soldiers, just seem to fade away. Once the term is over and the titles are gone, it's back to reality. No so with Governor Carey. He thrived perhaps more than ever during his post-governor years.

One night we were out very late. Evangeline Gouletas was with us. He insisted on driving because it was his car and his city. It would have been a wiser choice to hand me the keys. We were headed south on Park Avenue when a taxi pulled out right in front of us. The cabbie had just closed the door after his occupants had gotten out. The brake lights were not on and Mr. Carey didn't see him. We came within inches of being sideswiped. I grabbed the wheel, we swerved away, Hugh hit the brakes and we came to a screeching halt. It could have been a disaster. Nervously, he pulled over to the curb, unstrapped himself, and asked me to pilot his vehicle to his garage.

Hugh and Evangeline had an apartment near the United Nations building. They invited me up for a nightcap. I didn't need it, but I wanted to see how they were re-decorating since I had heard about it all during dinner. It was high in the sky overlooking the East River and beyond. It had a breathtaking view with the sparkle of the moon and the reflection of city lights on the river, in a city that never sleeps. There were still all kinds of tools and paraphernalia scattered about, as it was a work in progress. I stayed about 15 minutes and quietly descended to street level for a short walk to where I was living at the time. I later learned that much of the debris was broken dishes and other things that might have been hurled in dissatisfaction by the one with a Mediterranean temper.

Evangeline owned several properties and after I had lost my lease on 36th and Lex, she offered me an apartment that was open on the Upper Eastside. It was 86th Avenue with a doorman, a workout room and a spa on the top floor. It was more room than I ever had in a place by myself. She even gave me an old bed she had. Unfortunately, it was USED, with a cushioned headboard, all nice except the cushions were stained with hairy grease spots from the previous occupier. I never was sure who it was but knew it was someone from the family. When I showed the bedroom to guests who visited it was a sore sight for any eyes. They would react with facial expressions that encouraged me to return the bed. I could not, as it was a gift and came with the furnished apartment. It was one of those, "Don't look a gift horse in the mouth" things.

My longtime friend Barbara "Baby" Thieriot, mother of Kip, was flying back home to San Francisco and happened to be seated next to Hugh Carey. They chatted about many things. Baby could converse with anyone about myriads of things, as she was an untiring reader and a person who retained what she read. The governor told her he and Evangeline wanted to get married, but they couldn't find a priest in New York who could do the deed. "Oh," she said, "I have a close priest friend, Father Harry. I'm sure he could help you out."

"It wouldn't be the same Father Harry who does radio and television and lives in New York?" he asked.

"That's him," she replied with a smile.

So Mrs. Thieriot threw a dinner party for the governor at the Menlo Park Country Club. There were about 20 of us there. After dinner the governor sang, to everyone's delight. It was a Saturday night and I left before brandy and cigars. I had an early Mass the next morning. Hugh wanted to know where and would it be okay if he came.

A black limo showed up right at 11:00 a.m. with two motorcycle cops leading the way. After Mass, one of the neighbors hollered out the window across the street, "Hey Father who was in the big car in front of the church?" I told him it was the governor of New York. He yelled back, "He sure came a long way for church." By the way, the governor greeted all the people in front of the church and took his time with each one of them. He really had a special gift with people of all kinds and colors. I stood there with Evangeline admiring his pleasant and giving demeanor with some very, very poor people.

After Mass we went to brunch and the governor introduced the plans for their marriage. "We both would very much like you to perform the service," he said. I put down my fork with the sand dabs I was demolishing. They are small flatfish and so tasty. My mouth had to first connect with my brain. Once the synapses were all firing, I responded. "You know there will be paperwork and some kind of instructions and where exactly did you plan on doing it?" I knew the wife of the governor had passed some years ago, but I knew nothing of the marital status of Evangeline. When I introduced the question of time and place, they both said whatever would be convenient for you.

"Me? You are ones who are making the commitment and I would prefer you make all the decisions. Evangeline, have you ever been married?" "Oh yes," she said with a smile, "but I'm Greek Orthodox and it should not be a problem." Little did I suspect that I might be leaping into the unknown with a huge millstone attached. The governor of New York, who was touted as presidential material, and a Greek real estate mogul, who was excited about the chance to be First Lady of the United States of America, were asking me to witness their vows.

The better part of my brain took over as I gently said I would have to give it some thought and maybe ask a couple of priest friends how this might play in the press. I knew she would have to initiate a privilege of the faith request in order for this to happen.

Two days later I called Hugh and said I must decline, but thank you for having the confidence in me to celebrate the love the two of you have for one another. After an ever so brief conversation, I was out of the limelight for the public spectacle that might be their wedding. The following week or two there was an article in on the front page of the *New York Times* about their marriage and it mentioned that she had been divorced twice. Then a friend told me that they used to have a bumper sticker in Albany, the New York state capital, that read: HONK IF YOU WERE MARRIED TO ENGIE.

I'll never know what led me into all this, or out of it, but I'm grateful for the guidance.

CHAPTER 53

Renda Clark
1952-2020

I HAVE SEVERAL nephews and nieces and the oldest of my nieces recently passed away. I was close to her in her younger years, as she was like a little sister to me. She took the train with me to Dubuque, Iowa, when I bought my first car from Wayne Ressler's father. I can still hear her giggling as the little white Camaro slid across most of the icy roads in the Midwest. What I thought was precarious, she enjoyed. She confided in me on many different occasions and I was able to guide her through some trying times.

At her funeral I recalled the scripture about, "Take care of the present, forever will take care of itself." As is said, the past is history, the future is mystery and the present is a gift. Renda was indeed a gift to my brother and his wife, her brothers, and a treasure to her husband and daughter. Everyone dies, not everyone lives. As the wise man said, "I'm not afraid of death, it's just the dying part."

With death comes fear. When I'm at the pulpit, I often knock on the wood as if fear were knocking. I say when faith answers, the fear goes away. It's our Christian way of seeing life after death. On Ash Wednesday as the season of Lent begins, we remind ourselves again from the scriptures that, "We are dust and unto dust we shall return." Think of all the dirt around us that didn't have the chance to get up, dance around and be beautiful as Renda did. She traveled, she cooked, she sewed, she counted money at the bank, she carried mail, she honed her hospitality skills as an airline attendant and saw the world as well. She gave birth to a beautiful girl and lived to see her grandchildren. A whole new world awaited her as the wife of a successful oilman. Her role was social and diplomatic, serving alongside her husband meeting, dining and attending parties with the king and queen of Malaysia. She hosted famous people in Equatorial Guinea, in central Africa. She was called "First Lady" when her husband became president of the oil company in that part of the world.

Renda was just 15 when she and her girlfriend drove to Dallas from Missouri to visit some friends of mine. My buddy there had once played baseball with the Chicago White Sox. He was selling those little yellow ear tags that you see on livestock. They each have a number and take the place of branding. We spent a couple of days with the girls. Driving down there I got a speeding ticket in a small town and paid $25 instead of waiting to see the judge. My niece's girlfriend later became a law enforcement officer and at Renda's funeral reminded me of it.

But the highlight of our trip was going to a grill and club in Dallas where they had music. The girls were having Shirley Temples, when a very large man approached the table and asked Renda if she would like to dance. He looked familiar to me and when he spoke it was obvious that Dandy Don Meredith was in the house and thought my niece was old enough and pretty enough to be seen on the dance floor with him. He was quarterback for the Dallas Cowboys at that time. He went on to do color commentary on Monday Night Football. I can still see him on TV with Howard Cosell and Frank Gifford singing "The party's over . . ." as one or other of the teams was about to lose a game. After the dance, like the gentleman that he was, he returned Renda to our table and her soft drink. Her eyes were big as saucers when I told her who he was and how much he must have admired her to ask her for a dance.

God's resources are greater than our needs. We are all sources of comfort and compassion to one another at the loss of a friend or relative. I will always feel comforted by the life and smile of my dear niece as I read the poem *The Day God Called You Home* (paraphrased):

"GOD looked around his garden and he found an empty place. He then looked down on his earth and saw Renda's tired face. He put his arms around her and lifted her to rest. God's garden must be beautiful, he always takes the best. He knew that her heart had not been well; he saw the road was getting rough and her pain she would not tell. So he closed her weary eyelids and whispered, 'Peace of heaven be to you' and never mentioned hell. It broke our hearts to lose her, but she didn't go alone, for part of us went with her, the day God called her home."

CHAPTER 54

Father Kirk

THE DAY AFTER I returned from my niece Renda's funeral, we buried a brother priest, Father Kirk John Ullery. He was my peer and one of the remaining brethren from my time in active service to the Archdiocese of San Francisco. He'd been my housemate at St. Vincent de Paul when I'd moved there three years earlier but had since moved to Nazareth House. Tall, red-haired (in his prime) and possessing a deep commanding voice, Father Kirk was once mistaken for me when the good people of St. Elizabeth Ann Seton parish in Springfield, Missouri, pulled his photo instead of mine from the internet. They printed posters touting Father Harry's book-signing weekend, emblazoned with a huge photo of my colleague Kirk. I was at first confused, then amused, when I visited that parish in my home diocese to promote my memoir, *I'll Never Tell*, to see Father Kirk smiling out from poster after poster lining the halls and gracing the doors.

His funeral was memorable, befitting the man. The casket was draped with the American flag and the book of the Gospels. He had served his country and had preached the Gospel in several parishes, but his real love and shepherding was to the African-American community in the Bayview/Hunter's Point parish of Our Lady of Lourdes. It was directly across the street and a field from the naval shipyards, which have often been criticized for the polluted land left there by the U. S. government. It was not an expensive neighborhood and it's where many African-American families were forced to live because they could afford it. Today it is quite different as the Navy has disappeared and developers have renewed the space. The sun is often present because the hills hide the wind and the fog, which generally covers most of San Francisco in the summer. It's also on the Bay with a beautiful view of the water.

Father Kirk asked me to celebrate Mass in his parish a few times, when he was on vacation or sick. It was an active parish where the community responded to everything. Alleluias and amens abounded. It took me back to the time I served at Sacred Heart parish with its gospel choir and the same kind of celebrations. Father Kirk would often comment to me about the people at St. Vincent de Paul when we both lived there. "Are they alive or just taking up pew space?" If you are used to active responses, saying Mass in that parish was like talking to the tombstones in the yard for the dead. There was hardly ever a reaction whether something was good or bad, unusual or funny. We have the expression "deadpan." The assembly in this parish was a whole kitchen cabinet of them. Of course, let's be fair, it wasn't the people of God's problem. It was the way they were asked to comport themselves inside that church by previous pastors. They were simply following orders, traditions, or customs. Some guys think that complete silence is what should prevail at all times inside of every church. I believe that when a community comes together to celebrate life, death, or the life and death of an individual, the expressions should be voiced and sung with gusto.

There was no shortage of that in the parish as Kirk was honored by two choirs, the African-American ensemble as well as the Samoan group that had celebrated with him every Sunday at Our Lady of Lourdes. Both these choirs are of color. Father Ken remarked in the eulogy before the ceremony that Kirk saw every color and God in every person. It was obvious to us all that he was pleased that he had been chosen to serve both these communities, whose choirs filled the church with sustained and beautiful music throughout the ceremony.

My early encounter with Kirk had to do with his inimitable voice. He had the bass pipes of a baritone that could rattle any loose screw or piece of wood that wasn't nailed down. My radio experience led me to encourage him to take voice lessons with a commercial friend of mine in order to procure some extra money that could be used to supplement fish fries and bingo at his parish. He did so for a couple of years but failed to interest anyone in the same tones that I heard in his everyday speech. He was also an English teacher so it didn't hurt that he could pronounce almost any word with the correct emphasis on each and every syllable. I spoke to my friend who was instructing him and she, too, was surprised that in the call-backs he received, no one ever hired him. Strange. I often wondered whether it had anything to do with him being a priest. I too had felt that initial prejudice when I approached a voice agent in Hollywood, who said he would like to represent me. He had been a broadcaster in the Armed Forces and had followed my radio career. He spoke about my work on Armed Forces Radio and had great praise for my God Squad radio spots but still no call-backs, no jobs. No mon, no fun, I'm done!

Father Kirk's flaming red hair of his youth had mostly turned white at the end of his life, but nothing could stop him from leading any march or cause because, as Father Ken said, "He was a person who did not NOT see your color. He saw your color and appreciated every single one of the versions of God that he saw in you."

CHAPTER 55

Whoever Loses His Life for My Sake

Father Harry's Sunday Sermon
St. Vincent de Paul Church, June 28, 2020

Some of you at home or watching by the live streaming may not have heard nor seen the news that happened this week.

Father Ken was very exhausted after the passing of his very close friend Father Kirk Ullery. And in the preparation for that funeral service, which was held here in our parish on Tuesday, it was emotionally very draining for him. He had mentioned to Father Roy that he wasn't feeling well and Tuesday night he said he didn't feel very well and he was going to retire early. When I was leaving Wednesday morning, Ken hadn't made an appearance. We knocked on his door with no response. And then at one o'clock or thereabouts, Father Michael and Father Roy once again knocked on his door only to find no response. The door was unlocked and they found him on his bed. The coroner suspected he had been dead for perhaps eight hours or more.

Whoever loses his life for my sake will find it.

Father Westray loved every ministry that he was involved in and he loved this parish very much. He loved the people here. And like the good woman in the first reading today who showed hospitality, this could have been Father Westray's middle name. He was a great host. Those of you in the Men's Club and the Seniors Club would realize how he would hardly ever be able to sit and enjoy, as most there would, but rather he would have to be moving around to make sure everyone had enough food, everyone had enough drink, everyone was enjoying themselves. He always had to be popping up to make sure everyone else was served or skipping his place altogether and grabbing a tray of this or that and passing it around. He did this even when he wasn't the host.

Hospis, *the Latin word, means host, from which we get hospitality, from which we have the word hospital, all of which denote taking care of others. We even call the consecrated bread from this altar a host. A host because Jesus comes to us, he gives us himself. He hosts us in our spiritual life. Ken consecrated those hosts on a daily basis and said the blessing over the wine in the chalice just as he had been instructed to do from the scriptures: "Do this in memory of me." When Jesus took the bread and broke it with his apostles and shared the cup of wine as it came around the table at the last supper, it's the very same thing that Father Ken, a priest of God, did until the day he died.*

And just as the lady said to her husband in the first reading today (2 Kings 4:8-10), "Give him a bed so he can rest. Give him a table that so he can sit down and pray. Give him a chair so that he can read and understand. Give him a lamp that he might see." All of these little things. And then at the end of the gospel (Matthew 10:42), "Whoever gives this small child a cold drink of water does so for me and in my name."

This is a sad day for St. Vincent de Paul parish because we have lost our pastor.

As a practical memory of Father Ken Westray, we intend later on, once the virus subsides, to have a proper ceremony in this parish involving the entire parish. Unfortunately on Tuesday of this week we will not be able to have guests in our parish. We will have the family and some close personal friends of his and some priests. We'll have lines marked out in the middle aisle and the body of Father Westray will be here at 10 o'clock Tuesday morning, so if any of you at home want to come and pay your respects, come at that hour and you will be able to view the body and walk back out, but no one will be able to stay for the Mass. Because Father Ken's mother is elderly and, obviously, broken up at this time, the family has requested a very simple Mass and hopefully one that will be full of the spirit of God in prayer. Bishop McElroy was a close friend of Father's and will be the principal celebrant and the homilist. Also Archbishop Cordileone will be here.

I think I've said about everything. Did I miss anything?

So as we pray this Mass, we pray for the people of God in this parish, but we also remember our dearly beloved host. Hospitality, sine qua non, without which there is no other, Father Ken Westray.

* * *

Hospitality is an outward expression of an inward love. Some people are kind, polite and sweet until you take something from them. Not so with Ken. Many folks want to serve God and their neighbors but usually in an advisory capacity. Not so with Ken. Over the years I saw him reach out to the poorest of poor and to smile at the most wretched, crooked, con artists and beggars who rang our doorbell. Ken spent 15 years as pastor of Sacred Heart parish. In fact, I recommended him to Archibishop Quinn who made the assignment. He was only ordained two years when asked to lead a parish with almost no resources, a struggling school, a massive inner city plant with numerous deficiencies, and a neighborhood torn apart by gentrification. Ken was just a joy-filled human being who handled all this with virtue and ease.

When Covid-19 forced us all to wear masks and he had to take the Sunday collection to the bank, he asked if I might go along. This was just after all the demonstrations across the country, which had begun in Minneapolis with the death of George Floyd. He told me that I would not understand how it feels for a black man with a mask when he steps in the bank and up to the teller to make a deposit. His eyes would dart about in hopes that he might see a person from the parish who would acknowledge his presence, while the bank personnel kept a sharp eye on his every move. Really, it sounds strange to me, but that was the case that summer.

His good friend Bishop Robert McElroy, now the Bishop of San Diego, commented at the funeral service that Ken had been evaluated after six years of being pastor at St. Vincent de Paul. He had scored the highest on all categories except for one. He seemed to have a problem with being on time for almost everything. He didn't wear a watch and it really didn't bother him personally. So the good bishop remarked that God might have to wait a bit for Ken to show up in heaven, as he could easily be on the street somewhere helping some indigent find food for the day. Ken loved every kind of food, the hotter the better, both in temperature and taste. Fire and spicy sauce were two of his absolute musts before he cared to put any morsel between his teeth.

* * *

Father Harry's email to a friend, July 7, 2020:

I had been at my desk, working on *I'll Never Know*, writing the chapter about Father Kirk's death then sending it to my editor. There was a knock on my door and it was Father Roy. He told me that Ken was expected at the school at 10:30 for a meeting and he had not yet come down from his room. He asked me to walk down the hall and knock on his door. I did. Three times. No answer. I recalled that the night before, he told me he didn't feel good and would probably sleep in on Wednesday morning.

Bert Keane picked me up at 11:00 a.m. to go to Holy Cross to have the service for his father-in-law, who had passed a week before. Bert had brought sandwiches and a Diet Pepsi for me and we were going to eat in the schoolyard on one of the benches. Father Roy called about 12:55 p.m. and said that he and Father Michael were going to knock once again on Ken's door. I told them I would be home in a few minutes and I hoped that they would wait for me. They didn't. When Bert turned the corner onto Green Street, I saw the firetruck and an ambulance in front of the rectory. I figured they were going to take him to the hospital. I raced in the house and the parish secretary told me Father Ken was not breathing. I ran up the three flights of stairs to find two paramedics and three firemen just walking out of Ken's room. They said it was too late.

When the Medical Examiner came and did his investigation, he told us Ken had been dead about eight hours. According to the coroner, Ken died of a heart attack. I had to answer all the questions in the hall with a flurry of men around. Father Ray Reyes and Father Andrew Spyrow, who had succeeded Father

Ray as Vicar for Clergy, had come over as soon as they heard what happened. Ray called the archbishop and Andrew called his secretary Annabelle, then along with Father Labibi from Nigeria they sprinkled Ken's body with holy water and read the prayers from the ritual book. When they all had gone, Roy, Michael and I stood around the body and prayed. Nothing formal, just our simple goodbye and thank you for being a good housemate and a wonderful pastor and priest.

Meanwhile, after all had left I waited alone for the funeral director and his mate to wrap the body in a white sheet and then another covering that was of a different color but was not a body bag. They had to unbend his legs and arms in order to fit him on the stretcher. They wheeled him into the small elevator for his final trip down from the third floor, standing the body upright, as it was strapped onto the gurney. A photo of Ken's mother adorned the elevator door, something he saw first thing every morning. I never went down with them.

I returned to the room and then called Father Roy to help me get the mattress off the bed and onto the elevator. Ken had bled a bit from his nose and mouth. Once that was done I asked both Roy and Father Mike to meet after breakfast the following morning and we would clean out his room. It was a total mess. The police arrived in short order to do their investigation. They pretty much followed the instruction of the medical examiner. They did ask more questions and wanted to make sure that the next of kin had been contacted. I spoke to his brother, Kevin, on the phone and he would then pass along the information to their mother and sister. It was a shock to all.

The next morning Roy and I did some more work in that beautiful suite that overlooks San Francisco Bay. We pulled up the rugs. One of our workers is coming in tomorrow to give the room a thorough cleaning and re-carpet. I forgot to tell him about the drapes. They too are dirty and smell of smoke.

At five o'clock we're going to have a cocktail and toast the man.

* * *

Ken was a good guy. I always like to say with any of my friends, "He was one of us." It didn't matter what his color or where he came from. Of course, his smile and his laughter could affect anyone. I believe his happiness came from the heart in his fervent desire to serve his God and his conviction that Jesus Christ could overcome every form of human suffering.

Speaker of the House of Representatives, Nancy Pelosi, a member of St. Vincent de Paul parish, recognized Father Ken in the Congressional Record. Here's what she included about her pastor in the annals of the history of the United States:

CELEBRATING THE LIFE OF FATHER KENNETH WESTRAY

HON. NANCY PELOSI of California in the House of Representatives

Monday, June 29, 2020

Ms. PELOSI. Madam Speaker, I rise to pay tribute to Father Kenneth Westray, pastor of St. Vincent de Paul Parish in San Francisco and a civil and human rights champion in our city, who sadly passed away last week, on June 24, 2020.

Father Westray was a pillar of the San Francisco community whose selfless leadership was a tribute to the mission of the namesake of our parish, St. Vincent. He ministered to the poor and the most vulnerable in our community with great love, respect and faith. We all will remember and be inspired by the unwavering compassion and courage he showed in the face of the AIDS epidemic, which brought strength and solace to so many during one of the darkest chapters of our city's and country's history.

Personally, my husband Paul, my family and I were deeply saddened to hear of Father Westray's passing. Our family have been parishioners at St. Vincent de Paul for generations, since Paul's parents John and Corinne Pelosi became parishioners in the 1930s. We count ourselves blessed to have known Father Westray, beloved by all for his kind and gentle soul, who strengthened our church as he built community and inspired love for service and love for God. We enjoyed being with Father Ken in San Francisco and even in Washington. I had the privilege of welcoming Father Ken and his family to the U.S. Capitol for the visit of Pope Francis. His mother, Jean, was beaming with pride in him that day and on her visits to San Francisco. We shared a dedication to the San Francisco Interfaith Council and the San Francisco 49ers. Over forty years, Father Westray was a powerful force for good in our community, lifting up the lives of so many.

Although born in our nation's capital, Father Westray was proudly claimed by San Franciscans as a son of our city. He completed his seminary studies at St. Patrick's Seminary in Menlo Park and dedicated the rest of his life to ministering to the needs of our Bay Area community. After being ordained to the priesthood by Archbishop Quinn at St. Mary's Cathedral, Father Westray began his first assignment as associate pastor at Sacred Heart Church in San Francisco. Over the next forty years, he would serve in parishes throughout our city: at St. Elizabeth Parish, on the Council of Priests, at Sacred Heart Grammar School where he would minister for 14 years, at St. Sebastian Parish in Greenbrae, at St. Isabella Parish in San Rafael, and at our St. Vincent de Paul Parish. He served several terms on the Board of Directors of the San Francisco Interfaith Council, a powerful force for healing and unity in our community, including on its inaugural Board.

Father Westray served our community and country in so many ways, including both in the church and in uniform. Before entering seminary, he was a Merchant Marine and later served with the Military Vicariate as chaplain in the United States Navy Inactive Reserve.

May Father Westray's lifetime of compassionate leadership to lift up the least of these continue to be a blessing to our community. May it be a comfort to Father Westray's family, his mother Jean, sister Cecilia, brother Kevin and nephew Vonty, that Archbishop Cordileone, the entire St. Vincent de Paul Parish and so many others mourn their loss and pray for them during this sad time.

Daughter Christine Pelosi posted this touching tribute on Instagram:

"Heartbroken at the death of St. Vincent De Paul Pastor Fr. Ken Westray. Father Ken led worship and gave comfort at the church where my Nana attended and my parents call home. We loved him so much. I will never forget Father Ken's joy and incandescence at Pope Francis' 2015 visit to Washington DC and his patience with Bella being nervous about going to SVDP after I took her to the Lincoln Memorial Easter Sunrise Mass when she was 4 and the preacher screamed about the sacred bleeding heart of Jesus to where she was terrified of church even at Xmas. A godly man — I hope his faith is a comfort to his family and congregants. May his memory be a blessing."

Losing Ken and Kirk in pretty much the same time span left me with an emptiness I can't describe. From what I had written about Kirk would only be a ditto to what I write about Ken. The two "Ks" were similar in joy with their priesthood and generosity with sharing the Gospel with others.

CHAPTER 56

Priestly Advice for the Year 2000

TWENTY YEARS AGO I recall clipping this information from some publication. It was authored by Father Eugene Hemrick:

"PRIESTS
who hold on to an old system,
discontinue their education,
neglect their spiritual life,
work alone with little lay assistance,
and who are insensitive to other cultures
will most be frustrated and either leave
or become very ineffective."
"PRIESTS
who are flexible,
continue their education,
renew their spirituality,
and sensitivities,
and who capitalize on the moment
will grow, be very happy
and of great service."

I typed it and put it in a conspicuous place where I might now and again make reference. It was kind of a measuring stick, a barometer, or something more concrete than looking at the horoscope in the paper every day. You know I like to boast but, if it's in the Lord, it's okay, because I'm bragging about what I've been able to do with God's guidance.

Years ago when I was doing radio and television broadcasts all over the world, I would never have thought doing the Mass, our Eucharistic celebration, on television would be worth the transmission. It just wasn't exciting or a good use of the airtime. And yet, each day as I go through my mail I hear from people who are so grateful that I celebrate the Mass on television each week. I can't express the chills and the goosebumps that come over my body as I read day after day letters from people whom I never met, nor ever will. They send me gifts, greetings and a good word or two that reflect what I'm doing by coming into their homes, their rooms, their cells, their facilities. It means so much for people who have grown up with the Mass and with the Catholic Church and are now only able to participate through the media.

I'm grateful for the flexibility I've had to go right into the TV Mass after I retired from my active ministry in the Archdiocese of San Francisco. It forces me to continue my education by reading and rewriting all my homilies from years gone by. It forces me to pray, even more, while I'm reading the scriptures and trying to adapt what Jesus did and said those many years ago, and be sensitive to the times in which we now live and breathe and have our being.

Fatherharry.org has helped me capitalize on the moment and encouraged me to continue to minister through the new media. Some of you might remember my radio days when I called myself "The mass media minister with much more music in my message, moving my mouth to motivate you." Back then I was reaching hundreds or thousands, but today my reach is global thanks to the internet. When Vatican II sanctioned the use of media in promulgating the message of Jesus, I never would have known how dynamic and vital my ministry would still be today.

I would much rather be watering a garden and digging around plants than I would be dusting pictures and statues in a museum. That's really the difference in the Church today for me. Some people continue to hang on to the old system making sure that no one breaks in and steals the treasured artifacts nor destroys the statues of people who have had their time and made their mark. Some refuse to recognize that the cultures of the world are indeed coming closer and closer to that melting pot where we know each other better and will work to make sacrifices to respect and acknowledge our differences and applaud our likenesses. We will always have with us those who like to stir the pot, thinking that the continual vortex of mores will never be able to come together in anything solid, tasteful, or treasured.

I have spent the last month going through a priest's "things". He was a black man and was raised and lived in a whole other world than I could imagine. His library and his unique collection from various conventions, meetings, seminars, and sacramental life left a room so full of memorabilia that I couldn't begin to know where it all came from. But it was easy enough to realize what it meant to him and how steeped he was in the plight of the Black man in America. Now we have BLACK LIVES MATTER. It always mattered to him and I feel blessed to have been part of his life, ministry and happiness as a priest, even when it didn't favor celebration for who he was or who we were. He always told others how I influenced him in his early days as a priest. Regrettably, God took him before me. Now I have to say what a tremendous influence he was on me, and how much more does the expression Black Lives Matter mean because of him.

CHAPTER 57

Christmas Eve

IN MY MEDITATION this morning I was thinking about the Mass I said 56 years ago in the little village of Dollnstein, in Bavaria. It's about 40 clicks from *Munchen* (Munich). My classmate Father Erich Zenger had invited me to celebrate a "first Mass" in his parish church. We were good friends in Rome. I also had spoken at his first Mass banquet to the whole Bavarian village earlier in the year. It was then that I met the Bittlmayer family. Hildegard Bittlmayer was and has remained a good friend for all these years. They still live in Dollnstein. I remember when Father Erich first drove me into the town. There was a rather large building right outside of the main street. It said something like "founded in 1492". It was a brewery. Erich looked at me with a grin and said, "Isn't that the year your country was founded? Our brewery has been here as long as your country." I thought I came from a historical town. Yeah right!

Erich took me to his family home. They lived on the second floor of a small house with the farm animals on the first floor. It wasn't really a floor but a stable where the beasts lived and were fed during the cold months. The heat from their bodies would keep the people who lived on the second floor warm. As you travel around the rural area, this was typical in many of the houses we saw.

I didn't spend the night there. I was taken to Hildegard's home. Her family owned a stone factory. They made concrete blocks. Hilde was quite the beauty in her younger years and completely amazed and befuddled by Erich's friend, the Yankee priest from Rome. My close friend Roy Riedy was travelling with me, as he had come to Rome for my ordination. He also had been a classmate at the seminary but was asked to leave because he was gay. It was the 23rd of December, 1964, just one week after I received Holy Orders. Roy and I had spent the day in Munich shopping before taking the train to Dollnstein. The Bittlmayer family treated us to a traditional Bavarian Christmas dinner complete with *feuerzangenbowle*. It was a mulled white wine with a candle under it and a *zuckerhut*, or rum-soaked sugarloaf, melting into it. I'm not sure how it all worked but there was no cold even though the house was not heated. It was quite an evening — *gemütlich*, that wonderful German word meaning coziness, warmth, friendliness, good cheer, peace of mind and a sense of belonging and well being. We all went to bed with a smile and red cheeks. Sleeping in heavenly peace was a reality. I remember pulling up that huge *Jungfrau*, a featherbed blanket that enveloped the entire body. Never had I experienced a cold night with such warmth.

The next day was Christmas Eve. We walked to the parish church in the early morning dark. I vested with my friend Erich who would translate for me, as I had prepared the talk for the congregation in English. Little did I know nor expect that most of them would be *kleine kinder* with lighted candles in their small gloved hands, their smiles sparkling through the soft candlelight with only the breath of their voices moving the darting flames of the candles. *"Stille nacht, heilige nacht,"* they sang as I came to the altar, like a choir of little angels. There was no electricity in the church as it was over 900 years old but, like at the Bittlmayer's the night before, the light and warmth came from those gathered. The church was famous, as one of its parishioners had become a priest and later a pope. Pope Victor II had said Mass here nearly ten centuries ago and there I was at the same altar.

I studied for 12 years and put up with a lot of offal matter to be able to go to the altar of God and say my "first Mass". It follows the true belief that you take bread and wine and change it into the body and blood of Christ by doing what the scripture says. It's a faith thing that few are allowed to appreciate to the hilt. Some still walk away because it's just too difficult to make that leap of faith and believe. The rest continue to be nourished spiritually for the journey of life. It couldn't be more evident than it is now during this time of Covid, when so many are upset with the government and local politicians who close churches but allow strip joints and casinos to remain open for business.

Christmas Eve 2020 could not have been farther away, in time and dimension, from that blessed time in Bavaria. The only exception being that when Roy and I returned to Munich, after breakfast with the pastor and lunch with Erich's family and the Bittlmayers, everything was closed. And, for once, San Francisco was quiet.

I said my three Masses which were livestreamed from the parish. Facebook instead of faces, cyberspace not blessed space. Yet, later that evening I was reminded of the love of God for his people, even in times of pandemic. News came from my sister, Della, that she had become a great-grandmother for the first time at age 87 and once again I was a great-great-uncle. The Christmas blessing came in the form of a baby named Jack and, not unlike the *Christkindl*, he brought radiance into a dark world yearning for peace and joy.

My sister has these beautiful children, who had children who are now having children. It's that old thing about being a priest and not being able to procreate or father a child and still be called "father", so that in your old age you have others who are kin and who you would like to take into your arms and know they are flesh of your flesh and blood of your blood. *Sic transit gloria mundi* (So passes the glory of the world).

CHAPTER 58

Wilton Smith 1932-2021

I'M SURE I'VE TALKED about my good friend and priest Wilton Smith. I had the privilege of conducting his funeral and it had so many unusual twists that I can't help myself in passing them along.

He died on February 12, 2021, in the midst of Covid, so I had not been able to visit him in person for almost a year. He had moved to Golden Home Extended Care just a few months earlier, when Nazareth House was forced to close due to financial difficulties brought on in part by Covid. Upbeat as always, Wilt didn't mind the move because the food was better in the new place and he had more space.

Wilt's brother-in-law called to let me know he passed quietly early one morning, with his cousin who is a religious (sister) there to hold his hand and tell him that he was loved. Nobody should ever die without being loved. Saint Mother Teresa probably said it first or at least demonstrated it. But it's so true. It makes me sad to know all those people in quarantine who die without family or close friends. Sure they have the dedicated hospital staff but, after all, they are essentially strangers and doing their job, their work. A good friend told me that his son and his son's wife are both doctors in Brooklyn, New York. They both contracted Covid while on the job. They took time to recover and went back to work. He is now instructing new physicians what to do with Covid patients. He told his dad, "I'm telling all the newbies that they must use their hands and give hugs. It means so much more than all the medication and the air pumped into their lungs for life. Hold and hug with open arms and let them know that they are loved." As I said, NOBODY SHOOULD EVER DIE WITHOUT BEING LOVED.

Father Wilt, in his plans for the future, had ordered a coffin from the Trappist monks somewhere in Iowa. It was a very simple pine wood box with metal handles and a cross carved on the top. The drawback was that they were unable to ship such a coffin unless the person is dead, measured and weighed. This gives them the exact specifications they need to make the box. It doesn't take that long after they receive the order. But in this case, there is a winter storm in Iowa that prohibits normal shipping activities. So here I am with the family, trying to pick a date for the service and making sure we have the availability of a church. During this phase of the Covid pandemic we are only allowed 25% of the capacity of the church, so a big crowd is out of the question, even though Wilt served in a number of assignments where people would still remember him and would like to attend his service.

So, we end up planning the service for 10:30 on a morning even though the pine box had not yet arrived. A call came from the Trappists saying it was shipped. A second call came an hour later saying it should be there tonight. If the funeral director can receive it from the truck after dark, they will have time to place the body in the box and get it in the wagon to make sure it's at the church on time. When I saw it being rolled up on the funeral dolly, I wanted to break into applause. There were only about 15 of us there so it seemed foolish, but I still wanted to do it. Now we have the box, the body and the mandate to honor Wilt as best we could

Wilt was the slowest of human beings in all that he did. The only exception to that would be his speed to get to the ball on the tennis court. He was a wonderful player and an exceptional talent on the courts. So was Miles Riley, my erstwhile best friend and housemate, who gave a beautiful eulogy for Wilt using two props. He walked to the pulpit with a tennis racket and a small prescription bottle. He remarked that he first met Wilt on the seminary tennis courts and later became close friends, as Wilt had developed Parkinson's disease and now Miles had the same challenge. And they were both popping the same kind of pills.

When you speak at a funeral of a priest you have to be careful, as there are usually many of the clergy all willing to be critical of what you might have to say about the deceased. There are usually bishops as well as important people from the community. So it's good to make the meditation beforehand that assures you that this funeral and what you have to say is not about you but about the person lying in state. The best advice I ever had was from an old guy who told me when I asked what I should talk about. He replied, "Harry, talk about God and talk about five minutes."

As I said, Wilt was slow. In fact, when I brought him a burger at Nazareth House I always cut it in half before I unwrapped it and served him. I knew I would finish all I had before he was even close to being done. It never bothered him. He always said, "I've no place to go and I'm in no hurry to get there." I think I told you about the time I visited him in the hospital and he had wires and tubes coming out of everywhere. He opened his eyes and said, "Harry, I think I hear God calling." I said, "You better pick up Wilt, because from where I'm standing it looks like he really wants you this time."

So, when it was my turn to speak, I took the word S-L-O-W and tried to apply each letter to his life. S was for spiritual. The man was flat out holy. He had a great relationship with God. He was also my confessor and vice versa. One time he actually fell asleep while I was confessing. It didn't sit well with me for a while and then after that I always saved my worst faults for the end when I thought he might be napping.

L was for loving. That man could not help but love and be loved. His best years as a priest were when working with students at San Francisco's City College. He was the Newman Center chaplain there and really appreciated young people making their way through the challenges of growing up.

O was for obedient. The man kept the rules. He didn't always agree with the archbishop, but he never did anything to get in his way. He was a dedicated priest, fashioned by the thought and practice of Vatican II almost 60 years ago. He was committed to the Jesu Caritas group to which he and I both belonged. I wrote about it before.

W was for worthy. Lots of guys who are priests have humility with a hook. "Oh Lord, I am not worthy!" Right! Wilt was truly worthy of who he was, as an ordained priest to serve the needs of others. Nobody should ever die without being loved!

The service went well and next was a long trip to the cemetery where he was to be buried. From the chapel in Marin to Holy Cross in Colma would be about an hour and a half. So I'm speaking to anyone who would listen and the pine box with Wilt aboard is loaded in the hearse and on its way. I come out from the church to my car only to discover that it's locked tighter than a drum. I retrace my steps to and from the sacristy of the chapel and look under and all around the car. No keys. I asked the attendant to call Triple A. They can be there in less than an hour. The service is scheduled for 12:30 p.m.. It's now 11:20 a.m. and no keys. Finally, it's noon and the car is open but still no keys. I phone a friend who came over and picked me up. She says we'll be there by one. We call the family and Holy Cross to let them know the predicament and they are understanding. They will be patient and wait the 30 minutes. My driver was correct. We made it with one minute to spare. During the rites at the graveside, I noticed that my coat was way over my hands. Who bought this for me? Have I gotten that much smaller with age? I looked inside the coat and the label was one I recognized, but the coat didn't fit.

On the way to pick up a second set of keys, I got a phone call from the only other priest who attended the funeral. We both wore black coats and hung them over chairs. He picked up my coat with my keys. It was such a relief to know what happened, but really! The other guy was almost a foot taller than me and a few pounds heavier. I don't know why he didn't feel he was being squeezed into my coat nor feel the pockets to see that my keys were not his keys.

I chalked it up to Wilt being SLOW. He was in no hurry to have his remains go down into the ground and thought he would detain me a bit so I might learn a lesson about retirement. No sense in running to your end when you can take your time and smell the tulips. After all, nobody should ever die without being loved or laughed at!!!

CHAPTER 59

Promitto

I WENT TO A barbeque for retired priests today. I haven't been for a few years. I think I always felt it was for the "old guys". Now I'm one of them.

I was right. Everyone there was old. They were all kind of shapes, sizes and colors. One of my students of years ago when I taught homiletics at the seminary, was the first to sidle up and in his best Chinese/English wanted to know how his old professor was doing. Fortunately, for most Asian men, they don't show their age as much as Caucasian men. When I taught him, I gave him a passing grade but asked him to continue working on his second language and never go in the pulpit without a prepared text that would last no more than three minutes. Then carefully read it to the congregation. I thought for sure he would seek more help, but I stood there and he spoke to me for five minutes. The only words I could really understand were "old" and "professor". Don't get me wrong. He's a good priest and I'm sure he assists many people on their faith journey. But his English, like my Chinese, should not be more than three minutes, if it's preached.

My second encounter was with an elderly priest in a wheelchair who sat opposite me. His food was all brought to him and he didn't say a word. I tried a couple of times but realized that either his hearing or his mind was not attuned to the same wavelength that would allow me to have a conversation. We both smiled a lot. He chewed his burger as I used my teeth to skin the meat from the ribs that were so well prepared and just the food for a Fourth of July meal.

My other Jesu Caritas brother told me he could no longer drive. He gave up his keys and put his car in the garage. It seemed like only yesterday when he insisted that Father Wilt Smith not be allowed to drive. He told me he had bad eyesight and had a tendency to forget what he was doing. Then he asked if we could go out for dinner soon. I knew it was going to be my treat, as he would easily forget his wallet. So be it! I love the guy and could not find a better way to part with a few dollars for a dinner that could easily be the Last Supper for both of us.

The next encounter was with a guy who has had Giants baseball season tickets for 20 years. I asked him if he was still going to the park. "As often as I can and, wow, what a year we're having!" I must have gone to games with him 30 yeas ago. Time flies when you're having fun.

My final visit was to a hospital bed on the second floor of the Serra Clergy House for retired priests, where lay my dear and good friend Warren Holleran. He was my teacher at North American College those many years ago. He is the priest who asked me to say his funeral Mass and preach the homily. He warned me not to go on long and "for God's sake don't 'canonize the corpse' lying in the box before you." I'll never forget that one. Warren is 90 and bedridden. But he has all his marbles and can exchange pertinent comments about what is happening. Like many of us, he repeats himself. It was a blessing for me to be in his presence and it will be a privilege to pray the Mass for him. But who knows, I could go first. By the way, I made notes for that homily some five years ago when he asked me to celebrate his death. He wants it to be fun and fruitful for the many who don't understand that, with death, life just changes for us.

I had a telephone call earlier today from a close friend who asked if I was dying. "Of course I'm dying, aren't we all? We just don't know the when, where, or how." Whatever prompted her to telephone me about dying, I wondered. She said her favorite priest (besides me) announced that he was leaving the active ministry and would be getting married in a month. The parish was taking up a special collection for him as a going away gift. She thought the rule had changed and priests were now allowed to marry in the Roman rite. My friend reminded me that I'd often said the pope would change the rules and permit priests to marry . . . about five minutes after I was dead. I almost died, laughing!

Being around my retired brothers brought me back to the day I became a priest. *"Promitto."* I promise. The newly ordained priest puts his hands folded in the hands of the ordaining bishop and assents to his words: "Do you promise obedience to me and my successors?" *"Promitto."* I promise. I did this on December 16, 1964, at St. Peter's Basilica in Rome to Bishop Francis Reh. For these many years it has not really been a major problem.

There were those early days when the bishops were threatening to suspend priests if they didn't go along with the document from Rome that forbade the use of birth control (like my late North American College friend Jim Kogler, who walked away from the priesthood). It was called *"Humanae Vitae"* (Of Human Life). It had the result of turning many young couples away from the Catholic Church and regular attendance, for it carried with it the tag of serious sin if they were practicing birth control. There were a couple of options. The first, of course, was total abstinence. The second was almost as strange. It was called the "rhythm" method. One of my brothers and his wife attempted to practice it. It wasn't until years passed that I learned why they named their children Ronald, Renda, Roger, Ricky, Randy (and the final one John). The use of the letter "r" wasn't just a thing. What was I to think when all of this was happening in my own family? I recall serious conversations with them when I advised that I thought they had done their part in propagating the world for the Catholic faith. It never really dawned on me until I was working with people in the parish, or with parents of the kids I taught in high school, how problematic it might be for the formation of a clean conscience. It turned a number away, I'm sure. No one likes to think they are living in sin, especially if they're just trying to raise children and make ends meet.

I don't think it's comparable to what we're experiencing now in 2021 as our U.S. bishops have voted to deny the Eucharist to certain politicians who have supported women's right to make their own reproductive choices on the abortion issue. The official document has not yet been released. I'm sure it will be here by the time this book is published. You will then have the choice of reading and seeing how you feel about it and how you fit in or where you stand. It's not a real choice for me.

Nancy Pelosi is a practicing Roman Catholic at the parish where I live. On numerous Sundays I have given her the Eucharist. She is small in stature and so is hardly seen near the back of the church, but the dead giveaway is the black limo that is double parked directly in front of the church and the rather large man who stands near the rear entrance with a wire attached to his ear. He is always very smartly dressed. I would never think to deny her the Eucharist. There are a number of reasons, the most important being that I do not know her conscience nor her degree of culpability in this political football that gets kicked around with every election. For me, it's more important that she comes to pray and to stay united to the community of faith that gathers here each week. I'm sure there are those who feel the same way as many of our bishops but who are glad to see the pews occupied by such successful government officials who have given their lives to work for others. I have never gotten to know Speaker Pelosi. More often than not, she is in a hurry and boards her limo that might be blocking traffic. Jesus was pretty adamant about people following cults and taking sides. He called the Pharisees and others hypocrites and whited sepulchres because they stood on street corners and called attention to themselves as holy people. You have to stand for something or you'll fall for anything. These are not my words but apropos.

While university professors and professional theologians can argue and discuss all of this ad nauseum, it makes more sense to me not to use a sacrament like the Eucharist as a ticket for whether you gain admittance or are told to wait at the door until there is a final solution. My Vatican II experience forged me to be a pastoral kind of guy with a positive bent to all we do in the Church.

Now back to the *promitto*. I made a promise to the present archbishop, as the successor of Bishop Reh and in the Archdiocese of San Francisco where I am now retired. I'm not sure I could have made that promise today, knowing what I know and how I feel about such theological thought that is so negative. After all, it doesn't take long to realize that all of life does not depend on how you judge life in the womb. There I said it. There are many other life issues that are just as important. But the anti-abortion tag has finally a sizeable following and those who need a cause can easily board that bus. That's my belief and opinion. Abortion will be with us as long as there are unwanted pregnancies. So will prostitution, lying, stealing, and cheating. None of these practices should be judged by people who do not know what's in the conscience of an individual when such acts occur.

Politicians are called that because they must serve the people. The word comes from the Latin *populus*. People are of all makes and models and places where they live and cultures that they come from. All have a valid say about what they believe and feel about what is right and wrong.

"If today you hear his voice, harden not your hearts." This little scriptural phrase is repeated over and over again in the prayer of the priest each day. It's called the Divine Office. I often wonder if, when I put my hands in Bishop Reh's as he said to me, "Do you promise respect and obedience to me and my successors?", I would have done it today. The respect and obedience shows itself in your loyalty in word and deed. But it's been almost 60 years ago when I made that promise. I had no idea who the successors would be and what might be their ideology or understanding of the Church. And more to the point, how does he, the succeeding bishop, understand the teachings and work of Vatican II? I don't see it today. I have to admit it is confusing. But here's the kicker. I pray for my bishop. Every day I make a special effort to remember him to God. And I hope to God there will be a different understanding. I could be more specific with examples, but I choose to take the high road. Maybe I'll outlive this bishop and the next one will be like the ten or 12 that I knew before and to whom I made that same promise. *PROMITTO!*

Priest, mystic and martyr Charles de Foucauld put it this way:

"Father, I abandon myself into your hands;
do with me what you will.
Whatever you may do, I thank you:
I am ready for all, I accept all.
Let only your will be done in me,
And in all your creatures —
I wish no more than this, O Lord
Into your hands I commend my soul;
I offer it to you with all the love of my heart.
For I love you, Lord
And so need to give myself,
To surrender myself into your hands,

Without reserve,
And with boundless confidence,
For you are my Father.

IF TODAY, YOU HEAR HIS VOICE, HARDEN NOT YOUR HEARTS.

Epilogue

SLEEPLESS NIGHTS CAN often lead to profitable mornings. Last night was an example. I could not sleep and was thinking about an ending to this effort.

One of the really beautiful prayers of the funeral liturgy comes in the preface, where the Church says:

> "For your faithful, Lord,
> life is changed, not ended.
> And when this earthly dwelling turns to dust,
> an eternal dwelling is   -
> made ready in heaven."

The "changed not ended" part really reverberates in my brain. The way I feel today I wish it would go on and on, but I'm realistic enough to know it won't, it simply won't. One day I, too, shall be laid away. When, where, I haven't a clue. I do know that it wouldn't be for lack of trying that I've dedicated my life to helping others and doing my best to widen the narrow path, remove the beams from my own eyes and not worrying about the splinters, and at the same time doing my best to open the gates to all, like a Good Shepherd. Yes, it's much easier to make an adjustment to change, than to end . . . but then I'LL NEVER KNOW.

CPSIA information can be obtained
at www.ICGtesting.com
Printed in the USA
JSHW062144160922
30645JS00001B/2